Creating Mobile Apps with Sencha Touch 2

Learn to use the Sencha Touch programming language and expand your skills by building 10 unique applications

John Earl Clark

Bryan P. Johnson

[PACKT] open source *
PUBLISHING   community experience distilled

BIRMINGHAM - MUMBAI

Creating Mobile Apps with Sencha Touch 2

First published: April 2013

Production Reference: 1280313

Published by Packt Publishing Ltd.
Livery Place
35 Livery Street
Birmingham B3 2PB, UK.

ISBN 978-1-84951-890-1

www.packtpub.com

Cover Image by Avishek Roy (roy007avishek88@gmail.com)

Credits

Authors
John Earl Clark
Bryan P. Johnson

Reviewer
Kristian Kristensen

Acquisition Editor
Usha Iyer

Lead Technical Editor
Sweny Sukumaran

Technical Editors
Jalasha D'costa
Saumya Kunder

Project Coordinator
Amey Sawant

Proofreaders
Maria Gould
Kate Robinson

Indexer
Tejal Soni

Graphics
Ronak Dhruv

Production Coordinators
Manu Joseph
Nilesh Mohite
Nitesh Thakur

Cover Work
Nitesh Thakur

About the Authors

John Earl Clark holds a Master's degree in Human Computer Interaction from Georgia Tech and an undergraduate degree in Music Engineering from Georgia State University. John and his co-author, Bryan P. Johnson, worked together at MindSpring and later EarthLink, starting out in technical support and documentation, before moving into application development, and finally management of a small development team. After leaving EarthLink in 2002, John began working independently as a consultant and programmer, before starting Twelve Foot Guru, LLC with Bryan in 2005.

John has been working with Sencha Touch since the first early beta releases. He has also worked with Sencha's ExtJS since the early days when it was still known as YUI-Ext. John has also written a previous book with Bryan Johnson called *Sencha Touch Mobile JavaScript Framework* by Packt Publishing.

When he is not buried in code, John spends his time woodworking, playing the guitar, and brewing his own beer.

I would like to thank my family for all of their love and support. I would also like to thank Bryan for his help, his patience, and his continued faith in our efforts.

Bryan P. Johnson is a graduate of the University of Georgia. Bryan went on to work for MindSpring Enterprises in late 1995, where he met his co-author John Clark.

At MindSpring, and later EarthLink, for over seven years, Bryan served in multiple positions, including Director of System Administration and Director of Internal Application Development. After leaving EarthLink, Bryan took some time off to travel before joining John in starting Twelve Foot Guru.

Bryan has worked with Sencha's products since the early days of YUI-EXT, and has used Sencha Touch since its first betas. Last year, he and John wrote their first Sencha Touch book, *Sencha Touch Mobile JavaScript Framework* by Packt Publishing.

I would like to thank my friends and family for their support and my co-author John for his patience during the creation of this book.

About the Reviewer

Kristian Kristensen is an independent software development consultant. Through his company Kristensen Inc., he takes on the role of teacher, coach, facilitator, and anything in between to help software shops improve their processes and skills. He is particularly interested in languages and how they shape our thoughts and problem solving abilities.

He worked as a consultant for Microsoft before embarking on the journey of freelance consulting. He holds a Master's in Software Engineering from Aalborg University and currently lives in Brooklyn, NY with his wife.

For Heather…

www.PacktPub.com

Support files, eBooks, discount offers and more

You might want to visit www.PacktPub.com for support files and downloads related to your book.

Did you know that Packt offers eBook versions of every book published, with PDF and ePub files available? You can upgrade to the eBook version at www.PacktPub.com and as a print book customer, you are entitled to a discount on the eBook copy. Get in touch with us at service@packtpub.com for more details.

At www.PacktPub.com, you can also read a collection of free technical articles, sign up for a range of free newsletters and receive exclusive discounts and offers on Packt books and eBooks.

http://PacktLib.PacktPub.com

Do you need instant solutions to your IT questions? PacktLib is Packt's online digital book library. Here, you can access, read and search across Packt's entire library of books.

Why Subscribe?

- Fully searchable across every book published by Packt
- Copy and paste, print and bookmark content
- On demand and accessible via web browser

Free Access for Packt account holders

If you have an account with Packt at www.PacktPub.com, you can use this to access PacktLib today and view nine entirely free books. Simply use your login credentials for immediate access.

Table of Contents

Preface

Welcome to *Creating Mobile Apps with Sencha Touch 2*. The goal of this book is to help you learn the Sencha Touch mobile development platform by guiding you through a series of complete applications. Each application will focus on a different aspect of the language and show off many of the capabilities of Sencha Touch.

The Sencha Touch language is an HTML5 framework that uses JavaScript and CSS to create powerful and flexible mobile applications. These applications can be hosted like a regular website, or compiled into apps (applications) which can be sold on the Apple or Android app stores.

What this book covers

Chapter 1, A Simple Task List, walks you through the use of Sencha Architect, a graphical application development tool for the Sencha Touch framework.

Chapter 2, A Feed Reader, continues our exploration of Sencha Architect and explores using external data in your application, as well as creating complex layouts with xTemplates.

Chapter 3, Going Command Line, we step away from Sencha Architect and explore the power of the Sencha Cmd tool for creating applications. We also cover compiling a basic application so we can use additional features of your mobile device.

Chapter 4, Weight Weight, is an exercise and weight tracking application that uses the powerful Sencha Charts package to create visual displays for our data.

Chapter 5, On Deck: Using Sencha.io, explores the use of the Sencha.io framework to store data on a remote server.

Chapter 6, Catalog Application and API, builds on our use of APIs in the previous chapter to show how we might design and build our own custom API.

Chapter 7, The Decider: External APIs, covers the use of multiple external APIs (Google Maps and FourSquare) to create a single application.

Chapter 8, Evolver: Using Profiles, uses the Sencha Touch profiles to create a unique interface based on the mobile device you are using. It also covers pulling in data from WordPress to create a mobile version of your traditional website.

Chapter 9, Workbook: Using the Camera, shows you how to use the camera on your mobile device from inside the Sencha Touch Framework.

Chapter 10, Game On, shows you how to create a simple turn-based game. This can be used as a basis for creating your own turn-based games.

What you need for this book

The tools required are as follows:

- Sencha Touch 2.1 (Commercial or GPL).
- Sencha Cmd 3.
- Sencha Architect 2.1 (used in *Chapter 1, A Simple Task List* and *Chapter 2, A Feed Reader*).
- Touch Charts (used in *Chapter 4, Weight Weight.* This is included in Sencha Touch 2.1 GPL or available as a separate commercial purchase).

Who this book is for

This book is for people who have a basic knowledge of Sencha Touch and want to see how the features of Sencha Touch can be used as part of a complete application.

Conventions

In this book, you will find a number of styles of text that distinguish between different kinds of information. Here are some examples of these styles, and an explanation of their meaning.

Code words in text, database table names, folder names, filenames, file extensions, pathnames, dummy URLs, user input, and Twitter handles are shown as follows: "As with our previous iOS configuration file, we create a JSON file called `packager_android.json`."

A block of code is set as follows:

```
listeners: [
  {
    fn: 'onStartButtonTap',
    event: 'tap',
    delegate: '#startButton'
  }
]
```

Any command-line input or output is written as follows:

```
sencha generate model Contact --fields=id:int,firstName,
lastName,email,phone
```

New terms and **important words** are shown in bold. Words that you see on the screen, in menus or dialog boxes for example, appear in the text like this: "The **Toolbox** section of Sencha Architect is where you will find all of the components offered by Sencha Touch."

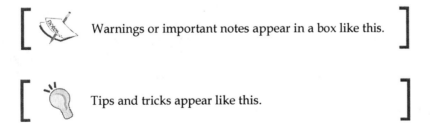

Warnings or important notes appear in a box like this.

Tips and tricks appear like this.

Reader feedback

Feedback from our readers is always welcome. Let us know what you think about this book—what you liked or may have disliked. Reader feedback is important for us to develop titles that you really get the most out of.

To send us general feedback, simply send an e-mail to feedback@packtpub.com, and mention the book title via the subject of your message.

If there is a topic that you have expertise in and you are interested in either writing or contributing to a book, see our author guide on www.packtpub.com/authors.

Customer support

Now that you are the proud owner of a Packt book, we have a number of things to help you to get the most from your purchase.

Downloading the example code

You can download the example code files for all Packt books you have purchased from your account at http://www.packtpub.com. If you purchased this book elsewhere, you can visit http://www.packtpub.com/support and register to have the files e-mailed directly to you.

Errata

Although we have taken every care to ensure the accuracy of our content, mistakes do happen. If you find a mistake in one of our books—maybe a mistake in the text or the code—we would be grateful if you would report this to us. By doing so, you can save other readers from frustration and help us improve subsequent versions of this book. If you find any errata, please report them by visiting http://www.packtpub.com/submit-errata, selecting your book, clicking on the **errata submission form** link, and entering the details of your errata. Once your errata are verified, your submission will be accepted and the errata will be uploaded on our website, or added to any list of existing errata, under the Errata section of that title. Any existing errata can be viewed by selecting your title from http://www.packtpub.com/support.

Piracy

Piracy of copyright material on the Internet is an ongoing problem across all media. At Packt, we take the protection of our copyright and licenses very seriously. If you come across any illegal copies of our works, in any form, on the Internet, please provide us with the location address or website name immediately so that we can pursue a remedy.

Please contact us at copyright@packtpub.com with a link to the suspected pirated material.

We appreciate your help in protecting our authors, and our ability to bring you valuable content.

Questions

You can contact us at questions@packtpub.com if you are having a problem with any aspect of the book, and we will do our best to address it.

1
A Simple Task List

At its core, most programming tasks fall into three categories: data display, data entry, and data storage. We will start our first project with the goal of covering how Sencha Touch handles each of these three basic categories. To do this, we will create a common programming application, the to-do list, or task list.

In this application, we will use the local storage available in HTML5 to store tasks including a name, description, creation date, completing date, and priority. We will then create a task list for displaying the current tasks as well as our completed tasks. We will discuss ways to test your display and to manage errors. We will then create the forms for entering in new tasks, editing existing tasks, and marking a task as complete.

Finally, we will explore some of the possible additional features for this type of application in our Extra Credit section.

A brief overview of Sencha Architect

Sencha Architect is a cross-platform visual development tool for Sencha Touch and Ext JS. Sencha Architect is available for Mac, Windows, and Linux, and it can be downloaded at the following link:

```
http://www.sencha.com/products/architect
```

For most of the chapters in this book we will be using a combination of Sencha Architect and standard coding to create our projects. This will give you an idea of some of the powerful advantages of the designer, while not hiding any of the actual code.

This is actually one of the key benefits of Sencha Architect; while it allows you to rapidly create interfaces and test them, behind the scenes the designer is generating standard JavaScript files, which you can edit with any text editor. This advantage allows you to quickly assemble the basic elements of your application, while maintaining the ability to tweak the code by hand as needed. We will cover this a bit more later on, but for now let's take a look at how Sencha Architect is set up.

When you first launch Sencha Architect, you are presented with a dialog box where you can choose to work on a new Ext JS project or a new Sencha Touch project, or you can choose from a list of existing projects:

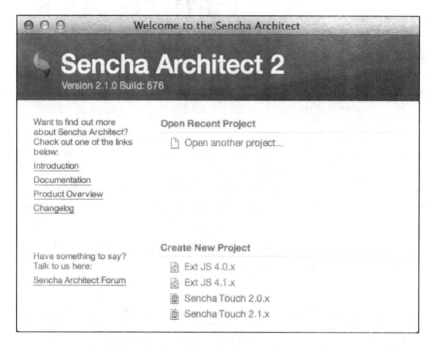

Since we are concerned with Sencha Touch in this book, you should select a new Sencha Touch 2.1 project.

The difference between Ext JS and Sencha Touch

Both ExtJ S and Sencha Touch are products created by the company Sencha Inc. Where Sencha Touch is used to develop mobile applications for various devices, Ext JS is used to create web applications for desktop browsers such as Firefox, Chrome, or Internet Explorer. For this book, we'll stick with Sencha Touch.

Once you have chosen your new project type, the Sencha Architect window will open. This window contains a visual display of the application and allows us to modify the application using drag-and-drop as well as directly entering code.

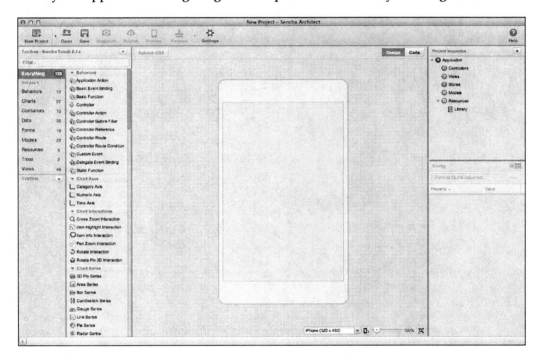

The Toolbox

The **Toolbox** section of Sencha Architect is where you will find all of the components offered by Sencha Touch. These components are listed in alphabetical order on the right side of the **Toolbox** section, while the basic types of components are listed on the left side. Clicking on one of these component types will limit the list to that particular type.

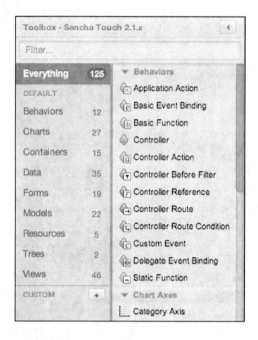

The following types are provided by default:

- **Behaviors**: It provides empty containers for functions and controllers
- **Charts**: It is a collection of graphs and charts that can pull data directly from a store
- **Containers**: It contains elements such as panels, tab panels, carousels, and field sets

- **Data**: It contains data-driven pieces such as stores, proxies, readers, writers, and filters
- **Forms**: It contains basic form elements such as text fields, radio buttons, select fields, and buttons
- **Models**: It includes the basic data model, validations, fields, proxies, readers, and writers
- **Resources**: It allows you to add external files for JavaScript and CSS, as well as packaging files for compiled applications
- **Trees**: Trees are the store types needed for nested tree components
- **Views**: It contains all of the basic viewable components in Sencha Touch such as containers, form fields, media, pickers, toolbars, lists, and buttons

There is also the **Everything** option to show all the types in the list.

You can also use the **+** button in the **CUSTOM** section to add your own custom types for limiting the list. This is very helpful for frequently used components, or simply for customizing the lists to fit your own personal habits.

Once a custom type is created, you can just drag components over from the list on the right, and drop them into your custom type.

Components can also be searched directly by name using the **Filter...** field at the top of the toolbox area.

The help section

When any component is selected from the toolbox the help section directly below it will display information for the component.

There is also a blue link at the bottom of the help area that says **See Class Documentation**. Clicking on this link will take you to the Sencha website documentation for the specific component that you have selected. This documentation is an invaluable source of information and you should familiarize yourself with it as quickly as possible.

The design area

The design area is where we will begin creating our first application. By default, a Sencha Touch application starts out with an iPhone 320 x 480 layout. This layout can be changed to be displayed as an iPad, Nexus S, or Kindle Fire display size. This allows you to look at your design under multiple devices. You can also set the orientation of the device and zoom in and out of the design view area.

The design area also offers an option to view and work with the code behind the design. This is a great learning tool if you're just getting into mobile programming. By switching between the **Design** and **Code** view, you can examine complex layouts and see exactly how the JavaScript code is used to create them.

The Project Inspector area

The Project Inspector area provides an alternative view to your project's code. As you drag components onto the design area they will also appear in **Project Inspector**. The **Project Inspection** area will display these components as a hierarchical list. This is often very helpful in seeing which components are nested inside of other components.

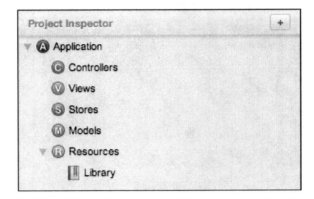

Components can also be dragged from the **Toolbox** list into **Project Inspector**. It is often easier to manage certain components by dropping them into **Project Inspector**, rather than the design area. This can ensure that you correctly position the component within the required container.

The **Resources** section is a new addition in Version 2.1, and it allows you to add external files to your project. If you have an older Version 2.0 Sencha Touch project, you can right-click on **Library** and select **Upgrade** to change the project to a newer Sencha Touch 2.1 project.

The Config area

The **Config** area will display all the configuration options for any component selected in the design area or in **Project Inspector**. All of the typical configuration options, such as height, width, layout, ID, padding, margin, events, and functions can be accessed from the **Config** area.

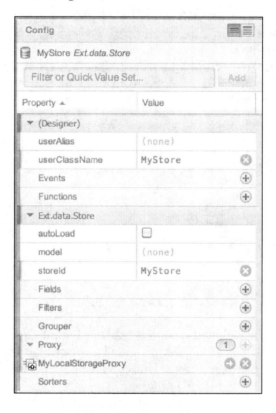

The configuration name is listed on the left and the value is on the right. Clicking on the value will allow you to edit it. You can also click on the + next to certain sections such as **Functions** and **Events** to add new items to **Config**.

Getting started with the task list

To see how all of these pieces work together to create an application, let's start by creating our data store for the Task Manager application. Save the new file you have opened as TaskList and let's get to work on adding some components.

Creating the data store

To add a component to the project, we need to drag the component from the toolbox and drop it on the project or onto the proper section of the project inspector. For our first component, let's choose a plain data store.

From **Toolbox**, select **Data**, and then click on **Store** and drag it onto our iPhone in the design area. You should now see a store called **MyStore** appear in the **Property Inspector** under the **Stores** list:

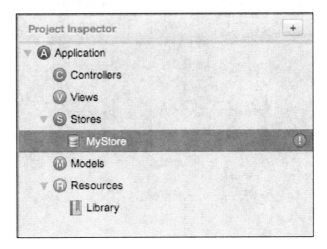

You will also notice that there is a red warning icon next to our store. This tells us that our store is missing a few of its required components. In this case, the store needs a proxy to control how the data is sent and received and it needs a model to tell it what data to expect.

From the **Toolbox** list, select a **LocalStorage Proxy** object and drag it over onto our store.

You will probably notice that some components can only be placed within other components. For example, when you drag the proxy over, you can't just drop it into the iPhone diagram like we did before. A proxy component will only exist as part of a data store. This means that you have to drop a proxy component onto a data store in **Property Inspector** in order for it to correctly add itself to the store.

Once you have dropped the proxy onto the store, we need to add a model, and link it to our store.

Adding a Model, Fields, and Field Types

In the **Data** section of our **Toolbox**, scroll up to find the listing for **Model**. Drag the **Model** object over to the **Models** section of our **Project Inspector**. This will create a new model called **MyModel**.

Select **MyModel** in **Project Inspector** and look at the **Config** section. The first thing we probably want to change here is the name. Click on the value listed for **userClassName**, change **MyModel** to `Task` and press *Enter* on your keyboard. The model should now be listed as **Task** in both **Config** and **Project Inspector**.

Next, we need to add some fields to our model. With the **Task** model selected, you should see a listing for **Fields** in the **Config** area. Click on the **+** button next to **Fields** and enter `id` into the text area that appears. Click on **Finish** on the screen or press *Enter* on your keyboard.

Your **Config** area should now look something like this:

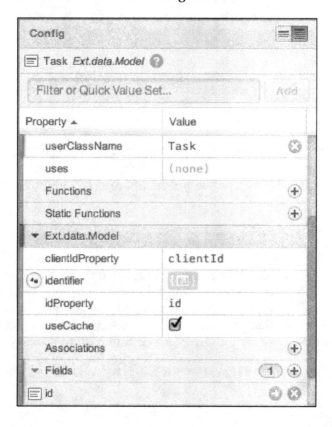

Repeat the previous steps to add the following fields to the task model:

- **name**
- **description**
- **create**
- **completed**
- **priority**
- **isCompleted**

Now that you have all of your fields, we need to define the data types for each field.

In **Project Inspector**, click on the field called **id**. This will open the configuration for that field and you should see that there is currently no value listed for **type**. Click on the value next to **type**. A drop-down menu will appear and you can select **int** from the list.

Now we need to do the same thing for our other fields. Select each field in turn and set them as follows:

- **name**: Set it as **string**
- **description**: Set it as **string**
- **create**: Set it as **date**
- **completed**: Set it as **date**
- **priority**: Set it as **int**
- **isCompleted**: Set it as **boolean**

Now that you have all of the model fields and types defined, we need to add the model to the store.

Adding the model to the store

Click on **MyStore** in **Project Inspector**. As we did with our model, we probably want to change the name of the store to make it easier to refer to and keep track of in our code. Click on the values next to **userClassName** and **storeID** and change both to say **taskStore**.

Next, you will need to click on and edit the model **Config** in the store to select our **Task** model. Once complete, your store configuration should look something like this:

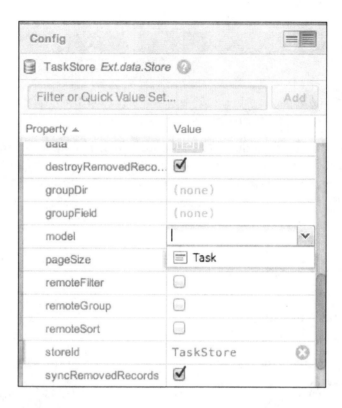

Making copies

Now that we have our store and model, we need to make a copy of it to hold our completed tasks. Both stores will use the same model and most of the same setup information. We only need to duplicate the store and change the **id** and **userClassName** values. Once we finish that, we will create filters for the store so that it only grabs the data we need.

To duplicate **TaskStore**, right-click on it in **Project Inspector** and select **Duplicate**. A new store will appear called **MyStore2**, with the same proxy and model information. Select **MyStore2** in **Project Inspector** and change both the **id** and **userClassName** values in the **Config** section to CompletedStore.

Adding filters

Now that we have our two stores, we need to set some filters to make sure that **TaskStore** only loads current tasks and **CompletedStore** only loads completed tasks.

You can add filters in the **Config** section for each of our stores. First, select **TaskStore** and then click on the **+** button next to **Filters** in the **Config** section. This will add a new filter called **MyFilter**. Click on the arrow next to **MyFilter** to reveal its **Config** options.

We need to add a function to this filter in order to tell it what records to grab. Click on the **+** button next to **filterFn** to add a new filter function. Up in the **Project Inspector** area, **filterFn** should appear beneath **MyFilter**. Click on **filterFn** in **Property Inspector** to bring up the code editor for the function.

The editor should appear with the following code:

```
filterFn: function(item) {

}
```

This sets up the basic function for the filter and passes us each record in the store as **item**. If our function returns `true`, the record is included in the store and if it returns `false`, the record is ignored.

Our model has a Boolean value called `isComplete`. We can check this value in our function like this:

```
return !item.data.isComplete;
```

This takes the record we were passed as `item`, and checks the record's data for `isComplete`. If a task record is complete this will be `true`, so we put the `!` character in front to grab only the records where `isComplete` is `false`. The filter is now complete.

Take the same steps to add a filter to `CompletedStore`:

1. Add a filter to `CompletedStore`.
2. Add a function to the filter using `filterFn`.
3. Add the code for the filter function.

In this case, our function just needs to look for tasks where `isComplete` is `true` (just drop the `!` character this time):

```
return item.data.isComplete;
```

Both stores will now correctly filter the tasks based on completion.

While we have been moving these components around on screen, Sencha Architect has been doing a bit of heavy lifting for us on the backend. Let's take a peek behind the curtain and see what's going on with the actual code.

Pay attention to the man behind the curtain

The first thing to look at is on your hard drive where you saved the Task Manager project file. You will notice that the designer has created a number of files here: `app.html`, `app.js`, and `TaskManager.xds`. We also have folders for app and metadata.

Sencha Architect uses both `TaskManager.xds` and the `metadata` folder. The `TaskManager.xds` file is the main project file you are currently working in and the `metadata` folder contains resources for that project file. We can ignore those files for now because the interesting stuff is in the other files.

Let's start with our `app.html` file. If you open this file in your favorite code editor, you should see something like this:

```
<!DOCTYPE html>

<!-- Auto Generated with Sencha Architect -->
<!-- Modifications to this file will be overwritten. -->
<html>
<head>
    <meta http-equiv="Content-Type" content="text/html; charset=utf-8"
/>
    <title>Chapter1</title>
    <link rel="stylesheet" type="text/css" href="http://extjs.
cachefly.net/touch/sencha-touch-2.1.0/resources/css/sencha-touch.
css"/>
    <script type="text/javascript" src="http://extjs.cachefly.net/
touch/sencha-touch-2.1.0/sencha-touch-all-debug.js"></script>
    <script type="text/javascript" src="app.js"></script>
    <script type="text/javascript">
        if (!Ext.browser.is.WebKit) {
            alert("The current browser is unsupported.\n\nSupported
browsers:\n" +
                "Google Chrome\n" +
                "Apple Safari\n" +
                "Mobile Safari (iOS)\n" +
```

```
                "Android Browser\n" +
                "BlackBerry Browser"
            );
        }
    </script>
</head>
<body></body>
</html>
```

This should look pretty familiar to anyone who is used to dealing with HTML and JavaScript. The file creates a basic HTML page, includes the JavaScript and CSS files for Sencha Touch, and also includes our `app.js` file (which we will get to in a second).

The file then sets up some browser detection so that if the user attempts to access the application with a non-WebKit browser, they will be told that their browser is incompatible and will be given a list of compatible browsers.

 Chrome and Safari are WebKit browsers and are available for Windows and Mac. Chrome is also available on Linux. In this book we will be using Safari for our testing, but the examples will work in Chrome as well.

One other thing to note is the message in the comments at the top of `app.html`. This particular file is autogenerated each time you save the TaskManager project. If you make changes to it in your code editor, they will be overwritten the next time you save.

 A word about CacheFly

CacheFly is a **CDN** (**Content Delivery Network**). They have computers all over the world, and can send files to your users from a server that's close to them, so that the files take less time to travel across the Internet, and therefore less time to load. That also means that you save on your own server bandwidth by not serving those files yourself.

Next, let's take a look at our `app.js` file:

```
/*
 * File: app.js
 *
 * This file was generated by Sencha Architect version 2.0.0.
 * http://www.sencha.com/products/designer/
 *
```

```
   * This file requires use of the Sencha Touch 2.0.x library, under
independent license.
   * License of Sencha Architect does not include license for Sencha
Touch 2.1.x. For more
   * details see http://www.sencha.com/license or contact license@
sencha.com.
   *
   * This file will be auto-generated each and every time you save your
project.
   *
   * Do NOT hand edit this file.
   */

Ext.Loader.setConfig({
    enabled: true
});

Ext.application({
    models: [
        'Task'
    ],
    stores: [
        'TaskStore', 'CompletedStore'
    ],
    name: 'MyApp'
});
```

Like our HTML file, we start out with a stern warning at the top about hand editing the file.

A word about hand editing

Sencha Architect does a lot of work for you, but that means that it can also accidentally overwrite code that you've written by hand. Your best bet is to wait to add any code yourself until you've fully laid out and configured all of the components for your application with the Architect first.

If we skip down past that section, we have a setup function for the Ext.Loader followed by a definition of our application. This includes links to all of our models and stores, as well as the name of our application (which we should probably change once we finish snooping around in the code).

Ext.Loader is a special part of Sencha Touch that will load JavaScript files as they're needed. Rather than include all of your JavaScript files in the HTML file, Ext.Loader will only load them as they're needed. This drastically cuts down on your application's startup time. You can learn more about Ext.Loader at `http://www.sencha.com/blog/using-ext-loader-for-your-application`.

Close the `app.js` file and open up the `app` folder. As you can see we have two folders called `model` and `store`. These, of course, contain our code for the model and the store.

Open the `store/TaskStore.js` file first:

```
Ext.define('MyApp.store.TaskStore', {
    extend: 'Ext.data.Store',
    requires: [
        'MyApp.model.Task'
    ],

    config: {
        autoLoad: true,
        model: 'MyApp.model.Task',
        storeId: 'TaskStore',
        proxy: {
            type: 'localstorage',
            id: 'Tasks'
        }
    },
        filters: {
            filterFn: function(item) {
                return !item.data.isComplete;
            }
        }
});
```

Beyond the ever-present warning about hand editing, you will see our store definition written out in plain JavaScript. Note that the store definition not only contains the code for our proxy, it also includes the filter function and it lists our task model as the model for the store.

Why is it "MyApp.model.Task"?

Ext.Loader turns the name of your components into a filename by turning the periods into slashes. This means that if your component is `MyApp.model.Task` then Ext.Loader will look in your application folder for a folder called `MyApp`. It will look inside that `MyApp` folder for a `model` folder that has a `Task.js` file in it.

This is also a good way to keep your application folder organized. If you put all of your models in a `model` folder and all of your views in a `view` folder then you'll know where to find them when you need to find them later.

Close the `TaskStore.js` file and let's look at the last file, `model/Task.js`. This is the file for our model:

```
Ext.define('MyApp.model.Task', {
    extend: 'Ext.data.Model',
    config: {
        fields: [
            {
                name: 'id',
                type: 'int'
            },
            {
                name: 'name',
                type: 'string'
            },
            {
                name: 'description',
                type: 'string'
            },
            {
                name: 'created',
                type: 'date'
            },
            {
                name: 'completed',
                type: 'date'
            },
            {
                name: 'isCompleted',
                type: 'boolean'
            }

        ]
    }
});
```

Notice that there is a fair amount of overlap between what's in the store and what's in the model. This duplication allows the model and store to act independently of each other while still maintaining consistency for the data itself. We will look closer at that when we deal with the forms for our application.

Architect versus coding by hand

As you can see, Sencha Architect generates code for us, but we could also choose to create this exact same code by hand. Sencha Architect offers benefits to the novice coder by allowing applications to be built visually and allowing the coder to explore the code as needed. The designer also generates code according to Sencha Touch best practices. This keeps the novice user from learning bad habits and encourages cleaner code when the coder needs to begin programming by hand.

For the seasoned coder, Sencha Touch offers ways to rapidly prototype interfaces and create mockups for clients. The code behind these mockups can then be used outside the designer to create complex applications that might be problematic if not impossible for Sencha Architect to accomplish.

By using a combination of Sencha Architect and traditional text-based coding, we hope that this book will offer additional benefits to the reader both in terms of speed and consistency.

Creating the views

So far, none of our code has actually created anything on the screen. Now we need to create some visual components for the user to interact with, starting with the main panel that will contain our application.

Drag a **Tab Panel** object out of the **Toolbox** list on the left and drop it onto the iPhone screen in the designer. A **Panel** option will now appear in **Project Inspector**. Select **Tab Panel** and add the following information to the **Config** area:

- Make sure the **initialView** checkbox is checked
- Change **userClassName** from **myTabPanel** to `mainView`
- Delete the third tab by right-clicking on it and choosing **Delete**

Save the project and let's take another look at the code for your project. In the `app.js` file, you will now see the following code:

```
Ext.Loader.setConfig({
    enabled: true
});
```

```
Ext.application({
    models: [
        'Task'
    ],
    stores: [
        'TaskStore'
    ],
    views: [
        'MainView'
    ],
    name: 'MyApp',
    launch: function() {
        Ext.create('MyApp.view.MainView', {fullscreen: true});
    }
});
```

The designer has now added a launch function that creates an instance of our MainView panel and sets it to fullscreen.

If we take a look in our app folder, we now see a folder called view. This folder contains our file for MainView.js:

```
Ext.define('MyApp.view.MainView', {
    extend: 'Ext.tab.Panel',

    config: {
        items: [
            {
                xtype: 'container',
                title: 'Tab 1'
            },
            {
                xtype: 'container',
                title: 'Tab 2'
            }
        ]
    }
});
```

Right now this file simply defines MainView as an extension of the standard Ext. tab.Panel function and sets the Config containing our two tabs. As we add additional pieces to the panel, they will appear here in the code. Let's head back to the designer and do just that.

Configuring the Tab Panel

The first thing we should probably do is rename the tabs. Select **Tab 1** in the **Project Inspector** and then click on the value for **Title** in the **Config** section. Change the title from **Tab 1** to Current and press *Enter* on your keyboard. Do the same thing for **Tab 2**, changing its title to Completed.

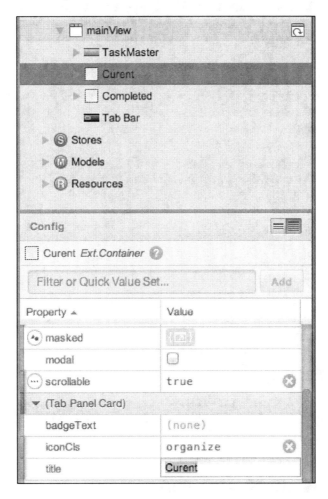

One additional thing we should do is change the tabs to appear on the bottom. This will give our application a more classic iPhone look. To make this change, select **mainView** in **Project Inspector** and find the **Tab Bar Config** listing in the **Config** section. Click on the + button next to **Tab Bar Config** and a new **Tab Bar** option will appear below. Click on the arrow next to the new **Tab Bar** option and the configuration options for it will appear.

Locate the docked **Config** area and change it from top to bottom. The tabs should drop down to the bottom and give us the large icons familiar to most iPhone users. You can change these icons by clicking on the **Current** or **Completed** tab in **Project Inspector** and changing the **Config** value for **iconCls**. Select the icons you like and save the project (I chose **organize** for the **Current** tab and **delete** for the **Completed** tab).

Once you are finished, select **MainView** in **Property Inspector** and then click on **Code** in the upper-right side of the designer. This will change the designer over into code view, showing us the contents of our `MainView.js` file.

```
Ext.define('MyApp.view.MainView', {
  extend: 'Ext.tab.Panel',
  config: {
  items: [
    {
        xtype: 'container',
        title: 'Current',
        iconCls: 'organize'
    },
    {
        xtype: 'container',
        title: 'Completed',
        iconCls: 'delete'
    }
  ],
  tabBar: {
    docked: 'bottom'
  }
  }
});
```

You can now see that the tab panel and its two tabs have been added to our `MainView.js` file. We also see our `tabBar` configuration and the `iconCls` values we selected.

Adding the lists and details

Next, we want to add a list and a panel to each of our tabs. The lists will display the names for our current and completed tasks. The panels will display details for the task when we click on it in the list.

Let's start by selecting each tab and setting the **layout** property in **Config** to **card**. This will let us easily switch between the **List** and **Details** sections for each tab.

Next, take a **List** component from the **Toolbox** list and drop one on each tab in **Property Inspector**.

Dropping items in Property Inspector

While most components can be dropped directly onto the design area, it is often better to drop components into **Project Inspector**. It's much easier to ensure that you are putting the component within the correct container using **Property Inspector**.

Next you will need to take a panel from **Toolbox** and drop one onto each tab, just like we did with the list. This panel will be our details container and it will not appear in the design view because the list is in front. We will create some code later on to swap the list and the container when the user clicks on a task in the list.

Your **Property Inspector** area should now look something like this:

Notice that the tabs (**Current** and **Completed**) are both indented under the **mainView** tab panel. Each tab also has a list and a panel beneath it. The tabs are children of the **mainView** tab panel and each tab has two child items; a list and a panel.

Since we will need to address the lists and the panels in our code, we should probably name them something a bit more descriptive than **MyList** and **MyPanel**. In order to do this, you will need to select each of these items and change the **id** property in **Config**. Let's rename them as follows:

In the **Current** tab, we will call them CurrentList and CurrentDetails and in the **Completed** tab, we will call them CompletedList and CompletedDetails.

Setting up the templates

Next we need to set up the templates (called **itemTpl** in the **Config** area) for our lists and our details. These templates control how our data will be laid out on the screen. Remember that we have the following data items:

- **id**
- **name**
- **description**
- **created**
- **completed**
- **priority**

We can use any of these values by including them in our template by placing them in curly braces like so:

```
<div>{name}</div>
```

We can also use any HTML styling or tags as part of our template. This gives us a great deal of flexibility in controlling the layout of our application.

To edit the template for our **CurrentList** component, select it in **Project Inspector** and a gear icon will appear next to the list in our **Design** view. Click on the gear and you will see a pop-up window with a few configuration options including **Edit Template** at the bottom of the pop-up window.

When you click on **Edit Template**, a text area will appear over the list with the following text:

```
<div>List Item {string}</div>
```

Change this text to:

```
<div class="priority_{priority}">{name}</div>
```

Click on **Done Editing** when you are finished. The list items will appear empty for now, but we will fix that a bit later.

Next, click on the **CurrentDetails** panel in **Project Inspector** and edit the template the same way you did for **CurrentList**. Set the template for the **CurrentDetails** to:

```
<div class="taskName">{name}</div>
<div class="taskDescription">{description}</div>
<div class="taskCreated">Created: {created}</div>
```

Click on **Done Editing** when you are finished.

When you are finished with the **CurrentDetails**, we want to follow the same steps for **CompletedList** and **CompletedDetails**. You can keep the list template the same but we should include the completed date on our details page like so:

```
<div class="taskName">{name}</div>
<div class="taskDescription">{description}</div>
<div class="taskCreated">Created: {created}</div>
<div class="taskCompleted">Completed: {completed}</div>
```

Testing with starter data

You will notice that since we have no records, we have nothing to display. This can make testing our application difficult, so we are going to add a few test records to our application using the `launch` method.

Select **Application** in **Project Inspector** and then locate **launch** down in the **Config** section. Click on the **+** button next to **launch** to add a new launch function, and then click on the arrow next to our new launch function to open it. This will open the code editor with:

```
launch: function() {

}
```

Add the following code inside the `launch` function:

```
var TaskStore = Ext.data.StoreManager.lookup('TaskStore');
var CompletedStore = Ext.data.StoreManager.lookup('CompletedStore');
if(CompletedStore.getCount()+TaskStore.getCount() === 0) {
    console.log('we have no records');
    TaskStore.add({name: 'Here Is A Task', description: 'You can mark
the task complete by clicking the Completed button below.', priority:
1, created: Date.now(), completed: '', isComplete: false});
```

```
    TaskStore.add({name: 'How To Edit A Task', description: 'You
can edit the task by clicking the Edit button below.', priority: 2,
created: Date.now(), completed: '', isCompleted: false});
    TaskStore.add({name: 'How To Add A Task', description: 'Add a task
by clicking the Add button in the upper right corner.', priority: 3,
created: Date.now(), completed: '', isComplete: false});
    TaskStore.sync();
} else {
    console.log('we have records');
}
```

This code will grab our two stores, TaskStore and Completed Store, and check to see if there are any records. If there are no records, the function will add three new records, and then sync the store to save the records. These task records can also serve as a set of three instructions to new users opening the application for the first time.

Console logs

The console.log command is your best friend when programming. It will print text and objects to the error console in Safari or Chrome. This is critical for debugging any issues you have. In the previous code, the console logs will print based on whether we get back records or not. We could also use console.log(TaskStore) to get a display of every attribute of that store object. This is really handy for making sure you actually have the object you think you have.

Now when you open up the app.html file in your browser, you should see the following in the **TaskMaster** application:

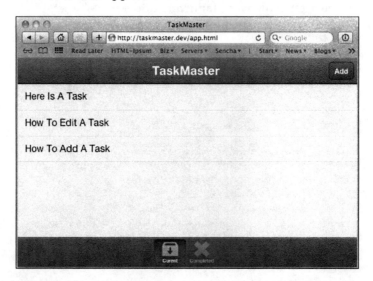

We now have tasks to view, but we still can't get to the details. We need to add a function to switch the view between our list and our details.

Back in Sencha Architect, click on **CurrentList** in **Project Inspector** and then look for **Events** at the top of the **Config** section. Click on the **+** button next to **Events** to add a new event listener. Use the menu that appears to choose the **select** event. Click on the arrow next the new **select** event to edit the code. The code editor will appear with the following code:

```
onCurrentListSelect: function(dataview, record, options) {

}
```

Add the following code to the `select` event:

```
var currentTab = this.getActiveItem();

var currentDetails = currentTab.down('panel');

currentDetails.setRecord(record);
currentTab.setActiveItem(currentDetails);
```

The first line grabs our `Current` tab and the second grabs our `CurrentDetails` panel. We then set the record on the details panel to the record we are passed as part of the `select` function (the record from our list). Finally, we switch the card layout of our current tab to the `CurrentDetails` panel, hiding `CurrentList`.

We need to do the same thing with our `CompletedList` component. Add the new **select** event and set the code to:

```
var completedTab = this.getActiveItem();

var completedDetails = completedTab.down('panel');

completedDetails.setRecord(record);
completedTab.setActiveItem(completedDetails);
```

If we test this in the browser we should be able to see our details panel when we click on an item in the list. This also brings us to our next challenge; we need a way to get back to our list.

In this chapter, we will create the back button manually and in the next chapter we will highlight a different approach to this same problem. For now, let's add a new button to our toolbar.

Adding the back button

Grab a **toolbar** object from **Toolbox** and drag it over onto the **mainView** tab panel. Grab a **button** object from **Toolbox** and drag it onto the new **toolbar** panel.

Next, we want to give our toolbar a title. Let's select the toolbar and change the title in the **Config** section to `TaskMaster`.

Next we need to change a few things with our button. Select the **Button** object and make the following changes to its **Config** section:

- Change **text** to **Back**
- Change the **id** to **backButton**
- Change the **ui** to **back** (this will make it look like a typical back button)
- Check the box next to the **hidden** property (we want the button hidden by default)

I can't find one of the Config options

If you are unable to find some of these properties, you may need to toggle the **Config** section between **Show Common Configs** and **Show All Configs** using the two buttons in the upper-right corner of the **Config** section.

Now that we have a back button, we need to make it do something. Add a tap listener by clicking on the **+** button next to events in the button's **Config** section. Select **tap** and then click on the arrow next to the tap event that appears.

Edit the back button code to look like this:

```
onBackButtonTap: function(button, e, options) {
  var currentTab = this.getActiveItem();
  currentTab.setActiveItem(0);
  button.hide();
}
```

By grabbing `this.getActiveItem()` we grab the active tab in our `MainView` tab panel, which makes sure that the button will work correctly for both of our lists. We set the active item to the first item in the active tab. Finally, we hide the button so that it does not show up in our list view.

The last part we need to take care of is showing the button when we click an item in the list. Click on the **select** event for our current panel and add the following to our `select` function:

```
var backButton = Ext.getCmp('backButton');
backButton.show();
```

You will want to add the exact same button code to our **select** event in the **CompletedList** component. Just copy, open the select event for **CompletedList**, and paste.

Our lists and details are now complete. Now we need to be able to add, edit, and mark tasks as complete.

Creating the forms

Before we start creating forms we need to add a button to our **MainView** toolbar that will display the form for adding new tasks.

Drag a **Button** object out from the **Toolbox** list and drop it on the **TaskMaster** toolbar. The new button should appear next to **backButton**. We probably want to move that over to the other side of our title, so we need to drag a **Spacer** out of **Toolbox** and drop it between our new button and **backButton**. **Spacer** will push the new button to the right side of the screen.

Next we need to change the following **Config** properties for the new button:

- Set **text** to **Add**
- Set **itemId** to **addButton**

We will come back and add a `tap` function once we complete our forms.

Add Task form

To create our Add Task form we will add a new form panel to the **Current** tab. Drag a **Form Panel** from the toolbox and drop it on our **Current** tab. The panel should appear below our **CurrentList** and **CurrentDetails** panels.

Next we need to drag some fields into our form so let's start with dropping a **Text Field** object on the **MyFormPanel** panel and changing the following **Config** properties:

- Set **name** to **name**
- Set **label** to **Name**

- Set **id** to **name**
- Set **margin** to **3**

Next, add a **Text Area** object to our **MyFormPanel** panel and set the following **Config** properties:

- Set **name** to **description**
- Set **label** to **Description**
- Set **id** to **description**
- Set **margin** to **3**

Now, we need to add a **Select Field** object to **MyFormPanel** and set the following **Config** properties:

- Set **name** to **priority**
- Set **label** to **Priority**
- Set **id** to **priority**
- Set **margin** to 3

We also need to add some options for **Select Field**. Locate **Options** in the **Config** properties and click to edit. The **Options** property expects an object as its value, in this case an array of name-value pairs like this:

```
[{text: 'High',   value: 1},
{text: 'Medium', value: 2},
{text: 'Low',    value: 3}]
```

By default, the **Select Field** uses text for display and value for the submitted value. You can change this by editing the **displayField** and **valueFields** in the **Config** properties, but we can leave these as the defaults for our application.

We can save ourselves a lot of work if we use this form for both adding new tasks and editing existing ones. To do this we also need to add a hidden field to hold the ID value of any existing tasks that we edit.

Add a **Hidden Field** object to **MyFormPanel** and set the properties for **id** and **name** to **id** in the **Config** section. We will use this later when saving the form.

The last thing we need in our form is two buttons; one for save and one for cancel. Add the buttons and make the following changes:

- Set **text** for **button 1** to **Save**
- Set **itemID** for **button 1** to **SaveButton**

- Set **margin** for **button 1** to **10**
- Set **text** for **button 2** to **Cancel**
- Set **itemID** for **button 2** to **CancelButton**
- Set **margin** for **button 2** to **10**

The structure and the form should look something like this:

Next, we will add a tap event handler to each button using the **Event** section of the **Config** as before.

For our **Cancel** button, set the event function to:

```
var currentTab = this.getActiveItem();
currentTab.setActiveItem(0);
```

This code grabs our **Current** tab and sets the active panel back to **CurrentList**.

The **Save** button is a bit more complex. As we mentioned earlier, we want to use this form for both adding new tasks and editing existing ones. This means we need to check to see if the **Hidden Field** value of our form is set and save the task correctly.

Add the following code to the **SaveButton** tap event function:

```
var currentTab = this.getActiveItem();
var formPanel = currentTab.getActiveItem();

var values = formPanel.getValues();

var store = Ext.data.StoreManager.lookup('TaskStore');

if(values.id === null) {
    var record = Ext.ModelMgr.create(values, 'MyApp.model.Task');
    record.set('created', new Date());
    store.add(record);
} else {
    var record = store.getById(values.id);
    record.set('name', values.name);
    record.set('description', values.description);
    record.set('priority', values.priority);
}

store.sync();
formPanel.reset();
currentTab.setActiveItem(0);
```

Our first two lines grab `currentTab` and `formPanel`. We then get the values from `formPanel` and `store` that we need to save our data to.

We check the value of our hidden field to see if it has been set. This will be `true` if we are editing, but not if we are adding a new task.

If we are adding a new task, we create a new `record` option using the `values` form in the form field, we set a create date, and add `record` to `store`.

If we are editing an existing record, we use the `id` value from our `store` to get the `record` from the `store`. We then set the `name`, `description`, and `priority` values of `record` from our form `values`.

Finally, we sync our `store` to save the `record`, clear out our form `values` and close the form by setting the active item back to our `CurrentList` view (`0`).

Editing and completing a task

For editing a task, we are going to use the form we just created, but we need to load it up with the currently selected record. For completing a task, we just need a button.

To do this we will add a toolbar with two buttons to our **CurrentDetails** panel. We should probably add a **Spacer** object between the two buttons like we did with our previous toolbar.

Each button also needs a **tap** event added to it in the **Config** section, under **Events**.

For the **Edit** button, set the **tap** function to:

```
var currentTab = this.getActiveItem();
var DetailsPanel = currentTab.getActiveItem();

currentTab.setActiveItem(2);
var formPanel = currentTab.getActiveItem();
formPanel.setRecord(DetailsPanel.getRecord());

this.setActiveItem(currentTab);

var backButton = Ext.getCmp('backButton');
backButton.hide();
```

This code grabs `record` from the `DetailsPanel` panel and loads this into `formPanel`. Setting this `record` on the form also sets the value of our hidden field to the correct `id` value for our record. We then display the form as before and hide the **Back** button.

For our Complete Task button, we need to get `record` from `DetailsPanel` and set the values for `completed` (a date) and `isCompleted` (a Boolean). We do that by setting the tap event function to this:

```
var currentTab = this.getActiveItem();
var detailsPanel = currentTab.getActiveItem();

var record = detailsPanel.getRecord();

record.set('completed', new Date());
record.set('isComplete', true);

var store = Ext.data.StoreManager.lookup('TaskStore');
store.sync();

this.setActiveItem(1);
var completedList = this.getActiveItem();
var completedStore = completedList.getActiveItem().getStore();
```

```
completedStore.add(record);
completedList.getActiveItem().refresh();

currentTab.setActiveItem(0);

var backButton = Ext.getCmp('backButton');
backButton.hide();
```

This gets our `record` as before, sets our two values, and syncs `TaskStore`. This sync will also cause the filter on `TaskStore` to prevent the record from displaying in our `Current` list.

Next we add the record to `CompletedStore` and refresh the view for our `completed` list. We finish up by returning the user to the **Current** list and hiding the **Back** button.

Testing the application

If we did everything correctly, you should be able to open the `app.html` file in Safari (or Chrome) and test the application. Try putting the editing and marking tasks as completed. Be sure to use the JavaScript console in your browser to track down issues and view errors.

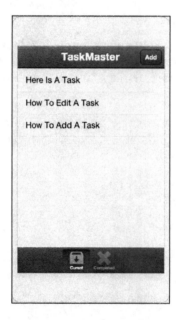

Extra credit

Task managing applications come in a variety of designs, with a wide variety of features. Everyone seems to have their own preference for tracking tasks. You can use this application as a base for your own personal task management application. These are a few ideas for taking the application to the next level:

- Add styles in the CSS file based on the priority of the tasks in the list and details
- Add a way to sort the tasks by date and priority
- Customize the `CurrentDetails` and `CompletedDetails` templates to add icons for priority

Summary

In this chapter we discussed the basic setup for an application using local storage, including:

- The basics of the Sencha Architect application
- Creating data stores to use local storage and a task model
- Creating lists and details for our data stores to use
- Creating events to switch between the **List** and **Details** views
- Creating buttons to control navigation and launch our forms
- Creating forms for editing and adding new tasks

In the next chapter we will take a look at using layouts and templates to create a more complex and visually appealing application.

2
A Feed Reader

In our first project, Task Manager, we explored some of the basics of Sencha Architect. We also covered some of the ways to store, edit, and display data in Sencha Touch.

This chapter will explore three new areas:

- The NavigationView
- Loading remote data
- Creating complex layouts with Sencha XTemplate

In this chapter we will build an RSS reader to grab news feeds from a list of sites and display the contents of those feeds in a complex pattern of columns and rows:

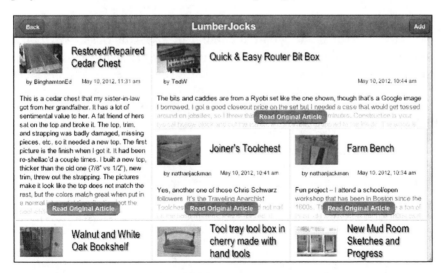

The newsreader will also build on the Sencha Touch `NavigationView` component to automate a number of helpful navigation elements for touch devices.

The basic application

Our basic application will start off much the same way as our previous application:

- A `NavigationView` component to hold all our view components
- A list to display feeds
- A store to hold the list data
- A model to describe the data
- A form to add items to the list

We will spend most of our time setting up `NavigationView` and a much briefer time covering the additional components, since these are very similar to what we did in *Chapter 1, A Simple Task List*.

An overview of NavigationView

In *Chapter 1, A Simple Task List*, we manually coded a Back button into our Details view. The Back button was hidden by default and only displayed when an item in the list was clicked on and the Details view appeared. The Back button returned our user to the main list of tasks and then hid itself until it was needed again.

In our new Feed Reader application, we will use `NavigationView`, which handles all of this functionality automatically. `NavigationView` functions similar to a card layout where a number of panels can be hidden or displayed based on the active item for the view.

However, unlike a card layout, where the items are typically declared when the layout is created, `NavigationView` typically adds items dynamically using the `push()` function to add panels and other items for display. For example, let's assume we have a `NavigationView` component called `MainView` that contains a list view with a list of items. We also have a details panel called `Details`. When the user clicks on an item in the list, we can call:

```
var main = Ext.getCmp('MainView');
var details = Ext.create('MyApp.view.Details', {
    title: 'Something Cool'
});
main.push(details);
```

This code will push a copy of our Details view onto `NavigationView` (`MainView`). `NavigationView` will use an animation transition to slide the new Details panel into place, automatically create the Back button for us, and then set the title of our Navigation bar to `Something Cool`. It also handles all of the behind-the-scenes code for taking us back to our main list when the Back button is clicked.

This makes `NavigationView` a very handy component to serve as the foundation for our application.

Let's begin by creating a new Sencha Touch application in Sencha Architect. For this application we are going to target the iPad tablet sized screen. This will give us more room to create an interesting display. We will also show you how to adjust the screen for iPhone and mobile phone users on the fly.

Use the **Size** menu at the bottom of the design area to select iPad as our screen size and drag a **NavigationView** object from the toolbox onto the iPad image in our display area. In the **Config** section, set **userAlias** to **MainView** so that we can reference it later.

Next, we need to add a **List** view to **MainView** and give it a **Store** (with a **LocalStorage** proxy) and **Model**, just as we did in *Chapter 1, A Simple Task List*:

1. Start by adding a model and configure it as follows:
   ° Set `userClassName` to `Feed`
   ° Add three fields:
       ° `id` **as** `int`
       ° `name` **as** `string`
       ° `url` **as** `string`

2. Next, add the store and configure it as follows:
   ° A `LocalStorage` proxy
   ° Set `userClassName` to `FeedStore`
   ° Set `storeId` to `FeedStore`
   ° Set `model` to `Feed`

3. Finally configure the list:

- ° Set `title` to `Feed Bag`
- ° Set `itemTpl` to `<div>{name}</div>`
- ° Set `id` to `FeedList`
- ° Set `store` to `FeedStore`

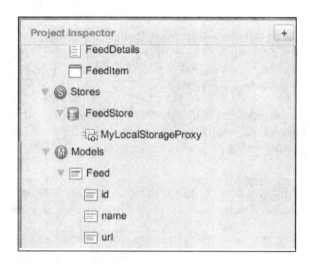

Adding the form

Since our form is pretty simple this time (and to add a bit of variety) we are going to use a sheet to display our form. The sheet can be set to slide in from the top, bottom, or sides of the screen. It can also be set to pop in from the center.

In this case, we do not want the sheet to be a child of our **MainView** container; we only want to create it when we need it, not when the application launches. To do this, we drag the **Sheet** object over to **Project Inspector** and drop it on the **Views** icon. This will create **Sheet** as a separate view from our **MainView** container.

Configure the sheet as follows:

- Set `userClassName` to `AddSheet`
- Set `enter` to `top`
- Set `exit` to `bottom`

- Set stretch to true
- Set stretchY to true

Next we will add a **Form Panel** object to our sheet with the following items: a **Container**, two **Text Field,** and two **Button** objects.

The container is simply a place to give the user some instructions. Set the **html** attribute to:

```
'Add an RSS feed URL and a Name. Feed URLs should be in the format:
http://feedURL.com'
```

Configure the two text fields as follows:

- For **Field 1**:
  - ° Set id to name
  - ° Set name to name
  - ° Set label to Name
  - ° Set margin to 3 0 3 0

- For **Field 2**:
  - ° Set id to url
  - ° Set name to url
  - ° Set label to URL
  - ° Set margin to 3 0 3 0

Configure the two buttons like so:

- For **Button 1**:
  - ° Set id to SaveButton
  - ° Set text to Save
  - ° Set margin to 10

- For **Button 2**:
  - ° Set id to CancelButton
  - ° Set text to Cancel
  - ° Set margin to 10

Next, we need to add tap listeners for our two buttons. In the **Event** section of **Config** for each button, click on the **+** button and select **Basic Event Binding**. When the menu appears, choose **tap**:

For the Cancel button, our tap function is pretty simple:

```
this.down('formpanel').reset();
this.hide();
```

Inside the function, `this` refers to our Sheet view. The code travels down into the sheet to find the form and then clears out all the field values. The sheet then hides itself.

The Save button works much the same way as the one from our previous chapter:

```
var formPanel = this.down('formpanel');

var values = formPanel.getValues();

var store = Ext.data.StoreManager.lookup('FeedStore');

var record = Ext.ModelMgr.create(values, 'MyApp.model.Feed');
store.add(record);
store.sync();

this.hide();
```

We move down from the Sheet view (`this`) to get our form panel. We then get the values from our form and find our store. Next, a new Feed record is created using the model manager and populated with the values from our form. Finally, we add the record to the store, sync the store to save it, and then hide the sheet.

Next, we need a way to show the sheet for adding Feed items.

Back to the navigation view

In our **MainView** component, we need to add a **Navigation Bar** object to the **Config** section using the + button next to **Navigation Bar**. This navigation bar will display our Back button and our titles. It will also give us a place to put the Add button that will show our sheet for adding feed items.

We don't need to change any configuration options for the navigation bar, so just drag a new **Button** object onto it for our Add button. Set the button's configuration like so:

- Set `align` to `right`
- Set `text` to `Add`
- Set `id` to `addButton`

Then we need to add a tap event listener like we did with our other buttons. The code for our tap event needs to create a new instance of `AddSheet` and display it. It also has to do a bit of thinking before it creates the sheet to make sure that there is no sheet that is existing already.

```
var sheet = Ext.getCmp('AddSheet');
if(!Ext.isDefined(sheet)) {
    sheet = Ext.create('MyApp.view.AddSheet');
    Ext.Viewport.add(sheet);
}
sheet.show();
```

The first thing we do is call `Ext.getCmp` to see if there is already an existing sheet. This is because we set up our Save and Cancel buttons to hide the sheet, which does not destroy it. It's still a part of the application (still in memory), but it is not being displayed.

If we have used the Add button previously, then `Ext.getCmp` will return a valid component. This is what we are checking on line two with `!Ext.isDefined(sheet)`. If the sheet is not defined yet (not created), we use `Ext.create('MyApp.view. AddSheet');` to make our sheet and then add it to the viewport.

At this point, we should have a valid component for our sheet and then we can just call `sheet.show();`.

Our application should now be able to add and display new Feed items to the list. Test the application to make sure everything is in working order by using Safari to open the `app.html` file in the folder where your project is saved:

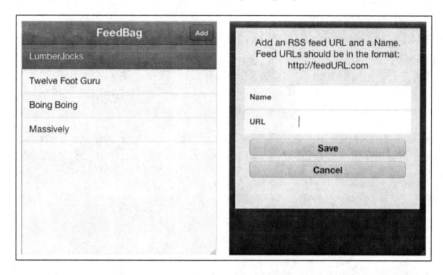

Next we need to add the logic for our MainView navigation view that will allow us to display a nice layout page for each of our feeds.

Adding the controller

Add a controller to the project by dragging it onto the **Controllers** section of **Project Inspector**. You can find it in **Toolbox** under **Behaviors**. Set the **userClassName** property of the controller to `FeedController`.

We also want to add a **Reference** property in the controller for **mainView**. Click on the **Add** button next to **Reference** and set the **ref** property to **mainView** and **Selector** to **MainView** (the selector needs to match our **userAlias** instance for the main navigation view).

Adding this reference will allow us to easily grab our MainView navigation by calling `this.getMainView()` anywhere inside the controller.

> **Wait, shouldn't it be getmainView instead of getMainView?**
>
> One of the things that should be pointed out in this example is that when the reference is created, Sencha automatically creates a "getter" function for the referenced component. Even though our reference has a lowercase m, the getMainView function changes this to uppercase, M. Given the case sensitive nature of JavaScript, this automatic case switch can lead to quite a bit of hair pulling and colorful language.

Now that we have our reference, we need to add an action to perform when the user taps on the list of feeds. Click on the + button next to **Actions** and set the following information:

- Set controlQuery to #FeedList
- Set targetType to Ext.dataview.List
- Set fn to onListItemTap
- Set name to itemtap

Next, we need to double-click on the **itemtap** action to bring up our code editor. This is the code that will be fired when the list is tapped. Notice that the function is already set up to pass us a number of useful items including the dataview itself and the record for the item the user tapped on. We will set this action to call another function like so:

```
onListItemTap: function(dataview, index, target, record, e, options) {
    this.createFeedDetailsView(record.get('name'), record.get('url'));
}
```

We will pass along the record name and url to our new createFeedDetailsView function using record.get().

If we take a look at our **Code** view for the controller, it should look something like this:

```
Ext.define('MyApp.controller.FeedController', {
    extend: 'Ext.app.Controller',
    config: {
        refs: {
            mainView: 'MainView'
        },
```

```
        control: {
            "#FeedList": {
                itemtap: 'onListItemTap'
            }
        }
    },

    onListItemTap: function(dataview, index, target, record, e,
options) {
        this.createFeedDetailsView(record.get('name'), record.
get('url'));
    }
});
```

Here we see that Sencha has set up our `FeedController` function to extend the main `Ext.app.Contoller` component. This means it inherits all of the basic functions for the `Ext.app.Contoller` component.

In the `config` section, we see our reference set up in the `refs` section. The `controls` section tells the controller which component to listen to (`#FeedList`), which event to listen for (`itemtap`), and which function to call when the event happens (`onListItemTap`).

The last thing we need to do here is create the code for our `createFeedDetailsView` function. This code needs to use the URL to grab the RSS feed, create a new view, and push it onto the main navigation view.

Before we do that, there are a few things that we need to consider: how do we get the data from the remote source and how can we format it in an easy-to-use structure (JSON)?

To answer these questions, we need to have a better understanding of how Sencha Touch communicates with external servers, and some of the limitations involved in these types of transactions.

Getting the data from a remote source

For security reasons, JavaScript (and thus Sencha Touch) is not allowed to make AJAX requests to other domains. This means that if your application resides on `myCoolApp.com` and you make an AJAX request to the RSS feed at `boingboing.net`, it will be denied.

The reason for this is the **Same Origin Policy**, which states that certain browser functions like cookies and AJAX requests can't be shared between different servers. The reasoning being that JavaScript executes within the browser on the end user's computer. This gives JavaScript some unique abilities to interact with the user without having to constantly be in contact with a web server. Once the web browser loads the initial JavaScript files, they are stored on the user's machine until the cache is cleared. This means the application can continue to function when offline.

However, as we all know, with great power comes great responsibility. The ability to run remote code on a user's computer can lead to people doing very bad things. AJAX requests in particular are problematic because they can happen without any direct request from the user.

For this reason, cross-domain AJAX requests in JavaScript are a very bad idea. While it may be easy enough to determine that your own code has honorable intentions, unchecked code from another domain can be potentially hostile.

If you would like to learn more about same origin policy, this Wikipedia article is a good place to start:
`http://en.wikipedia.org/wiki/Same_origin_policy`

Enter the JSONP proxy

We can get around the same origin policy by using Sencha's JSONP proxy component to send the request. This component injects `<script>` tags containing the proxy URL directly into the DOM to get around the cross-domain limitation. The script tag looks like a regular JavaScript embed tag, something like this:

```
<script src="http://somedomain.com/articles?callback=someFunction"></
script>
```

The response gets included as if it were any other JavaScript include. The JSONP proxy uses the `callback` function (which is generated automatically) to process this data and send it back to the proxy. The one caveat here is that the response has to be in JSON in order for the `callback` function to correctly process it.

A full explanation of cross-site scripting issues can be found here:
`http://en.wikipedia.org/wiki/Cross-site_scripting`
and an overview of the JSONP proxy component can be found
here: `http://docs.sencha.com/touch/2-0/#!/api/Ext.data.proxy.JsonP`.

This brings us to another issue that we will run into with RSS feeds: they are formatted in XML instead of JSON. Since we need the JSONP store for cross-site requests and a JSON-encoded response for our `callback` function to process, XML won't work for us without a bit more fiddling.

This basically gives us two options. The first option would be to use another programming language to write something that would make the proxy request for us. This would include languages such as PHP, Ruby, ASP, and Perl, which run on the local server along with our application and are not under the same security restrictions as JavaScript.

A local proxy would receive the request from our store along with the variables and make a request to the remote server with our variables. The remote server would then send the request back to our local proxy that would then pass it back to the store in whatever format we need. This is a fine enough way to accomplish the task, but it is also overkill for our simple application. Don't worry, we will get to the overkill later on.

We also have a second option called **YQL**, the **Yahoo Query Language**, which we will be using in our application.

Yahoo Query Language (YQL)

The **Yahoo Query Language** (**YQL**) was developed as a way to search open data sources in a language similar to **Structured Query Language** (**SQL**), a standard language for dealing with database information.

A typical SQL request might look something like this:

```
select * from users where lastname = 'Scalzi';
```

This would grab all the records in the `users` table where the last name was `Scalzi`. The * character tells our query to grab all the data for the record.

A YQL request is similar in structure and might look something like this:

```
select * from rss where url= "http://feeds.boingboing.net/boingboing/
iBag"
```

This request would return the RSS feed data from `boingboing.net`.

 YQL has access to a tremendous number of open data sources. To read up on the sources and get a better idea of what is possible in YQL, go to: `http://developer.yahoo.com/yql/`.

Now that we can get information from our data source, we need to figure out how to have it sent in a format our Sencha Touch application can understand.

One of the bonuses we get with YQL is that our results can be set up to return in a number of different formats, including the JSON format we want for our application. Before we set up the YQL query for our application we should take a look at the actual JSON that gets returned from the query. We can do this using the YQL console.

The YQL console

The YQL console (located at: `http://developer.yahoo.com/yql/console/`) offers an easy way to test the various YQL commands and immediately see the results:

Enter the the query shown in the previous screenshot into the console, select JSON, and click on the **TEST** button.

You will get back the results as a large bundle of JSON starting with:

```
cbfunc({
  "query": {
   "count": 30,
   "created": "2012-05-10T15:25:40Z",
   "lang": "en-US"...
```

The `cbfunc` header is the callback function our JSONP store is going to use to process the response. We don't need to worry about this since the store deals with it automatically. The first piece of information we need is the `count` parameter listed inside the `query` array. We can reference this in our code as `query.count`.

Further down in the results you will see the actual items we need to use for our dataview:

```
"results": {
   "item": [
    {
      "title": "Minecraft heads to consoles",
      "link": "http://feeds.boingboing.net/~r/boingboing/iBag/~3/
iyy5tLpUCpU/minecraft-heads-to-consoles.html",
      "category": [
       "Short",
       "Games",
       "minecraft"
      ],
      "creator": {
       "dc": "http://purl.org/dc/elements/1.1/",
       "content": "Rob Beschizza"
      }...
```

Since these results are nested down in the `query` array, we will need to tell the store to set our `rootProperty` property as `query.results.item`. This `item` array holds the 30 listings returned by our query.

When these items are part of the store we will have access to each of the individual pieces by name. For example, `title` from the previous code will give us `Minecraft heads to consoles` and `creator.content` will give us `Rob Beschizza`. All of this data will be accessible in the item template of our dataview.

You will need to set up a data model to grab the pieces of information you are interested in. For our purposes, we will be using the following data model:

```
Ext.define('MyApp.model.FeedItem', {
    extend: 'Ext.data.Model',
    config: {
        fields: [
            {
                name: 'title'
            },
            {
                name: 'link'
            },
            {
                name: 'pubDate',
                type: 'date'
            },
            {
                mapping: 'encoded.content',
                name: 'content'
            },
            {
                mapping: 'creator.content',
                name: 'creator'
            },
            {
                name: 'description'
            },
            {
                name: 'thumbnail'
            },
            {
                name: 'author'
            }
        ]
    }
});
```

Notice that we need to map some of the more deeply nested items such as `encoded.content` and `creator.content`. This model will give us all of the data items we need for our view.

Let's see how it all fits together.

Meanwhile, back at the controller

If you remember, back in our `FeedController` function we had a tap handler that looked like this:

```
onListItemTap: function(dataview, index, target, record, e, options) {
        this.createFeedDetailsView(record.get('name'), record.
get('url'));
    }
```

We now need to set up the `createFeedDetailsView` function and get it to create our data store for connecting to the YQL server.

Add the new function by clicking on the **+** button next to **functions** and setting the **Config** value for **fn** to `createFeedDetailsView`. Then add two **params**: `name` and `url`.

In the code editor, we want our function to grab the name and URL that we passed from our tap function and create a new data store. We will then load the store and use it to feed data into a new dataview. Lastly, we will push this new dataview onto our main navigation view for display.

The code looks like this:

```
createFeedDetailsView: function(name, url) {
    var newURL = 'http://query.yahooapis.com/v1/public/yql?',
        yql = {
            q: 'select * from rss where url="' + url + '"',
            format: 'json'
        };

    newURL += Ext.Object.toQueryString(yql);
    var details = Ext.create(
    'MyApp.view.FeedDetails', {
        title: name,
        store: Ext.create('MyApp.store.FeedItemStore', {
            proxy: {
                type: 'jsonp',
                url: newURL,
                reader: {
                    type: 'json',
                    rootProperty: 'query.results.item',
                    totalProperty: 'query.count'
                }
            }
```

```
      })
    });
    details.getStore().load();
    this.getMainView().push(details);
  }
```

Our first line sets up our URL to the main connection point for the YQL server:

```
var newURL = 'http://query.yahooapis.com/v1/public/yql?'
```

We then set up our variables using the format required by YQL. This includes a query string (q) and a format type for the return value, which will be JSON:

```
yql = {
q: 'select * from rss where url="' + url + '"',
         format: 'json'
};
```

Next, we convert our variables into a Query String and add them to our URL like so:

```
newURL += Ext.Object.toQueryString(yql);
```

Next, we need to add a new dataview to our main navigation view. We will create the actual view in the next section, but for now we can in put the code to display it here like so:

```
var details = Ext.create(
    'MyApp.view.FeedDetails', {
        title: name,
        store: Ext.create('MyApp.store.FeedItemStore', {
            proxy: {
                type: 'jsonp',
                url: newURL,
                reader: {
                    type: 'json',
                    rootProperty: 'query.results.item',
                    totalProperty: 'query.count'
                }
            }
        })
    });
```

This creates the `details` view using `MyApp.view.FeedDetails` (a view we will add a bit later) and set up the store for it with our `newURL` string that we created at the beginning of the function.

Our `reader` configuration is set for `json` and the `rootProperty` and `totalProperty` configurations are set to the default values that get returned from the YQL server for each of those attributes. `rootProperty` tells the reader where to start looking for results and `totalProperty` tells the reader how many results we have gotten.

Finally, we load our store and add the new dataview to our main navigation panel:

```
details.getStore().load();
this.getMainView().push(details);
```

Now that we have the store code in place, it's time to create the dataview for `MyApp.view.FeedDetails`, which is needed to display the feed data.

The details dataview

When using Sencha Touch, it's very easy to think of a dataview as just a fancy list. However, that tends to lock people into the list aspects of the dataview while ignoring the possibility of more complex layouts.

For example, a newspaper-style layout is a great use of a dataview. The layout is a collection of articles with titles, dates, authors, and content. However it sidesteps the standard concept of a list and replaces it with a more visually interesting layout:

A newspaper-style layout works well on a larger tablet-sized screen, but it would be difficult to read on a smaller phone screen. We need a way to change the layout of our application based on the user's device.

Fortunately for us, not only does Sencha Touch understand the difference between devices, it also leverages the power of the HTML5 standard, which also understands different platforms and devices.

We will cover how Sencha Touch manages the different devices in a later chapter. For now, we are going to use CSS media queries to load different style sheets based on the device. Before we get too deeply into that, we need to create the dataview and the XTemplate.

An **XTemplate** is basically an HTML template with a few extra bells and whistles. The XTemplate takes the data you supply and uses it to fill out the template by substituting any value in curly braces, with the corresponding value from your data.

For example, suppose that you have an XTemplate that looks like this:

```
<div class="name">{name}</div>
```

In this example, the XTemplate will search your data for a variable called name and insert it into the template where we have {name}. You can use these curly braces to reference any of the fields in a data record.

The XTemplate also offers us the opportunity to add logic (the "if...then" statements, simple math, and more) to the HTML template.

Let's create one for our dataview to see how it all fits together.

Create a new dataview in Sencha Architect and set userAlias to feeddetails and userClassName to FeedDetails. Set the store configuration to use our FeedItemStore we created earlier.

Next we need to create an itemTpl XTemplate. You should see a listing for **itemTpl** underneath the new **FeedDetails** dataview in the **Project Inspector** and if you select it, the **Code** editor will show the default **itemTpl** for editing.

Our itemTpl will need to account for any missing data in the RSS feed (RSS feeds are often missing things such as descriptions, icons, and other elements). We also need to translate the dates into something Sencha Touch understands, and we need to loop through some of the nested array elements returned by our YQL request.

Let's look at the full template first, and then we will go through the different sections to cover what we are doing:

```
itemTpl: [
    '<tpl if="thumbnail">',
    '   <article class="hasThumbnail">',
    '       <tpl else>',
    '           <article>',
    '       </tpl>',
    '       <header>',
    '           <div class="headline">',
    '               <tpl if="thumbnail">',
    '                   <tpl for="thumbnail">',
    '                       <img class="thumbnail" src="{url}" height="{height}"
width="{width}" alt="Thumbnail" />',
    '                   </tpl>',
    '               </tpl>',
    '               <h2>{title}</h2>',
    '           </div>',
    '           <tpl if="creator"><p class="creator">by {creator}</p>',
    '           <tpl elseif="author"><p class="creator">by {author}</p></
tpl>',
    '           <tpl if="pubDate"><time datetime="{pubDate:date("c")}">{p
ubDate:date("M j, Y, g:i a")}</time></tpl>',
    '       </header>',
    '       <div class="description">{description}</div>',
    '       <div class="content">',
    '           <tpl if="content.length &gt; 0">',
    '           <tpl for="content">',
    '               <tpl if="xindex == 2">{.}</tpl>',
    '           </tpl>',
    '           <tpl else>',
    '               {description}',
    '           </tpl>',
    '       </div>',
    '       <footer>',
    '           <a href="{link}">Read Original Article</a>',
    '       </footer>',
    '       </article>'
]
```

Our first section looks to see if we have a thumbnail for the article using `<tpl if="thumbnail">`. If we do, then we style the article container with a class of hasThumbnail, if not, we just use the basic `<article>` tag. This will let us do different things with CSS depending on if we have the thumbnail or not.

Next we begin constructing our header section, creating a `<div>` tag with a class of `headline` that contains our `thumbnail` and `title` variables for the article. We also check to see if we have a `thumbnail` and then loop through the data for thumbnails (using `<tpl for="thumbnail">`) to gain access to the individual elements (`height`, `width`, `url`) in the `thumbnail` array.

Next, we close out the headline `div` tag and add our author/creator and the date to our template. RSS feeds can use either author or creator to refer to the person who wrote the article. We use `<tpl if="creator">` and `<tpl elseif="author">` to make sure we get one or the other if they are available.

We then check to see if we have a date and convert it to a format we like using:

```
<tpl if="pubDate"><time datetime="{pubDate:date("c")}">{pubDate:date(
"M j, Y, g:i a")}</time></tpl>
```

Notice that we have also wrapped the date inside an HTML5 `<time>` element, which provides contextual data to the browser, allowing features such as localization, visual timelines, and adding events to calendars. We set `datetime` to a format the browser understands, and then we set the displayed date and time to something a bit more user friendly.

Next we format our description and content. The description is pretty straight forward, but the content is a slightly different matter.

Depending on the size of the device, we may not want to show the full content div, just the shorter description div. We can set our CSS to only show the `<div class="description">` or the `<div class="content">` block, depending on the device. However, the content element is also optional, so if we have no content we need to show the description in the `<div class="content">` block instead.

To make things more complicated, the content returned by our YQL query is a nested array with two elements: a content definition link, which we can ignore, and the actual content that we want. To do this, we loop through the content and count the loops using the built-in `xindex` variable to add the second data element to our XTemplate (`{.}` is the current data element in the loop).

```
'            <tpl for="content">',
'              <tpl if="xindex == 2">{.}</tpl>',
'            </tpl>'
```

Finally we close out our XTemplate with a footer and a link to the original article.

We will take a look at some other XTemplate options in later chapters, or you can see a full list of the options in the online documentation at:

```
http://docs.sencha.com/touch/2-0/#!/api/Ext.XTemplate
```

And now, the CSS

As our container currently exists, the display would not be very interesting. It's just simple blocks of data one after another. While this is fine for small devices such as phones, it's a bit dull for larger tablet displays.

We are going to address this by creating these three separate CSS files:

- `feedbag.css`
- `feedbag-tablet-portrait.css`
- `feedback-tablet-landscape.css`

We will link these files in our `app.html` file like this:

```
<link rel="stylesheet" type="text/css" href="feedbag.css"/>
<link rel="stylesheet" type="text/css" href="feedbag-tablet-
portrait.css" media="only screen and (min-device-width : 700px)"/>
<link rel="stylesheet" type="text/css" href="feedbag-tablet-
landscape.css" media="only screen and (min-device-width : 700px) and
(orientation : landscape)"/>
```

The first file, `feedbag.css`, contains all of our default styles for colors, font sizes, and so on. It also contains the small phone screen styles, which only show our image and header in the list view.

This set of styles gets overridden by the next file, which contains our portrait styles for tablet computers (minimum device width: 700 px). This file uses the same styles from the previous file, but organizes our content into two columns of blocks. It also displays the description block in the list view.

The last file is used for tablet devices in landscape orientation. As before, it will override some of the styles in the previous files to further enhance the layout. In this case, we will float all of the blocks and set them to different widths to give the layout a more organic feel.

Rather than dig through the entire CSS file, we want to focus on the last file, as it is the most complex of the files — `feedback-tablet-landscape.css`.

In this CSS file, we will take a series of steps to get to this layout, starting from a grid of 12 items and modifying the widths and heights to give us a more fluid layout. Take a look at the following figure to see what we mean:

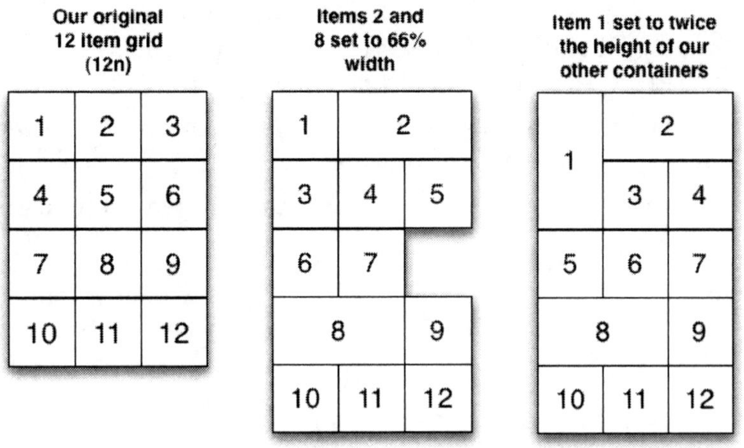

The CSS Layout Progression

In `feedback-tablet-landscape.css` our first block of CSS looks like this:

```
div.x-dataview-item {
    width: 33%;
    float: left;
}
```

We can fit three blocks of content across the screen in landscape mode, so we set each item to a default width of 33 percent.

The next block of CSS uses the nth-of-type selector to change the sizes of some of our item blocks:

```
div.x-dataview-item:nth-of-type(12n+2), div.x-dataview-item:nth-of-
type(12n+8) {
    width: 66%;
}
```

This rather complicated looking CSS says the following:

1. We are only looking at items tagged with `div.x-dataview-item` (which are our item blocks).

2. We want `nth-of-type(12n+2)`, which in this case means that we are looking at everything in blocks of 12 items (`12n`). Of those 12 items, we want to apply this style to the second (`+2`) of those items.

3. We also want to do the same thing for the 8th member of our set of twelve (`nth-of-type(12n+8)`).

4. For our two items, we want to set the width to 66 percent (twice our normal article width).

By dealing with these items in blocks of 12 we end up with a more random and natural feel to our layout, rather than if we had simply set every third item to a wider size.

The next two styles ensure that we don't end up with one or two items dangling off the end of our layout. First we give our last item in the list a width of 99 percent:

```
div.x-dataview-item:last-child {
    width: 99%;
}
```

However, if our last item is the last in a row of three, we don't want it to have a 99 percent width as this would push it down a row and make things look weird. It should just be the regular size (33 percent):

```
div.x-dataview-item:nth-of-type(12n+7), div.x-dataview-item:nth-of-
type(12n) {
    width: 33% !important;
}
```

The `12n+7` (the seventh item and the twelfth) items are the only two items in our set of twelve that may end up as the last item in a row of three.

We use `!important` in our CSS to make sure that our `width` definition overrides any other `width` values that might be applied by other (parent) classes.

We also don't want it to be 99 percent if it's the last item in a row with only two items. In this case, the last item just needs to have a width of 66 percent:

```
div.x-dataview-item:nth-of-type(12n+6):last-child {
    width: 66% !important;
}
```

Lastly, just to give us a break in the vertical rhythm of the layout, we make the first item in the set of 12 be twice as tall as the rest:

```
div.x-dataview-item:nth-of-type(12n+1), div.x-dataview-item:nth-of-
type(12n+1) article {
    min-height: 400px;
    max-height: 400px;
}
```

While these types of CSS selectors can seem a bit daunting at first, they offer a wide range of layout options beyond the standard Sencha Touch options.

If you look at the other two style sheets, you'll see that the styles get much simpler. The `feedbag-tablet-portrait.css` file is a simple two-column layout, while the plain `feedbag.css` file is a one-column layout with description content blocks hidden, for small devices such as iPhones. It would be possible to further customize the layouts based on device, or screen pixel density, but we'll leave that as an exercise for you.

Homework

In the support files for this chapter, we have also added a details view called `FeedItem.js`, which is a simple panel that is called from the controller when an item in our dataview is clicked on. The panel is pushed onto the navigation view in the same way as our feed details view. The panel contains a simple XTemplate loaded from the record passed in the tap function. If you explore this code, you will also see that we added a bit of animation to make the transition slicker.

This type of application can easily be modified to serve as a mobile version for any website with an RSS feed. You can also use the additional data in the RSS feed to add more information to the display, or modify the look and feel through CSS.

Summary

In this chapter we discussed:

- The basic application setup for the Feed Reader application
- Creating data to use a remote data source
- Potential issues with making Ajax requests to a remote server
- Using the YQL system to query data from the web and return it as JSON
- Setting up a complex XTemplate for our dataview
- Using CSS styles and selectors to create a visually interesting and adaptable dataview display

In the next chapter we will take a look at using a compiled Sencha Touch application to take advantage of features that are beyond a standard web based application.

3
Going Command Line

For our third project, we are going to change it up a bit from our reliance on Sencha Designer. In this chapter, we will explore the uses of Sencha's free command-line tool called **Sencha Cmd**. Using this new toolset, we can quickly generate the basic skeleton of a new application, create controllers and models, and compile our application into a native application for iOS and Android.

The application for this chapter is a simple time tracker for scheduling break times. We call it **TimeCop**.

The TimeCop application lets the user set an alert for a certain amount of time in the future (say 15 minutes for break time). Once the time is set, the start button is pressed, and an alert will appear after the appropriate delay. The simplicity of this application will allow us to focus on some of the details and issues involved in using Sencha Cmd and creating a compiled application.

In this chapter we will cover:

- Creating a basic application using Sencha Cmd
- Features of Sencha Cmd
- Creating a developer account for iOS
- Provisioning an application for iOS
- Creating the correct file configurations
- Adding native notifications
- Compiling the application

The basic application

The TimeCop application is designed as a simple way to track when your break or lunch time is over. The application consists of four main buttons labeled **5**, **10**, **30**, and **60**. Clicking on any of these buttons will cause a fifth button to appear in the center. This button will display the amount of time the user selected and serves as a start button. The user can add differing amounts of allotted time by clicking the four outer buttons multiple times.

For example, clicking on the **5** button twice will place 10 minutes on our allotted time in the center button. Clicking the **5** button once and then clicking the **10** button once will place **15** minutes on our allotted time. Once the desired amount of time is reached, the user clicks the center button and the countdown begins. When the countdown ends, the user is alerted via a device notification.

Installing Sencha Cmd

Sencha Cmd is a separate download from our Sencha Touch code and can be found at: http://www.sencha.com/products/sencha-cmd/download. The download is available for Windows, OSX, and Linux (32 and 64 bit). When you unzip the downloaded file, you can double-click on it to install Sencha Cmd.

For this book we are using Sencha Cmd Version 3 (at least 3.0.0.250 is required). Detailed installation instructions can be found at: http://docs.sencha.com/ext-js/4-1/#!/guide/command.

Once you have installed Sencha Cmd, you can open up the command line on your computer as follows:

- On Mac OSX, go to **Applications** and launch **Terminal**
- On Windows, go to **Start | Run** and type cmd

From here you will need to change to the directory where your Sencha Touch files are installed (not the Sencha Cmd files we just downloaded, but your original Sencha Touch 2.1 files):

```
cd /path/to/Sencha-touch-directory/
```

Once you have changed directories, type:

```
sencha
```

You should see something like the following screenshot in your terminal:

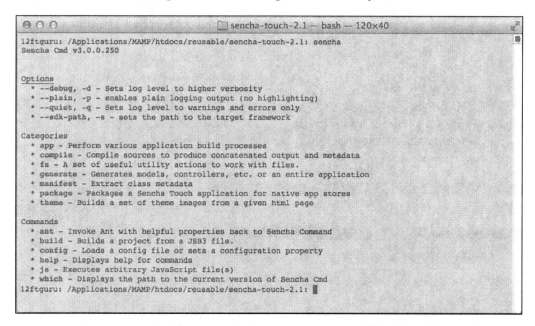

This text gives you a quick overview of the commands available and the version of Sencha Cmd you are currently running (this should be Version 3.0.0.250 or higher).

Advantages of Sencha Cmd

One of the big advantages of Sencha Cmd is that, unlike Designer, it is provided free of charge. Sencha Cmd can also handle a lot of our repetitive coding for us. For example, you can generate a complete application skeleton by executing the following command from your Sencha Touch 2.1 directory:

```
sencha generate app MyApp /path/to/www/myapp
```

This will create a new application called MyApp in the directory specified.

You can also create models from the command line using something like this in your new application directory:

```
sencha generate model Contact --fields=id:int,firstName,
lastName,email,phone
```

This will create a complete model for a user with the five specified fields, and will make sure that the id field is an integer.

A note about Sencha Cmd and directories

When generating the skeleton for an application, you will need to be in the Sencha Touch 2.1 directory. Once the application is generated, you will need to change to the new application directory to execute commands for generating models and controllers, or for building and compiling the application.

You can also use the build command to automatically optimize your application for production. This includes resolving dependencies so that your application only includes the code it actually needs. Additionally, the build command sets up HTML5 application caching, minimizes all the JavaScript and CSS, as well as other speed and caching enhancements.

Let's take a look at how this works by generating our TimeCop application.

Generating the application skeleton

We start with the create command in our previous example:

```
sencha generate app TimeCop /Library/Documents/Webserver/timecop
```

You will also need to make sure that you adjust the output path to suit your development environment.

As we noted previously, this command should be executed from your Sencha Touch 2.1 directory in order to work correctly. You can also specify the Sencha Touch directory by using the -sdk option like this:

```
sencha -sdk /Path/to /sencha-touch-2.1 generate app
AppName /path/to/your/app/directory
```

This will create the following files and directory structure in the timecop folder:

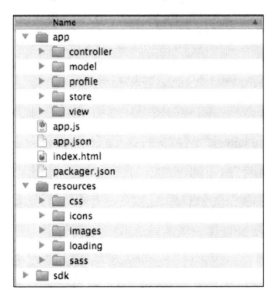

If you look at the index.html file, you will see that it already sets up the basic application and includes the following JavaScript:

```
<script id="microloader" type="text/javascript" src="touch/
microloader/development.js"></script>
```

This is the autoloader, which will automatically include the rest of the JavaScript we need. It also includes a loading indication in CSS. This will fire off while the application loads, to alert the user that things are happening behind the scenes. You shouldn't need to touch the index.html file.

The app.js file has a few more interesting pieces included:

```
Ext.Loader.setPath({
    'Ext': 'touch/src',
    'TimeCop': 'app'
});
```

```
Ext.application({
    name: 'TimeCop',

    requires: [
        'Ext.MessageBox'
    ],

    views: ['Main'],

    icon: {
        57: 'resources/icons/Icon.png',
        72: 'resources/icons/Icon~ipad.png',
        114: 'resources/icons/Icon@2x.png',
        144: 'resources/icons/Icon~ipad@2x.png'
    },

    phoneStartupScreen: 'resources/loading/Homescreen.jpg',
    tabletStartupScreen: 'resources/loading/Homescreen~ipad.jpg',

    launch: function() {
        // Destroy the #appLoadingIndicator element
        Ext.fly('appLoadingIndicator').destroy();

        // Initialize the main view
        Ext.Viewport.add(Ext.create('TimeCop.view.Main'));
    },

});
```

The `Ext.Loader.setPath` function at the top will point to our `touch` directory where all of our base Sencha Touch 2 library files are located.

The next section sets up the name of our application, our required components, our views, our icons, and the startup screens.

The `launch` section removes our loading indicator and then adds our `TimeCop.view.Main` to the viewport.

If you navigate to the folder in Safari and look at the application, you will see something like this:

Most of the actual display code for this application is contained in the `TimeCop.view.Main` file. This is the file we will modify to create our actual application.

Creating the TimeCop layout

The layout for this application consists of a vbox layout on our main container. Inside the main container is a set of three containers, each with an hbox layout and containing three additional containers. This gives us a flexible 3 x 3 grid where we can place our components:

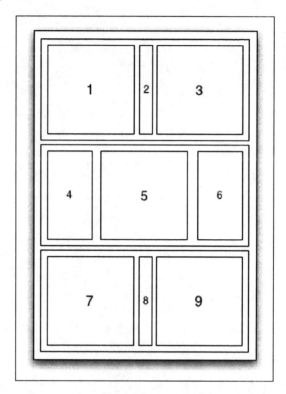

Inside of containers **1, 3, 7**, and **8** we need buttons with our four time increments. In container **5** we will place our start button. By using the vbox and hbox layouts as described later in this section we can keep our components centered regardless of the screen size.

The containers for our buttons can be given a fixed width (in this case we choose 120). The empty containers in the row are then given a flex value of 1. This will cause them to take up the rest of the available space and maintain an even spacing between our buttons regardless of screen size.

For example, our first row is laid out like so:

```
{
    xtype: 'container',
    layout: {
        type: 'hbox'
    },
    flex: 1,
    items: [
        {
            xtype: 'container',
            width: 120,
            layout: {
                type: 'fit'
            },
            items: [
                {
                    xtype: 'incrementButton',
                    text: 5

                }
            ]
        },
        {
            xtype: 'container',
            flex: 1
        },
        {
            xtype: 'container',
            layout: {
                type: 'fit'
            },
            width: 120,
            items: [
                {
                    xtype: 'incrementButton',
                    text: 10
                }
            ]
        }
    ]
}
```

You will notice that each of our buttons has an xtype type of incrementButton, but different values for text (5 and 10). We will come back to that in just a moment, but we need to take a look at our second row first.

The second hbox container row is a variation on the first row; a single fixed-width container in the center and a variable-width (flex:1) container on either side:

```
{
    xtype: 'container',
    layout: {
        type: 'hbox'
    },
    flex: 1,
    items: [
        {
            xtype: 'container',
            flex: 1
        },
        {
            xtype: 'container',
            width: '',
            layout: {
                type: 'fit'
            },
            width: 120,
            items: [
                {
                    xtype: 'button',
                    hidden: true,
                    id: 'startButton',
                    ui: 'roundStart',
                    text: 0
                }
            ]
        },
        {
            xtype: 'container',
            flex: 1
        }
    ]
}
```

Our `startButton` in the center starts out hidden by default and it will only appear when the `incrementButtons` are tapped. We set `ui` to `roundStart`, which we will use later on to style the button, and we set the `text` value of the button to `0` (we will use this value later in our `incrementButton` functions). We also add a listener for our `startButton` instance's tap event.

Our third row is simply a copy of our first row, with the button values set to `30` and `60` respectively. Both of these buttons will have `xtype:incrementButton` as in the first row.

Creating the theme

The base layout we currently have will give us a bunch of large, ugly, square buttons. We want something a bit cooler than that, so we are going to set a new theme for the application. Sencha Touch Themes use SASS and Compass to customize the user interface in a number of interesting ways.

 For more information on creating Sencha Touch themes, review the documentation and tutorial videos at: `http://docs.sencha.com/touch/2-0/#!/guide/theming`.

The first step in our theme is adding a `ui` configuration for our buttons. The four time increment buttons will have `ui: 'round'` added to their configuration options. This will give us a more pleasing circular button.

The center button will have `ui: 'roundStart'` added to its configuration options. We will make `ui` inherit all of our qualities from our original round ui and add some color changes to give us a green start button.

We can then add the following code to `app.scss`:

```scss
.x-button-round, .x-button-roundStart {
  background-color: transparent;
  background-image: none;
  width: 120px;
  padding: 10px;
  height: 120px;
  overflow:hidden;
  border: none;

  span {
    color:#333;
    font-size:24px;
    line-height:68px;
  }
}
```

```
span.x-button-label {
  display: block;
  background: -webkit-gradient(linear, left top, left bottom, color-
stop(0%,rgba(230,230,230,1)), color-stop(50%,rgba(168,168,168,1)),
color-stop(50%,rgba(168,168,168,1)), color-stop(100%,rg
ba(230,230,230,1))); /* Chrome,Safari4+ */
  position:relative;
  height:100px;
  width:100px;
  text-align:center;
  cursor:pointer;
  border:16px solid #e8e8e8;
  -webkit-border-radius: 60px;
  font-weight: 900;
  -webkit-box-shadow: inset 0 0 10px#C7C7C7, 0 0 1px 2px #bababa;
  }
}
```

The key pieces of this are -webkit-border-radius: 60px (half of our button
width/height), which makes the buttons circular, and background: -webkit-
gradient, which creates the gradient background of the buttons.

We do something similar with our start button, but we make the text white and
the background green:

```
.x-button-roundStart {
  span {
  color: white;
  }
  span.x-button-label {
  background-color: #0C0;
  background-image: -webkit-gradient(linear, 50% 0%, 50% 100%, color-
stop(0%, #1AFF1A), color-stop(50%, #00E600), color-stop(51%, #0C0),
color-stop(100%, #00B300));
  background-image: -webkit-linear-gradient(#1AFF1A, #00E600 50%, #0C0
51%, #00B300);
  background-image: linear-gradient(#1AFF1A, #00E600 50%, #0C0 51%,
#00B300);
  }
}
```

Running compass compile will regenerate the app.css file with our new styles in
it. Now that we have the basic look and feel of our application, we need to talk about
using the native APIs in a Sencha Touch application.

Creating the increment button

Since each of our increment buttons will do much the same thing, this becomes an excellent opportunity to create a button class.

To do this we will make a separate file on our view folder called `incrementButton.js`:

```
Ext.define('TimeCop.view.incrementButton', {
    extend: 'Ext.Button',
    alias: 'widget.incrementButton',
    config: {
        itemId: 'mybutton',
        ui: 'round',
        text: 5,
        listeners: [
            {
                    fn: 'onMybuttonTap',
                    event: 'tap'
            }
        ]
    }
});
```

This code extends the standard `Ext.Button` class and sets defaults for `itemID`, `text`, and `ui` (we will use `ui` later on to style the buttons). We also add a tap listener for when the user presses the button.

When our time increment button is tapped, we need to add the appropriate time to our start button in the center and display it (if it is hidden). We will do this by adding the following to our tap handler function after the `Config` section in our previous code:

```
onMybuttonTap: function(button, e, options) {
  var increment = button.getText();
  var start = Ext.getCmp('startButton');

  var startInt = start.getText();

  var total = parseInt(startInt, 10) + parseInt(increment, 10);

  start.setText(total);

  if(start.isHidden()) {
   start.show();
  }
}
```

This code grabs the text from our current button, which is 5, and then grabs the start button. We then add the values from the two buttons together and set this as the text on our start button. Since this function is now a part of the base `incrementButton`, each of our four buttons with an `xtype` of `incrementButton` will be able to use this same function. The only thing that will change is the text value of the button. This allows you to easily choose other time increments if you desire.

Using the buttons works like this: when the user first starts the application, the start button is hidden and has a text value of **0**. The user taps the **5** button and the start button appears, 5 is added to 0 and the start button's text is set to **5**. The user then taps the **10** button, causing the start button text to be increased to **15** and so on.

Creating the start button

Our start button uses a separate function to begin the timer countdown. In this case, we will add a listener to our main view:

```
listeners: [
 {
  fn: 'onStartButtonTap',
  event: 'tap',
  delegate: '#startButton'
 }
]
```

This will fire a function called `onStartButtonTap`. We add this new function after the `Config` section of our `Main.js` file. This is the function that starts the countdown for the timer:

```
onStartButtonTap: function(button, e, options) {
 var delay = button.getText();
 setTimeout(function() {
  Ext.Msg.alert('Back to work minion!',
  'The boss needs a new villa!',
  Ext.emptyFn);
 },parseInt(delay)*1000);
}
```

This function grabs the text of the buttons, which is now set for the total amount of time we want to set on our timer. We then create a `setTimeout` function that will display a message box after the timer finishes. For the purposes of testing, we have set the delay for delay *1000, which will actually give us our delay time in seconds instead of minutes. When we want to set the delay to minutes, the last line can be changed to:

```
setTimeout(function() {
 Ext.Msg.alert('Back to work minion!',
 'The boss needs a new villa!',
 Ext.emptyFn);
},parseInt(delay)*60000);
```

For testing purposes let's leave the code as is for now and test the functions.

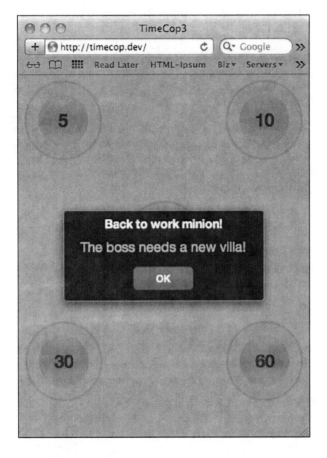

As we can see from our example, the alert appears once the delay time expires. However this doesn't currently use any of the native alerts available on the device. In order to do this, we need to take a look at Ext.device.

Using native APIs with Ext.device

By default, a Sencha Touch application is web-based. This means that a user on Android or iOS will use a web browser to access your application. You can add the web page to the desktop and it will look and behave very much like a compiled application. However, there are a number of features available on a mobile device that cannot be accessed through a web-based application; these include things like the camera, the device orientation, connection monitoring, native alerts, and some native geolocation features.

Sencha Touch offers a way around this issue by using Ext.device. This component accepts JavaScript commands, which will then be translated into native functions when the application is compiled.

 It should be noted that one essential consideration when using Ext. device is that the application has to be compiled each time in order to actually test the native application features. If you make changes, or need to do debugging, you will have to recompile the application and reinstall it on your mobile device.

Ext.device offers the following options:

- **Connection**: This allows you to check if the user is online using Ext.device. Connection.isOnline(). You can also check the type of connection using Ext.device.Connection.getType().

- **Notification**: This allows you to access native notification windows and the vibrate device option.

- **Orientation**: This provides the current orientation of the device tracked in three dimensions (alpha, beta, and gamma). These dimensions return values between 0 and 360 and can be used to calculate various device movements.

- **Camera**: This lets your application take pictures or select existing images from the camera library (with your user's permission).

For TimeCop, we will use a simple notification/vibrate alert. In later chapters, we will cover the other Ext.Device components. First, though, we will need to take a bit of a detour and explore some of the additional steps we need to take to test and run compiled applications under iOS.

Testing and running native applications

In order to run a native (compiled) application on iOS, you will need to take the following steps:

1. Register as an Apple iOS developer (cost is $99 annually as of this writing).
2. Enable your device for development.
3. Provision the application with Apple and create a P12 certificate.
4. Install the application on your device.

This process is not always intuitive, and can often seem more laborious than coding the actual application. If you would prefer to create an Android application, we will discuss building native Android applications later in this chapter.

Registering as a developer

In order to publish your application to the Apple Store, or even to simply test compiled iOS applications, you are going to have to sign up for a developer account. There is a fee to become a developer (the cost is $99 annually as of this writing), and Apple will require quite a bit of information about you. They require this information for several reasons. First, they have to know who you are so that you can get paid for apps that you sell in their store. Second, they need to know how to contact you if there's a problem with your application. And last, they need to be able to track you down if you try to do something evil with your app. Not that you would, of course.

Even if you are not yet ready to distribute your application, you will still need to register as a developer in order to install a compiled application on your iOS device.

Your iOS device will also need to be registered for development with Apple. This will allow you to install and test your own personal compiled applications directly from your development computer instead of going through the Apple store.

Becoming an Apple developer

To become an Apple developer, first you must go to: `http://developer.apple.com/programs/register/`.

You will either need to supply your existing Apple ID or sign up for a new one, fill out some lengthy profile information, agree to some legal documents, and then perform an e-mail verification. From there you will have access to the Apple Developer center. The two points of most interest to us as mobile developers are the iOS Dev Center and the iOS Provisioning Portal.

The **iOS Dev Center** is where you can download the iOS SDK (known as Xcode), as well as read documentation, see sample code and tutorials, and view some videos on iOS development.

The **iOS Provisioning Portal** is where you add your application to the Apple store or publish test versions of your application.

> Note that in order to use Xcode, install a development certificate, or publish your application to the Apple store, you must have a computer running OSX. Windows and Linux computers cannot run Xcode or publish to the Apple store.

The provisioning portal is the main area we are concerned with.

Provisioning an application

In order to run a compiled Sencha Touch application that you're developing for iPhone, iPad, or iPod touch, you must have a provisioning profile and a development certificate installed on your device and your Mac. (This is only true for compiled applications and not standard Sencha web applications.)

While the provisioning process can seem a bit complex, Apple has a very nice set of "How To…" videos listed on the right side of the provisioning portal, as well as a handy **Provisioning Assistant** setup wizard. The **Provisioning Assistant** wizard will guide you through the steps to create and install your development provisioning profile and iOS development certificate.

The first step in the process is to obtain a development certificate. The **development certificate** is an electronic document that links you as an Apple developer with your compiled applications. For testing purposes, the certificate gets loaded onto your iOS device and it lets the device know that it's okay to run your application.

The provisioning profile is used when your application is compiled. It contains a separate set of development certificates, a device ID, and an app ID. This is checked against the original development certificate to authorize the application to run on your device.

Meanwhile back in the code

Now that we have our certificates properly set up, we can get back to the business of writing code.

Using the native notifications

To use the native notifications we need to replace our original `onStartButtonTap` function with a new function that uses `Ext.device`. Aside from that, the code for native notifications looks almost the same as our previous code:

```
onStartButtonTap: function(button, e, options) {
    var delay = button.getText();
    setTimeout(function() {
        Ext.device.Notification.vibrate();
        Ext.device.Notification.show({
            title: ' Back to work minion! ',
            message: 'The boss needs a new villa!'
        });


    },parseInt(delay)*1000);
}
```

We still wrap the function in a `setTimeout` statement. We then call `Ext.device.Notification.vibrate` and `Ext.device.Notification.show`. This will cause the device to vibrate (if the device supports it) and then show our original message as before.

Also, `Ext.device` is not loaded by default, so we need to add it to our `app.js` file, in the `requires` configuration:

```
Ext.application({
    name: 'TimeCop',

    requires: [
        'Ext.MessageBox',
        'Ext.device.Notification'
    ],
```

Debugging problems with `Ext.device` is a difficult proposition. The `Ext.device` functionality is not available in desktop browsers, or when your app hasn't been compiled. However, if you need to debug an app running on your mobile device, there are some third-party solutions out there, one of the best being **weinre**, which stands for **WEb INspector REmote**. You can learn more about weinre at: `http://people.apache.org/~pmuellr/weinre/docs/latest/`.

For now, though, we need to compile the application for a native iPhone using Sencha Cmd.

Compiling the application

In order to compile an application you will need a few things from Apple first:

- A developer certificate in P12 format (for a walkthrough on this process go to `http://docs.sencha.com/touch/2-0/#!/guide/native_provisioning`)

- A provisioning profile (from Apple Provisioning Profile, launch the Development Provisioning Assistant: `https://developer.apple.com/ios/manage/overview/index.action`)

You will also need to know the application name, application ID, and bundle seed ID for your application. This information can be found by clicking on **configure** next to the application name in the **App ID** section of the portal. The format looks like this mockup:

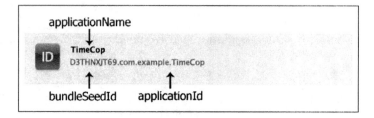

Once we have this information and the files, we need to set up our `packager.json` file.

Setting up packager.json

The `packager.json` file is in the root directory of our application folder and it is a template originally generated for us by Sencha Cmd. We need to change some of the default information in order to compile the application.

The `packager.json` file has extensive comments, so we will just take a look at some of the more critical settings in the file:

- `"applicationName":"TimeCop"`
- `"applicationId":"com.example.TimeCop"`
- `"bundleSeedId":"D3THNXJT69"`

This is where we use the values from our previous example mockup. You will need to change these to reflect your own application information.

 Please note that we are using example information for our `applicationID` and `bundleSeedId` values. You will need to change these values to the ones you get from Apple.

The next important section is:

```
"configuration":"Debug",
"platform":"iOSSimulator",
"deviceType":"Universal",
```

We can leave these as is for right now, but they control how the application is outputted and what devices it works on. The `Configuration` type should always be `Debug` until you are ready to distribute the application through the app store. This will help you track down any code errors that you might have.

The platform options are:

- iOSSimulator
- iOS
- Android
- AndroidEmulator

Using the `iOSSimmulator` or `AndroidEmulator` options allows you to test locally on your machine without an iOS or Android device. You will need to have Xcode and/ or the Android SDK kit installed on your machine to use this option.

`deviceType` is an iOS-only option that declares the application as `iPhone`, `iPad`, or `Universal` (meaning both).

The last critical pieces of information are:

```
"certificatePath":"/Users/12ftguru/Downloads/New_Cer/Certificates.
p12",
"provisionProfile":"/Users/12ftguru/Downloads/New_Cer/TimeCop.
mobileprovision",
```

Both `certificatePath` and `provisionProfile` should correspond to the correct paths to the converted P12 certificate mentioned earlier and the provisioning profile you downloaded from Apple.

Once you have the information in place, we are ready to compile the application.

In the command line, change to your application directory:

cd /path/to/your/application

And then type:

sencha app build -run native

This should compile your application into an executable file and launch the iOS simulator.

 The `-run` option is new in Sencha Cmd Version 3. Previous versions would launch the simulator by default. You can drop the `-run` option if you only want to build the application.

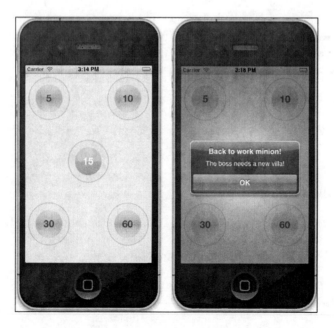

This looks more like a native iPhone app should, and if the application is run on an iPhone, the phone will also vibrate when the notification occurs.

The compiled application should now be in the `build/native` folder in your application directory. You can drag it onto iTunes to install it on your device.

Installing a native application

If your application fails to install, it is often helpful to try installing under Xcode. Connect your device and drop the application file on top of the Xcode application. This will launch Xcode and attempt to install the application on your mobile device. Xcode often gives back better error information than iTunes does.

Building native Android applications

Building compiled applications in Android follows a similar pattern as the one we used for iOS:

1. We create an Android signing certificate.
2. We create a package configuration file for Sencha Cmd to use.
3. We run the Sencha Cmd packager to create an `application.apk` file, which will run on Android devices or the Android emulator for testing.

The nice part is that we can still use the exact same code, all we need is a new certificate and some configuration changes.

Creating the Android signing certificate

Generating the Android signing certificate is significantly less complex than its iOS counterpart. All of our keys can be generated on our local machine and there is no provisioning process for Android applications.

The first thing we need to do is download the Android SDK from `http://developer.android.com/sdk/index.html`. Once the ZIP file is downloaded, we need to extract it and save it in an appropriate location. For this example, we have chosen our home directory in a folder called `development`. When we create our configuration files, your file path information may vary depending on where you place the SDK.

The Android certificate is generated from the command line using the following command (all on one line):

```
keytool -genkey -v -keystore time-cop.keystore -alias timecop -keyalg RSA
-keysize 2048 -validity 10000
```

The important parts of this command are the `keystore` name, `time-cop.keystore`, and the `alias`, which is `timecop`. We will need to have these values in order to correctly set up our configuration file.

When you execute this command, you will be prompted to create a password for the keystore. You will then be walked through a series of questions about your organization and location (these are optional, but probably a good idea).

Once you have answered all of the questions, a file will be generated called `time-cop.keystore` (or whatever you named your keystore).

Creating the Android configuration file

As with our previous iOS configuration file, we create a JSON file called `packager_android.json`. The format for this file will follow the same format as our previous iOS file:

```
{
  "applicationName": "TimeCop",
  "applicationId": "com.12ftguru.TimeCop",
  "outputPath": "/Users/12ftguru/Development/compiled/",
  "iconName": "timecop.png",
"versionCode": "1.0",
"versionString": "1.0 Release 1",
  "inputPath": "/path/to/your/application",
  "configuration": "Debug",
  "platform": "AndroidEmulator",
  "certificatePath": "/Users/12ftguru/Development/time-cop.keystore",
  "certificateAlias": "timecop",
  "sdkPath": "/Users/12ftguru/Development/sdk",
  "orientations": [
   "portrait",
   "landscapeLeft",
   "landscapeRight",
   "portraitUpsideDown"
  ],
  "deviceType": "<Not applicable for Android>"
}
```

`applicationName` will be the name of the `.apk` file that is created when we compile, which in this case, is `TimeCop.apk`.

`applicationId` is a unique identifier for your application, we recommend using something like `com.your_name.your_application_name`.

`outputPath` is where the `.apk` file will be saved and `iconName` is the file that will be used as the icon for your application. `versionCode` and `versionString` are up to you and should be used to differentiate which version of the software is being used.

`inputPath` is the full path to your TimeCop files (or a path relative to this configuration file).

`configuration` can be set to `Release` or `Debug` and `platform` can be set to `Android` or `AndroidEmulator`. These settings will typically be `Debug` + `AndroidEmulator` for testing and `Release` + `Android` for a finished application.

`certificatePath` is the location of the `keystore` file that we generated in the previous section and `certificateAlias` is the alias we supplied as part of our command-line arguments when we created `keystore`.

The orientations are the viewing positions available to your application. They will typically stay as the defaults listed before. The device type is ignored by Android, but the configuration manager will return errors if the configuration or value is left off. You can keep this value set as `<Not applicable for Android>` and it will be safely ignored.

Compiling and launching the Android application

Just like the previous iOS application, we will use the Sencha package command to compile the application. However, if you are testing in the Android emulator, you will need to start the emulator before issuing the command.

Once the emulator is running, enter the following command on the command line:

```
sencha package run packager_android.json
```

This will execute our `packagerAndroid.json` file we created in the previous section.

If you are creating a release version of the application, set `configuration` to `Release` and `platform` to `Android` in your `packager_android.json` configuration file. You can then execute the `package` command, but leave off the `run` command like so:

```
sencha package packager_android.json
```

This will compile the application without running it in the emulator.

> The Android emulator is capable of emulating a wide variety of hardware. For more information on the Android emulator, go to `http://developer.android.com/tools/devices/emulator.html`.
>
> For information on setting up different hardware profiles (sometimes called **Android Virtual Devices** (**ADVs**) with the Android emulator, take a look at the documentation available at `http://developer.android.com/tools/devices/managing-avds.html`.

Once the application is running, you can begin testing the different features and fixing any issues.

Summary

In this chapter we learned about:

- Generating an application skeleton with the Sencha SDK command-line tools
- Using Sencha's native `Ext.device` APIs
- Provisioning iOS applications through the Apple developer portal
- Compiling a Sencha Touch web application into a native iOS app
- Compiling a Sencha Touch web application into a native Android app

In the next chapter, we will take a look at the Sencha Touch Charts package. The Charts package is an add-on to Sencha Touch that will let us use charts and graphs in our applications. We will show you how to take a standard `datastore` instance and use it to feed data to your charts and graphs.

4
Weight Weight

In this chapter we will explore an optional add-on package to the Sencha Touch Framework. The package is called Sencha Charts and it enables us to create charts using a data store.

In this chapter we will cover:

- Building the basic application
- Defining the data stores
- Setting up the Sencha Charts package
- Connecting the stores to Sencha Charts
- Configuring and displaying the charts

Sencha Charts overview

The basic Sencha Touch Framework has a number of components for displaying data. However, business and other intensive software products often require something a bit more robust. By using Sencha Touch Charts, we can also display complex graphical data as part of our applications.

The following screenshot exemplifies an overview of chart and graph types for displaying data:

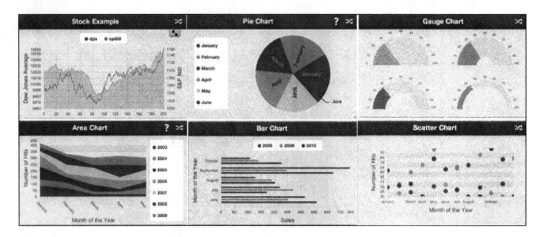

These new components use data stores to display a wide range of chart and graph types including:

- Pie
- Bar
- Line
- Scatter
- Area
- Candlestick
- Radar
- Gauge

We will be using a few of these charts to provide a more user-friendly display for our application.

 As of writing, the Sencha Charts package is only available as a part of Sencha Complete, or the open source version (GPL) of Sencha Touch 2.1 download. For this chapter, we will be using the open source version, which can be downloaded for free from the web page at http://www.sencha.com/products/touch/download/.

Later on in the chapter, we will cover the basic setup for using Sencha Charts, but first, we will take a look at setting up the basic application.

The basic application

We will use the Sencha Charts package to create a program for tracking weight, exercise, calories, and water consumption. We will also allow the user to tag entries for adding additional information to the charts.

The application consists of four basic pieces as follows:

- A form for entering data
- An overview that will provide a group of charts on a single page
- A details section for viewing a specific chart in greater detail
- A configuration section that will allow the user to set goals for our four categories, and define the units of measurement for weight and water consumption

We will start by setting up the basic application and building our form.

Setting up the application and building the form

We will be using the Sencha Command SDK to create the application as described in the previous chapter. You will need to execute this command from the `Sencha Touch` directory. The basic command is as follows:

```
sencha app create weightweight /Path/To/Your/New/Application
```

If you prefer, you can create the initial directories and files yourself. Your file and directory structure should look something like this:

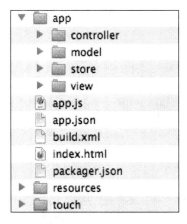

The previous screenshot shows the structure that is automatically generated with the sencha app create command.

- The touch directory contains a copy of the Sencha Touch Framework including our chart functions.
- The resources directory will contain our images and CSS files.
- The app directory will contain the bulk of our code.

To begin, we need to define our main view. This file will be called main.js and it belongs to the views folder. The main.js file is a simple tab panel with four items:

```
Ext.define("WeightWeight.view.Main", {
    extend: 'Ext.tab.Panel',
    requires: ['Ext.TitleBar'],

    config: {
        tabBar: {
            docked: 'bottom'
        },
        items: [
            { xtype: 'dataentry'},
            { xtype: 'overview'},
            { xtype: 'details'},
            { xtype: 'configform' }
        ]
    }
});
```

We also need to make sure that this component is added into our app.js file in the views section of our Ext.application function:

```
Ext.application({
    name: 'WeightWeight',
    views: ['Main'],
    ...
```

Remember that the name we list under the view is not the file name (Main.js), it's the last part of the define statement at the top of our code: WeightWeight.view.Main. Once we have this setup, let's create four placeholder files, one for each panel in our tab view.

We need to create a placeholder for dataentry, overview, details, and configform panels. These files will contain starter code for each panel or form in our application. This will let us test our application without getting errors for missing files.

Let's have a look at how to test our application by using the starter code for each panel:

1. Create a `dataentry.js` file in the `views` directory. This will be a form panel so the starter code should be set as follows:

```
Ext.define("WeightWeight.view.DataEntry", {
    extend:'Ext.form.Panel',
    alias:'widget.dataentry',
    config:{
        title:'Enter Data',
        iconCls:'info',
        html: 'Data Entry'
    }
});
```

2. Next, we need to create an `overview.js` file with a simple panel in the `views` directory and set the code as follows:

```
Ext.define("WeightWeight.view.OverviewChart", {
    extend:'Ext.Panel',
    alias:'widget.overview',
    config:{
        title:'Overview',
        iconCls:'star',
        html: 'Overview'

    }
});
```

3. The `view/details.js` file is also a panel like the previous `overview.js` file. The code is as follows:

```
Ext.define("WeightWeight.view.DetailChart", {
    extend:'Ext.Panel',
    alias:'widget.details',
    config:{
        title:'Details',
        iconCls:'locate',
        html: 'Details'

    }
});
```

4. And finally, the `views/config.js` file, which is also a form panel like the `dataentry.js` file. The code is as follows:

```
Ext.define("WeightWeight.view.Config", {
    extend:'Ext.form.Panel',
    alias:'widget.configform',
```

```
config:{
    title:'Config',
    iconCls:'settings',
    html: 'Config'

}
});
```

5. Once all the views are created, we need to remember to add them to the views section in our app.js file (where we added Main previously). In the app js file, set the views section as follows:

```
views: ['Main', 'Config', 'AddTag', "OverviewChart",
"DetailChart"]
```

We should now be able to load the code and test our panels.

Small steps

Creating code can be a very involved process. It is often helpful to make small changes and then test, rather than changing a few hundred lines of code and then testing. By changing small amounts of code, you should be able to track down problems quicker when they occur. In this case, by creating these starter files, we can test to make sure that Sencha is locating the files correctly and that the application starts without errors. We can then work on one file at a time and limit the places where we need to look when things go boom.

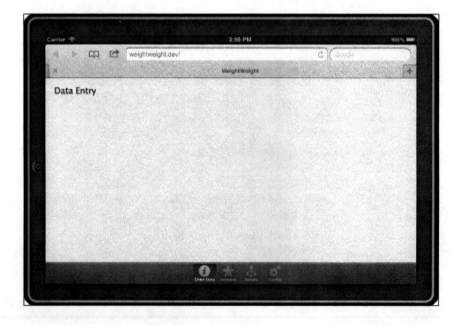

At this point, our application should simply start and allow us to switch between our views. This confirms that the application is working and then we can start creating our form.

Creating the data entry form

Our data entry form consists of:

- Three fields: `datepickerfield` for setting the date, `numberfield` for each of our four categories (weight, water, calories, and exercise), and `hiddenfield` for storing our tag value for the entry.

- Three buttons: One for adding tags, one for saving, and one for canceling and clearing the form.

- We will also place the **Cancel** and **Save** buttons inside an Hbox layout container. This will let us display the buttons side by side.

We will replace the line in `view/DataEntry.js` that says `html: 'Data Entry'` so that the code looks like this:

```
Ext.define("WeightWeight.view.DataEntry", {
    extend:'Ext.form.Panel',
    alias:'widget.dataentry',
    config:{

        title:'Enter Data',
        iconCls:'info',
        items:[
            {
                xtype:'datepickerfield',
                label:'Date',
                placeHolder:'mm/dd/yyyy'
            },
            {
                xtype:'numberfield',
                id:'weightField',
                margin:'10 0',
                label:'Weight'
            },
            {
                xtype:'numberfield',
                id:'waterField',
                margin:'10 0',
                label:'Water'
            },
            {
```

```
                    xtype:'numberfield',
                    id:'calorieField',
                    margin:'10 0',
                    label:'Calories'
            },
            {
                    xtype:'numberfield',
                    id:'exerciseField',
                    label:'Exercise'
            },
            {
                    xtype:'hiddenfield',
                    id:'hiddenTagField'
            },
            {
                    xtype:'button',
                    margin:'25 0 25',
                    text:'Add Tag',
                    id: 'addTagButton'
            },
            {
                    xtype:'container',
                    layout:{
                        type:'hbox'
                    },
                    items:[
                        {
                            xtype:'button',
                            margin:'0 10 0 0',
                            text:'Cancel',
                            flex:1
                        },
                        {
                            xtype:'button',
                            margin:'0 0 0 10',
                            text:'Save',
                            flex:1
                        }
                    ]
            }
        ]
    }
});
```

We have also provided margins for each of our items to add spacing to the form, making it more readable. The end result should look something like this:

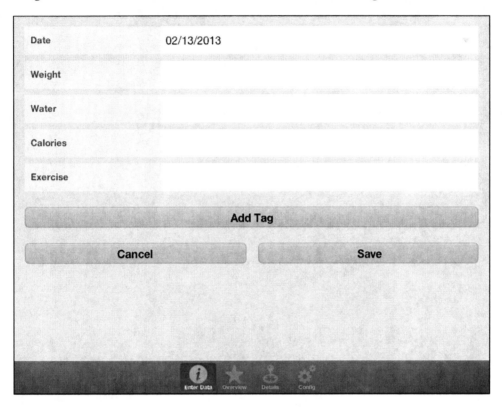

The next view we need to create is the one for adding our tags. We will use a sheet to achieve this.

Creating the AddTag view

The `AddTag` view is embedded in an `ActionSheet` component. This view will allow us to add new tags or select from the previous ones, and the `ActionSheet` component will display the view as an overlay that slides up from the bottom of the screen. The form contains a single field called `textfield`, a `list` view, and two buttons. Create the file in the `views` directory and call it `AddTag.js`:

```
Ext.define('WeightWeight.view.AddTag', {
    extend: 'Ext.ActionSheet',
    alias: 'widget.addtag',
```

```
config: {
    id: 'addTagSheet',
    items: [
        {
            xtype: 'textfield',
            label: 'Enter a New Tag',
            placeHolder: 'or choose a tag from the list below.'
        },
        {
            xtype: 'list',
            height: 300,
            itemTpl: [
                '<div>List Item {string}</div>'
            ]
        },
        {
            xtype: 'container',
            margin: 10,
            layout: {
                type: 'hbox'
            },
            items: [
                {
                    xtype: 'button',
                    margin: '0 10 0 0',
                    text: 'Cancel',
                    flex: 1
                },
                {
                    xtype: 'button',
                    margin: '0 0 0 10',
                    text: 'Save',
                    flex: 1
                }
            ]
        }
    ]
}
});
```

We have used the `alias` configuration to give this component an `xtype` property. This will let us quickly create and remove it within our program. We have also given the component an `id` property so that we can reference it in our controller.

The end result should look something like this:

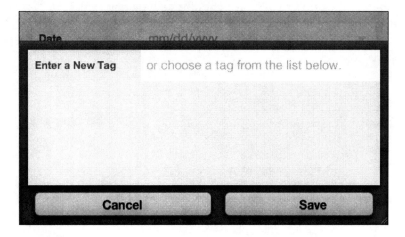

The list component is a placeholder for now. We will finish it later once we have our data stores set up.

The next view we need to set up is the config form. This will be similar to our data entry form with a few different field types.

Creating the config form

We will start by editing the Config.js placeholder file that we set up earlier in the chapter. The code for it is as follows:

```
Ext.define("WeightWeight.view.Config", {
    extend:'Ext.form.Panel',
    alias: 'widget.configform',
    config:{
        title:'Config',
        iconCls:'settings',
        items:[]
    }
});
```

The alias property allows us to call the panel by a custom xtype of config form. This is the xtype property we used in our Main.js file for the fourth panel. The title and iconCls properties control how the navigation for this panel appears in the main view.

Next, we need to add some items to our panel. We will start by adding number fields for Starting Weight and Target Weight. By using a numberfield component we make sure that the number keyboard will appear on most mobile devices. To keep the field organized, we will put them in a fieldset component. This will go in the empty items config:

```
{
    xtype:'fieldset',
    title:'Weight Loss Goal',
    items:[
        {
            xtype:'numberfield',
            id:'startingWeight',
            name:'startingWeight',
            label:'Starting Weight'
        },
        {
            xtype:'numberfield',
            id:'targetWeight',
            name:'targetWeight',
            label:'Target Weight'
        }
    ]
}
```

Next, we will add a set of spinner fields. The spinnerfield component allows the user to increment the field values using + and - buttons. These will also be in a fieldset component like the previous ones:

```
{
xtype:'fieldset',
title:'Daily Goals',
items:[
    {
        xtype:'spinnerfield',
        id:'exercisePerDay',
        label:'Exercise (minutes)',
        defaultValue:30,
        stepValue: 1
    },
    {
        xtype:'spinnerfield',
        id:'caloriesPerDay',
        label:'Caloric Intake',
        defaultValue:0,
        stepValue: 100
    },
```

```
        {
            xtype:'spinnerfield',
            id:'waterPerDay',
            label:'Water Consumption',
            defaultValue:8,
            stepValue: 1
        }
    ]
}
```

Notice that the `spinnerfield` component also allows us to set a `stepValue` configuration, which controls how much the field will increase or decrease when the buttons are pressed.

Lastly, we will add our units of measurement section with radio buttons for different selections as follows:

```
{
    xtype:'fieldset',
    title:'Units of Measure',
    padding:25,
    items:[
        {
            xtype:'fieldset',
            title:'Weight',
            items:[
                {
                    xtype:'radiofield',
                    label:'Pounds',
                    name:'weightUnits',
                    value:'lbs',
                    checked:true
                },
                {
                    xtype:'radiofield',
                    label:'Kilograms',
                    name:'weightUnits',
                    value:'kg'
                }
            ]
        },
        {
            xtype:'fieldset',
            title:'Water',
            items:[
```

```
            {
                xtype:'radiofield',
                label:'Glasses',
                name:'waterUnits',
                value:'glass',
                checked:true
            },
            {

                xtype:'radiofield',
                label:'Ounces',
                name:'waterUnits',
                value:'oz'
            }
        ]
    }
    ]
}
```

The end form should look something like this:

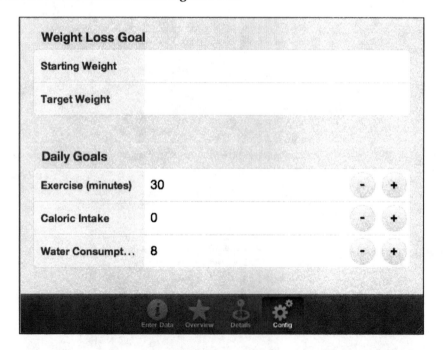

Now that we have our two forms, let's start working on the controllers for them. We'll start with the data entry controller.

Creating the DataEntry controller

Let's start off with a bare controller like so:

```
Ext.define('WeightWeight.controller.DataEntry', {
    extend: 'Ext.app.Controller',
    config: {
        refs: {

        },
        control: {

        }
    }
});
```

We start off by extending the basic controller and then adding a `config` section that will contain the rest of our initial setup code. The `refs` section will contain references to other components we need, and the `control` section will assign functions to our buttons and other components.

The `refs` section is where we will add a reference to our `AddTag` sheet:

```
refs: {
    tagSheet: '#addTagSheet',
}
```

This is occasionally written out in a longer form as follows:

```
refs: {
    tagSheet: {
        selector: '#addTagSheet'
    }
}
```

Both ways will work just fine. The reference looks for a component selector, in this case a component with an `id` value of `addTagSheet`.

By creating this reference using the `id` configuration of our `AddTag` sheet, we can access it anywhere in the controller by typing the following code:

```
var sheet = this.getTagSheet();
```

> Notice that despite the fact that we use `tagSheet` as the reference, the `get` function capitalizes the first letter in our reference to `getTagSheet`. Since JavaScript is case sensitive, if you tried using gettagSheet, JavaScript will return an error.

Now that we have our reference, we need to add controls to the **Add Tag** button in our `DataEntry` form and the two buttons on our `AddTag` sheet. The code is as follows:

```
control: {
    'button#addTagButton': {
        tap: 'showAddTag'
    },
    '#addTagSheet button[text="Cancel"]': {
        tap: 'cancelAddTag'
    },
    '#addTagSheet button[text="Save"]': {
        tap: 'saveAddTag'
    }
}
```

Each of our controls has three parts:

- A DOM selector that tells the program which component we want to bind to
- The event we want it to listen for
- The function to fire when the event occurs

We will add additional controls later on when we create our data stores. For now, let's add in the functions that need to fire when these three buttons are clicked.

The first is a `showAddTag` function. It calls our `AddTag` sheet and displays it. The function is added after the end of the `config` section and looks similar to the following code:

```
showAddTag: function() {
    var sheet = this.getTagSheet();
    if (typeof sheet == 'undefined') {
        sheet = Ext.widget('addtag');
        Ext.Viewport.add(sheet);
    }
    sheet.show();
}
```

First, we check to see if there is already a sheet in the memory (using the `this. getTagSheet()` function automatically created by our reference in the `refs` section), and if not, then we create a new one using the `Ext.Widget()` function to create a new component with an `xtype` property of `addtag`. We then add this sheet to the view port and show it.

The **Cancel** button in our `AddTag` sheet has a very simple function:

```
cancelAddTag: function() {
    this.getTagSheet().hide();
}
```

This is also used as our autogenerated reference function to grab the open sheet and close it.

For now, we will duplicate this function for our last `saveAddTag` function:

```
saveAddTag: function() {
    this.getTagSheet().hide();
}
```

This will simply hide that sheet as well. We will add the code to save our tag data once we get our stores created. For now, save and test the code to make sure that the sheet appears and hides as expected.

The end result should look something like this:

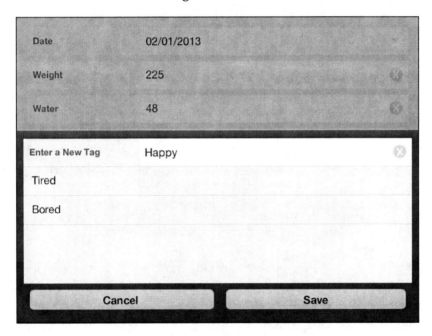

Now that we have the basic forms, we need to create our stores and models. This will provide us with places to store the data from our various forms.

Defining the models and stores

For this project, we will be using the local storage offered by HTML5 to store our data. We will begin by defining the model for our data entry form. We will just call this one `Entry.js` and it goes in the `models` folder. The code is as follows:

```
Ext.define('WeightWeight.model.Entry', {
    extend: 'Ext.data.Model',

    config: {
        idProperty: 'id',
        fields: [
            {name: 'id', type: 'auto'},
            {name: 'entryDate', type: 'date', dateFormat: 'm-d-Y'},
            {name: 'weight', type:'float'},
            {name: 'water', type:'int'},
            {name: 'calories', type: 'int'},
            {name: 'exercise', type: 'int'},
            {name: 'tag', type: 'string'}
        ],
        proxy: {
            type: 'localstorage',
            id: 'weightweight-entry'
        }
    }
});
```

The model is pretty straightforward, defining the various data types and names. One thing to be aware of is the `entryDate` field, which has a `type` field of `date`.

 When you use a date type in a model, you should always declare a `dateFormat` component. This tells the model how to store and retrieve the data. It also provides a common translation for the components that grab data from the model. Failure to set the `dateFormat` component often leads to foul language and extreme frustration.

The next model we need is a model for the tags. The `Tag.js` file goes in the `models` folder and it is pretty simple. It only has an `id` field and a `text` field:

```
Ext.define('WeightWeight.model.Tag', {
    extend: 'Ext.data.Model',

    config: {
        idProperty: 'id',
        fields: [
            {name: 'id', type: 'auto'},
```

```
                    {name: 'text', type: 'string'}
            ],
            proxy: {
                type: 'localstorage',
                id: 'weightweight-tag'
            }
        }
    });
```

As before, we just use a `localstorage` proxy and give it a unique ID. This ID makes sure that the data is stored in its own separate table.

The last model we need is our `Config.js` model. This model follows the same format as a local storage proxy and the fields from our `config` form. The code is as follows:

```
Ext.define('WeightWeight.model.Config', {
  extend: 'Ext.data.Model',
  config: {
   fields: [
    {name: 'id', type: 'int'},
    {name: 'startingWeight', type: 'float'},
    {name: 'targetWeight', type: 'float'},
    {name: 'exercisePerDay', type: 'int', defaultValue: 30},
    {name: 'caloriesPerDay', type: 'int'},
    {name: 'waterPerDay', type: 'int', defaultValue: 8},
    {name: 'weightUnits', type: 'string', defaultValue: 'lbs'},
    {name: 'waterUnits', type: 'string', defaultValue: 'glass'}
   ],
   proxy: {
    type: 'localstorage',
    id  : 'weightweight-config'
   }
  }
});
```

We also include some default values as part of the model. These values will get pulled into the form when we create a new config record.

Once we have our models, we need to create our data store. The `EntryStore.js` file is created and it goes into the `stores` folder. The code is as follows:

```
Ext.define('WeightWeight.store.EntryStore', {
    extend: 'Ext.data.Store',
     config: {
    model: 'WeightWeight.model.Entry',
    autoLoad: true,
     storeId: 'EntryStore'
     }
});
```

This is a very basic store that we will expand later. For now, we will be using the model to do most of the heavy lifting. We give the store a `storeId` value of `EntryStore`, so that we can easily address it with our `DataEntry` controller.

Next, we need a store for our tags. Since we only need very limited control over the tag store (it only feeds the list in our `AddTag` form), we are going to add the store as part of the component itself. Open the `AddTag.js` file and modify the `list` entry so that it looks similar to the following code:

```
{
    xtype: 'list',
    height: 300,
    store: {
        model: 'WeightWeight.model.Tag',
        autoLoad: true
    },
    itemTpl: [
        '<div>{text}</div>'
    ]
}
```

This simple store format creates the store as part of the `list` entry and does not need to be added to our `app.js` file.

Speaking of the `app.js` file, we should add other models and stores near the top of the `Ext.Application` function as follows:

```
models: ["Tag", "Entry", "Config"]
stores: ['EntryStore']
```

 If a model or store is within its own file, then it needs to be added into the `app.js` file. But, since the simple store format for our `list` is part of the component itself, we don't need to add it to the `app.js` file.

In the case of our `Config` model, there will only be one config record for the application. This means that we don't actually need a store to use it. We will take care of that back in our controllers.

Meanwhile, back in the controllers

Back in our controllers, it's time to put those stores to work for us, saving and displaying our data.

Let's start with our `DataEntry` controller. First, we are going to add a few more references, so that we can get to our components easier. Update the `DataEntry.js` references as follows:

```
refs: {
    tagSheet: '#addTagSheet',
    tagList: '#addTagSheet list',
    tagInput: '#addTagSheet textfield',
    tagButton: 'button#addTagButton',
    tagField: '#hiddenTagField',
    entrySaveButton: 'dataentry button[text="Save"]',
    entryCancelButton: 'dataentry button[text="Cancel"]',
    entryForm: 'dataentry'
}
```

This provides us with easy access to our tag adding sheet, the list of tags, the input and hidden fields, as well as the button that opens the sheet. We also add references to our data entry form and both of its buttons.

Here, in the `control` section we need to assign events and functions to each of these items. We can also use our reference names here to address the controls as follows:

```
control: {
    tagButton: {
        tap: 'showAddTag'
    },
    tagInput: {
      clearicontap: 'deselectTag'
    },
    tagList: {
      select: 'selectTag'
    },
    '#addTagSheet button[text="Cancel"]': {
        tap: 'cancelAddTag'
    },
    '#addTagSheet button[text="Save"]': {
        tap: 'saveAddTag'
    },
    entrySaveButton: {
        tap: 'saveEntry'
    },
    entryCancelButton: {
        tap: 'clearEntry'
    }
}
```

Notice that we used the reference name for most of these. However, for the `Save` and `Cancel` buttons on our `tagSheet`, we used the component query reference. This is because we don't really need any additional control over those two pieces. They are basically single purpose components.

For example, our `showAddTag` and `cancelAddTag` functions both need to be able to grab the sheet itself in order to show and hide it. Since we have a reference of `TagSheet` assigned to it, we can call it with the following code:

```
var sheet = this.getTagSheet();
```

Since we don't modify the `Save` and `Cancel` buttons once they have been created, there is no need to create a reference for them. However, we will be making some modifications to our `AddTagButton` when we save our tag, so we created a reference for that one.

Let's update our `saveAddTag` function and see how that's done. Change the function as follows:

```
saveAddTag: function() {
        var tag = this.getTagInput().getValue(),
            store = this.getTagList().getStore();
        if (tag != "") {
            this.getTagButton().setText('Tag: '+tag);
            this.getTagField().setValue(tag);
            if (store.findExact('text', tag) == -1) {
                store.add({text: tag});
                store.sync();
            }
        } else {
            this.getTagButton().setText('Add Tag');
            this.getTagField().setValue('');
        }

        this.getTagSheet().hide();
    }
```

Right from the start we begin using the `get` functions automatically created by our references. We get the value of the `textfield` in our form using `this.getTagInput().getValue()` and then we get the store we use for our tag list by calling the `this.getTagList().getStore()` function.

Remember, the list store is the one we created as part of the component instead of a separate `store.js` file. However, since we can get to the list, and the list knows what store it is using, we have easy access to everything we need. The reference to the parent also gives us quick access to its children.

Next, we check to see if the user entered anything into the field (if the value of `tag != ""`) and if so, we set the text on our button to say **Tag:** and whatever the user entered. This provides the user with easy feedback as to what tag is on the current entry, so if we tag our entry as **Tired**, then the button will look like this:

Tag: Tired

Next, we set the value of our hidden field to the same value. We do this because we will need to load our form into a record to save it. We can load values from a form field but we cannot load values from a button name. We use the hidden field to hold the value within the form for later use.

Next, we need to find out if the tag is the one that we have entered previously, or if it is something new. To do this, we need to search the store using `store.findExact('text', tag)`. This will return `-1` if the value of `tag` is not found in the `text` field for any of the store's data. If we don't find the tag, we add it to our store using the following code:

```
store.add({text: tag});
store.sync();
```

Lastly, if the user has cleared the `textfield` out leaving it blank, we remove the previous tag text from the button and clear out the value of the hidden field.

Our next function controls when the user selects an existing tag from the list of tags in the sheet (instead of entering a new one):

```
selectTag: function(list, record) {
this.getTagInput().setValue(record.get('text'));
}
```

When the user selects an item in the list, we put the text of the item in the text field for saving. The `saveAddTag` function will take care of the rest.

We have a similar function that deselects the items in the list:

```
deselectTag: function() {
  this.getTagList().deselectAll();
}
```

Our text field has a clear icon that removes the value of the field. We tie into the `clearicontap` event that we set up in our `controllers` section to fire this `deselectTag` function.

Now that we have our tags taken care of, we will be able to save the full entry. We do this by adding the following function:

```
saveEntry: function() {
    var values = this.getEntryForm().getValues(),
    store = Ext.getStore('EntryStore'),
    entry = Ext.create('WeightWeight.model.Entry', values);

    store.add(entry);

    store.sync();
    Ext.Msg.alert('Saved!', 'Your data has been saved.', this.
clearEntry, this);
}
```

This function grabs the values from our form and creates a new entry for our store. Since the form names match the names of our model, we can use `Ext.Create` to create a new entry record and assign the values directly. We then add the new record to the store and sync. Finally, we alert the user that the new data has been saved.

Our final function clears the fields in our form by using the following function:

```
clearEntry: function() {
    this.getEntryForm().reset();
    this.getTagButton().setText('Add Tag');
}
```

This function resets our form and the text of the button. This function will be fired by the **Cancel** button in our data entry form.

This wraps up the `DataEntry.js` controller. We can now move on to the `Config.js` controller.

Config.js

Create a new file in the `controllers` folder called `Config.js` (make sure to also add it to the `app.js` file in the list of controllers). We will start with just the basic controller:

```
Ext.define('WeightWeight.controller.Config', {
    extend: 'Ext.app.Controller',

    config: {
        views:['Config'],
        models:['Config'],
        refs: {
            form: 'configform'
```

```
        },
        control: {
            form: {
                initialize: 'getSavedConfig'
            }
        }
    }
});
```

This sets up the controller with our views, models, and references. It also assigns a function to our form so that when it is initialized it calls `getSavedConfig`. This function is also the first one we need to create.

Before we get started, we should keep in mind a few things about `config`. This will be like a set of preferences for the application. There will only be one record for `config`, which is why we don't need to create a store. We can use the `Config.js` model to create, load, and save the record directly. Let's take a look at how this gets done.

Beneath the `config` section, we need to add the following code:

```
getSavedConfig: function() {
    var config = Ext.ModelManager.getModel('WeightWeight.model.
Config');
    config.load(1, {
        scope: this,
        failure: this.createSavedConfig,
        success: this.bindRecordToForm
    });
}
```

Here, we create an instance of our `Config` model and attempt to load the first record from the HTML5 local storage (remember this should also be the only record). There are two possible outcomes here:

- If the load fails, it means that this is the first time the user has accessed the `Config` section and we have no record. In this case, we will call another function called `createSavedConfig`.

- If the load succeeds then we need to load the data into our form for display. This will happen in the `bindRecordToForm` function.

By setting the scope of the function to `this` (meaning the controller itself), we can make these two functions part of the controller and call them with `this.createSavedConfig` and `this.bindRecordToForm` respectively.

We'll start by adding our new functions beneath the previous `getSavedConfig` function:

```
createSavedConfig: function() {
    var config = Ext.create('WeightWeight.model.Config', {id: 1});
    config.save({
        success: this.bindRecordToForm
    }, this);
}
```

This function creates a new empty record with the default values we defined in the `config` object and then saves the record. If this is successful, we call our next function, which binds the data record to our form:

```
bindRecordToForm: function(record) {
    this.savedConfig = record;

    var form = this.getForm();
    form.setRecord(this.savedConfig);

    form.on({
        delegate: 'field',
        change: this.updateValue,
        spin: this.updateValue,
        check: function(field) {
            this.updateValue(field, field.getGroupValue());
        },
        scope: this
    });
}
```

This function is called by both `getSavedConfig` and `createSavedConfig`, which pass along the data record automatically. We set this record to be our `savedConfig`, which allows us to get at the config data from anywhere in the controller.

Next we grab the form and use `setRecord` to populate the form with our data. Once the form is populated, we also need a way to save the data. To do this, we are going to use an interesting technique called **delegate**.

Delegate allows us to set listeners and functions on specific children within the form. In this case, we do `form.on({ delegate: 'field',` which lets us set a group of listeners on every field in our form:

- The `numberfield` component understands the `change` event
- The `spinnerfield` component understands the `spin` event
- The `checkboxfield` component understands the `check` event

Each of these events will call `this.updateValue` to save the data. While the other fields pass along both the field and value automatically, the checkboxes actually only pass the field when the `check` event fires. This means we do a tiny bit of extra work to get them to pass both field and value to our next function.

Our `updateValue` function takes the field and value passed in our previous function, and saves the data for us:

```
updateValue: function(field, newValue) {
    this.savedConfig.set(field.getName(), newValue);
    this.savedConfig.save();
}
```

This saves our data to local storage. Now that we have a way to save data and our goals, we can start looking at the charting functions for displaying the data.

Getting started with Sencha Touch Charts

As we noted at the beginning of the chapter, Sencha Touch Charts is currently only available as part of Sencha Complete or the open source version of Sencha Touch 2.1. Previously, Sencha Touch Charts was a separate download, which had to be installed and configured as part of your application in order to function. This is no longer required.

 It should also be noted that if you are using the standalone commercial version of Sencha Touch 2.1 (which is not part of the Sencha Complete package), you will not be able to use the new Sencha Charts functions. While this standalone commercial version of Sencha Touch 2.1 includes an empty `src/charts` directory, it does not have any of the actual chart functionality.

Creating the overview chart

The overview chart is a single-line chart, tracking weight and exercise. Our chart will have three axes, with weight ranges displayed on the left, date ranges displayed across the bottom, and exercise time ranges along the right.

The following screenshot describes the preceding explanation in more detail:

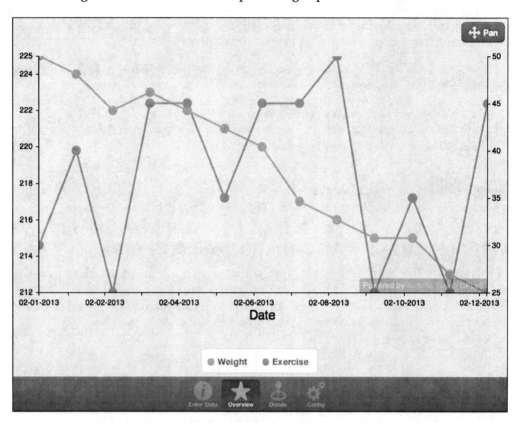

We will start with a few changes to our placeholder for the `OverviewChart.js` view:

```
Ext.define("WeightWeight.view.OverviewChart", {
    extend:'Ext.Panel',
    alias:'widget.overview',
    config:{
        title:'Overview',
        iconCls:'star',
        layout: 'fit',
        items:[{
          xtype:'chart',
          store:'EntryStore',
          legend:{
            position:'bottom'
          }]
        }
    }
});
```

Here, we've replaced the `html` configuration and included a single `chart` item as part of our panel.

 Previous versions of the Sencha Touch Chart software used a `chartPanel` object, which automatically included the `chart` item as part of the panel. The current Version 2.1 treats the `chart` item as a separate object, which allows the `chart` item to be embedded in a panel or a container.

We have given the `chart` item a `store` value to grab data from, and positioned the `legend` section at the `bottom` of the chart.

Adding the axes

The next piece we need to add is our axes. As we mentioned earlier, there are three for this graph. The code for them goes inside the `chart` section of the `config` definition (below our `legend` definition):

```
axes:[
  {
    type:'numeric',
    position:'left',
    fields:['weight'],
    title:{
      text:'Weight',
      fontSize:14
    }
  },
  {
    type:'numeric',
    position:'right',
    fields:['exercise'],
    title:{
      text:'Exercise',
      fontSize:14
    }
  },
  {
    type:'time',
    dateFormat:'m-d-Y',
    position:'bottom',
    fields:'entryDate',
    title:{
```

```
    text:'Date',
    fontSize:20
   }
  }
 ]
```

The first axis has a `title` section of `weight` and it's a `numeric` axis. We position it on the left-hand side and then tell the axis which fields we are tracking (in this case, `weight`).

As you might have guessed from the name `fields`, this means we can have multiple items tracked along the same axis. This works well if you have multiple items with the same numeric range of data. In this case, we have too much variation in the range of `exercise` and `weight`, so we keep them on different axes.

The `exercise` axis is set up in a similar fashion, but positioned on the right.

The `date` axis is a bit different. It has a type of `date` and a `dateFormat` for display.

Next, we need to set up the series.

Creating the series

The `series` section goes inside the chart configuration and beneath our axes section. The `series` section describes how the data points should align on the graph and how they should be formatted.

Our overview graph is a line graph display, tracking weight and exercise over time. We need one entry for weight and a second one for exercise:

```
series:[
 {
  type:'line',
  xField:'entryDate',
  yField:'weight',
  title:'Weight',
  axis:'left',
  style:{
   smooth:false,
   stroke:'#76AD86',
   miterLimit:3,
   lineCap:'miter',
   lineWidth:3
  },
  marker:{
   type:'circle',
   r:6,
```

```
      fillStyle:'#76AD86'
     },
    highlightCfg:{
      scale:1.25
    }
   },
   {
    type:'line',
    xField:'entryDate',
    yField:'exercise',
    title:'Exercise',
    axis:'right',
    style:{
     smooth:false,
     stroke:'#7681AD',
     lineWidth:3
    },
    marker:{
     type:'circle',
     r:6,
     fillStyle:'#7681AD'
    },
    highlightCfg:{
      scale:1.25
    }
   }
  ]
```

This defines our two series (`Weight` and `Exercise`). The `type` configuration defines which kind of series we are using. The `xField` configuration determines which data field is tracked along the horizontal axis (`entryDate` for both) and the `yField` configuration determines which field is tracked along the vertical axis (`weight` for the first series and `exercise` for the second). The `axis` configuration tells the series which part of the graph to map its values to.

The `style` section determines how the line for our series will appear. The `marker` section gives us the appearance of each data point along the line. The `highlightCfg` section uses `scale` to increase the size of a selected marker, so when the user clicks on a data point, the marker will increase to 1.25 times its normal size.

The `marker` section itself is actually a `sprite` reference, which means that we can use any of the available Sencha Touch `sprite` objects for our `marker`. These include things such as:

- Circles
- Ellipses
- Images
- Rectangles
- Text

A full list of available sprites and their configuration options can be found at `http://docs.sencha.com/touch/2-1/` in the **draw | sprite** section of the API. To use these sprites, you just need to set the type configuration to the sprite name. The name for each sprite can be found at the top of the documentation as seen in the following screenshot:

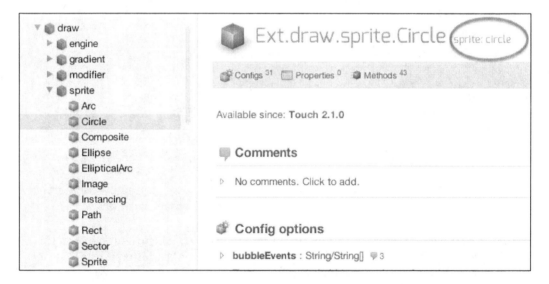

Once the `type` config is set for the `marker` section, you can use any of the sprite's configuration options to customize the marker's appearance.

Now that the series configuration is complete, we can also add some interactions to the graph to make it more interesting.

The interactions section

The interactions section allows us to respond to the user's taps and gestures to expand the amount of information we provide. The current types of interactions include the following:

- ItemCompare: This lets the user select two items and see a data comparison
- ItemHightlight: This lets the user tap and highlight a series of data items in the chart
- ItemInfo: This lets the user tap and get a detailed view of the data record
- PanZoom: This lets the user pinch the chart to zoom in and out, or let them tap and drag to pan
- PieGrouping: This lets the user select and merge consecutive pie slices
- Rotate: This lets the user tap and drag around the center of the pie or radar charts to rotate the chart
- ToggleStacked: This lets the user toggle between stacked and grouped orientations on a bar or column series chart

For this application, we will allow the user to tap the data points and get back all of the details for that particular day. We set up an interaction with a type value of iteminfo and define a tpl tag, which is used to display the data in the panel. The interaction receives the entire data record for the tapped data point so the tpl tag can use any of our values for weight, exercise, water, calories, or tags:

```
interactions:[
  {
   type:'iteminfo',
   panel:{
    tpl:[ '<table>',
      '<tpl if="weight"><tr><th>Weight</th><td>{weight}
({weightUnits})</td></tr></tpl>',
      '<tpl if="water"><tr><th>Water</th><td>{water} ({waterUnits})</
td></tr></tpl>',
      '<tpl if="calories"><tr><th>Calories</th><td>{calories}</td></
tr></tpl>',
      '<tpl if="exercise"><tr><th>Exercise</th><td>{exercise} minutes</
td></tr></tpl>',
      '<tpl if="tag"><tr><th>Tag</th><td>{tag}</td></tr></tpl>',
      '</table>'
    ]
   }
  }
```

This template will display our detailed item info. Next, we need to add the listener that will show the window when we click on one of the data points in our `OverviewChart`:

```
listeners:{
  show:function (interaction, item, panel) {
   var record = item.record;
   var dt = new Date(record.get('entryDate'));
   var config = Ext.ModelManager.getModel('WeightWeight.model.
Config');
    config.load(1, {
      scope:this,
      success:function (configRecord) {
       panel.setData(Ext.apply(record.getData(), configRecord.
getData()));
      }
    });

panel.getDockedComponent(0).setTitle(Ext.Date.format(dt, 'm-d-Y'));
    }
   }
  }
 ]
```

The listener starts by setting `var record = item.record;` and then getting the date out of the record so that we can format it properly for our `setTitle` function at the end of the listener.

Next, we grab our single config record so that we can get the units of measurement for weight and water consumption. Then we set the data for the panel to the combined `record` and `configRecord` objects (using `Ext.apply()`). This gets both sets of data into our `tpl` for display.

Lastly, since this is a special floating panel in Sencha Touch, it has no `title` attribute, but we can create one using the first docked component in the panel. We set this `title` to the formatted date we grabbed at the top of the function.

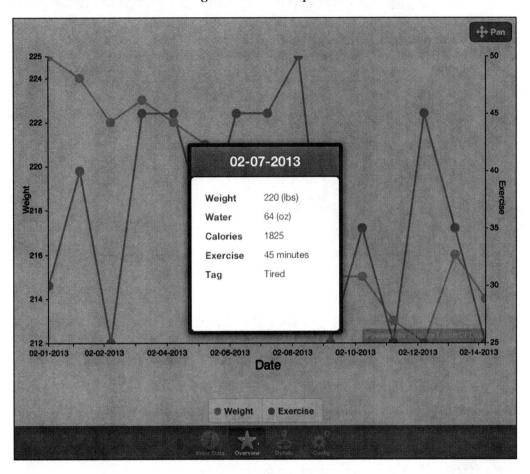

You should be able to save your work now and click on any of the data points to see our new detailed item info.

The last thing we want to cover is creating the details view.

Creating the details view

For the details chart, we have decided to make something a little more reusable. Our overall details view will contain three similar charts and a radar chart. Since we don't want to create the same chart over and over, we need a view we can call up with a different configuration for each of our charts. This will be a simple bar style chart with two axes; one for the date and one for the amount.

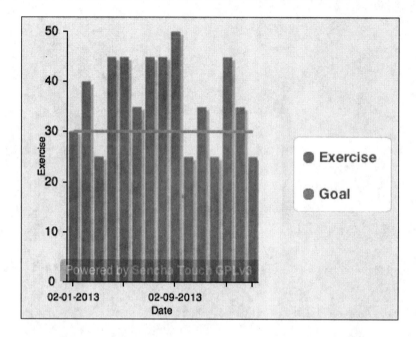

This reusable chart will be our goalChart view. We will create the goalChart view with its own xtype, which will allow us to reuse it with different configurations.

Creating the goalChart view

We start by creating a goalChart view and setting it up to load our config file when it initializes:

```
Ext.define('WeightWeight.view.goalChart', {
    extend:'Ext.Panel',
    alias:'widget.goalchart',
    config: {
        layout: 'fit'
    },
```

```
    constructor: function (config) {
        this.store = Ext.getStore('EntryStore');

        Ext.apply(this, config);

        this.callParent([config]);
        var configRecord = Ext.ModelManager.getModel('WeightWeight.
model.Config');
        configRecord.load(1, {
            scope:this,
            success: this.createChart
        });

    }
});
```

Here, we set our panel's store to the `EntryStore` that contains all of our data (this gives us access to every record). Next, our `constructor` function will take whatever configuration options are passed to it, and applies them to the panel using `Ext.apply(this, config);`. This is where we will set an individual `title`, `dataField`, `goalField`, and `colorSet` for each chart.

Once these options are set, the panel then loads the goals and measurements from our single `configRecord` in much the same way as our previous chart panel. This time when the `Config` successfully loads, we call a new function called `createChart`.

The `createChart` function comes right after our `constructor` function:

```
createChart: function(config) {
 this.configRecord = config;
 var goalStore = Ext.create('Ext.data.Store',{ fields: [
    'entryDate',
    {name: Ext.String.capitalize(this.dataField), type:'int'},
    {name: 'goal', type: 'int'}
  ]
 }
);
 this.store.each(function(record) {
 if (record.get(this.dataField)) {
  var values = {
  entryDate: Ext.Date.format(dt,'m-d-Y'),
  goal: this.configRecord.get(this.goalField)
  };
  values[Ext.String.capitalize(this.dataField)] = record.get(this.
dataField);
  goalStore.add(values);
  }
 }, this);
}
```

The `createChart` function starts by creating a second `store` called the `goalStore` and gives it three fields as follows:

- `entryDate`: This is the date field from our store
- `goal`: This is the the goal passed from our `configRecord`
- `this.dataField`: This will be passed to us as one of our config options when we use the `goalChart` view

We then loop through our data in the main store (`EntryData`) and look for any values in the field that match the value we received for `this.dataField`. As we find matches, we add them to our `goalStore`. The `goalStore` is the actual store that will feed the chart.

For example, we could use the following code to create a `goalChart` view:

```
{
  xtype: 'goalchart',
  chartTitle: 'Exercise',
  dataField: 'exercise',
  goalField: 'exercisePerDay',
  colorSet:['#a61120', '#ff0000']
}
```

The `goalChart` view would use the `dataField` value to look for any data we have for `exercise` and create the chart. It would also use the `goalField` value of `exercisePerDay` to grab that number from our config record and add it to the display.

The final part of our `goalChart` sets up the series and axes much like the previous one:

```
this.chart = Ext.factory({
 xtype: 'chart',
 store: goalStore,
 animate: true,
 legend: {
  position: 'right'
 },
 axes: [{
  type:'Numeric',
  position:'left',
  fields:[ Ext.String.capitalize(this.dataField), 'goal'],
  title: Ext.String.capitalize(this.dataField),
  decimals:0,
  minimum:0
 },
```

```
        {
          type:'category',
          position:'bottom',
          fields:['entryDate'],
          title:'Date'
        }],
        series: [
          {
            type: 'bar',
            xField: 'entryDate',
            yField: Ext.String.capitalize(this.dataField),
            style: {
              fill: this.colorSet[0],
              shadowColor: 'rgba(0,0,0,0.3)',
              maxBarWidth: 50,
              minGapWidth: 3,
              shadowOffsetX: 3,
              shadowOffsetY: 3
            }
          },
          {
            type:'line',
            style: {
              smooth: false,
              stroke: this.colorSet[1],
              lineWidth: 3
            },
            axis:'left',
            xField:'entryDate',
            yField:'goal',
            showMarkers: false,
            title:'Goal'
          }
        ]
      }, 'Ext.char t.Chart');
```

The main difference from the previous charts is that we have some values that
will be supplied by our `config`, and we use the `Ext.factory` function to create
the chart object.

> Here, our use of Ext.factory is equivalent to Ext.create, but
> Ext.factory can also be used to update the configuration of existing
> objects. We chose to use Ext.factory here, rather than Ext.
> create, solely because most of the Sencha Charts examples refer to
> Ext.factory when creating charts, and we wanted to be consistent.

Now we can re-use the chart for our exercise, water, and weight charts just by setting different `config` values for:

- `dataField`
- `goalField`
- `chartTitle`
- `colorSet`

Take a look at the `DetailChart.js` file in our example code to see how this works.

The last chart we need to touch on is the word chart.

Creating the word chart

The `wordChart` view is set up much like our `goalChart` with its own `constructor` and `createChart` function. However, the goal chart uses our tags to create a different type of chart called a radar chart. Our `wordChart.js` file checks for the number of occurrences of specific words and uses the information to draw our radar chart.

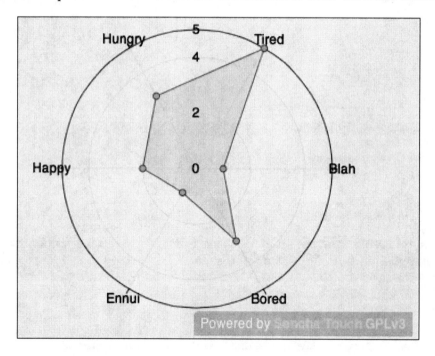

The beginning of the `wordChart.js` file looks almost the same as our `goalChart`:

```
Ext.define('WeightWeight.view.wordChart', {
    extend:'Ext.Panel',
    alias:'widget.wordchart',
    config: {
        layout: 'fit'
    },
    constructor: function (config) {
        this.store = Ext.getStore('EntryStore');
        Ext.apply(this, config);
        this.callParent([config]);
        var configRecord = Ext.ModelManager.getModel('WeightWeight.
model.Config');
        configRecord.load(1, {
            scope:this,
            success: this.createChart
        });

    }


});
```

After the end of the `constructor`, we set up our `createChart` function:

```
createChart: function(config) {
        this.configRecord = config;
        this.store.filterBy(function(record) {
            if (record.get('tag')) {
                return true;
            } else {
                return false;
            }
        });
        this.store.setGroupField('tag');
        this.store.setGroupDir('ASC');
        var groups = this.store.getGroups();
        this.store.setGroupField('');
        this.store.clearFilter();
        var wordStore = Ext.create('Ext.data.Store',
            { fields: ['name', {name: 'count', type: 'int'}]}
        );
        Ext.each(groups, function(group) {
            wordStore.add({name: group.name, count: group.children.
length});
        });
```

This grabs our `configRecord` like we did previously and then filters our `store` to find only the records that have `tag` data. We then `group` the fields by `tag` so that we can generate a `count` for each `tag`.

Next we create a second `store`, much like in our `goalCharts` and we transfer our tag names and our counts into the second `store`. This one is called our `wordStore`.

Now that we have a `wordStore` that consists only of the tag name and the number of times it occurs, we can use it to feed our new chart. Again, we use the `Ext.Factory` to create our store:

```
this.chart = Ext.factory({
 xtype: 'polar',
 store: wordStore,
 animate: {
  easing: "backInOut",
  duration: 500
 },
 series: [{
  type: 'radar',
  xField: 'name',
  yField: 'count',
  labelField: 'name',
  marker:{
   type:'circle',
   r:3,
   fillStyle:'#76AD86'
  },
  style: {
   fillStyle: 'rgba(0,255,0,0.2)',
   strokeStyle: 'rgba(0,0,0,0.8)',
   lineWidth: 1
  }
 }]
```

The radar style chart uses an `xtype` value of `polar` as part of its chart configuration.

 Polar charts include circular chart systems such as the pie and radar style charts, whereas **Cartesian** charts are line-based charts such as the area and bar charts.

In the `series` section, the `type` value for our chart is then set to `radar`, which gives us our specific chart appearance.

As with our previous charts, we also set `marker` and `style` configurations. Finally, we finish our `wordChart` by setting up the axes, closing out the chart object, and adding it to our panel:

```
axes: [{
  type: 'numeric',
   position: 'radial',
   fields: 'count',
   grid: true,
   label: {
    fill: 'black'
   }
  },{
   type: 'category',
   position: 'angular',
   fields: 'name',
   grid: true,
   label: {
    fill: 'black'
   },
  style: {
   estStepSize: 1
  }
 }]
}, 'Ext.chart.Chart');

this.add(this.chart);
```

We have two axes here: a `numeric` axis for our tag counts and a `category` axis for our tag names. We map these axes to the correct `field` and set `grid` to `true`. This will give us an underlying grid for our radar chart.

The `style` setting of `estStepSize: 1` ensures that all of our words will show up around the edge of our radar chart, without skipping any words.

Now that our `wordChart` is finished, we need to assemble all of our charts into a single page for our full details view:

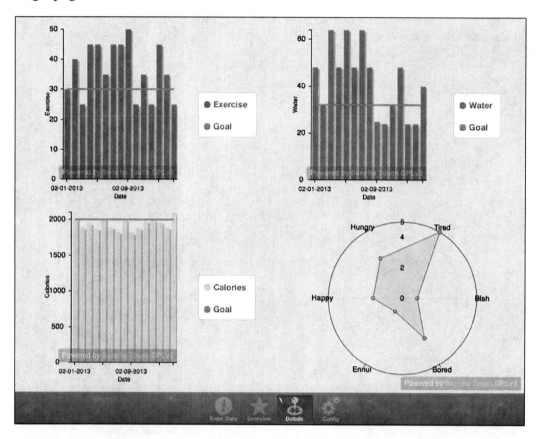

Back in our `details.js` placeholder file, we need to set up a new layout and add our four charts. As you can see in the screenshot, we have our four charts arranged in a square on the page with one chart in each corner. The easiest way to accomplish this is with a set of nested `hbox` and `vbox` layouts:

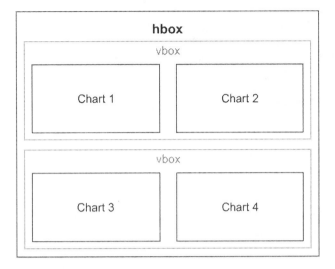

As you can see in the previous image, our details panel will have a `layout` section of `hbox`, with two containers inside, one on top of the other. In our `config` section, add the layout as follows:

```
layout: {
 type: 'hbox',
 align: 'stretch',
 pack: 'center',
 flex: 1
}
```

The `stretch` and `center` values ensure that our containers will expand to fill the available space and occupy the center of our details panel. The `flex` value makes the inner containers equal in size. These two containers will have a layout of `vbox`.

We add these two containers in an `items` section within our `config` section:

```
items: [
    {
        xtype: 'container',
        layout: {
            type: 'vbox',
            align: 'stretch',
            pack: 'center',
            flex: 1
        },
```

```
        items: [
                {height: 300, width: 400, xtype: 'goalchart', chartTitle:
        'Exercise', dataField: 'exercise', goalField: 'exercisePerDay',
        colorSet:['#a61120', '#ff0000'] },
                {height: 300, width: 400, xtype: 'goalchart', chartTitle:
        'Caloric Intake', dataField: 'calories', goalField: 'caloriesPerDay',
        colorSet:['#ffd13e', '#ff0000']}
            ]
        },
        {

            xtype: 'container',
            layout: {
                type: 'vbox',
                align: 'stretch',
                pack: 'center',
                flex: 1
            },
            items: [
                {height: 300, width: 400, xtype: 'goalchart',
        chartTitle: 'Water', dataField: 'water', goalField: 'waterPerDay',
        colorSet:['#115fa6', '#ff0000']},
                {height: 300, width: 400, xtype: 'wordchart', chartTitle:
        'Tags', dataField: 'tag'}
            ]
        }
    ]
```

The two containers form a top and bottom layout with two charts each. The goal charts each have slightly different configurations so that they display exercise, calories, and water consumption. We also color them differently to provide more visual appeal. The `wordchart` uses a similar configuration to include only the data from our tags.

With this last panel completed, you should be able to enter data into the application and test all of the charts.

Homework

Take some time to play around with the different types of charts and see what is available. The Sencha website has an excellent guide for using charts and interactions at http://docs.sencha.com/touch/2-1/#!/guide/drawing_and_charting.

Summary

In this chapter we talked about:

- Setting up the basic application to create the different views for the application
- Creating the stores that will hold the data and feed our charts
- Setting up the controllers for the application
- Creating the overview chart
- Creating the details chart

In the next chapter we will look at creating a simple application to work with an external API.

5

On Deck: Using Sencha.io

In our previous chapters we have typically used local storage for maintaining our data. This offers a number of advantages with its ease of use and simplicity. The store and the model do all of the heavy lifting for us.

However, there are a number of disadvantages to local storage as well. First and foremost, it is very much local to the device. This means that if your user has more than one device (a phone, desktop, and a tablet computer), then they will have a separate set of data for each device.

This can be confusing to the user and it negates the advantage of having a single application that is accessible from multiple devices. Additionally, the data can be deleted by the user when they clear the local browser data. This can make local storage a bit problematic for a robust application.

In this chapter we are going to look at solving this issue with an external API called Sench.io. Here's what we will cover:

- Setting up the basic application
- Getting started with Sencha.io
- Updating the basic application to work with Sencha.io

The basic application

Our basic application is designed to present a set of flash cards to the user in a random order. Each set of flash cards comprises a deck. The user can add new decks and new cards to each deck. The decks and the cards will reside in a remote storage service called **Sencha.io**. Using this service, the user will also be able to log in from any number of devices and access their cards and decks.

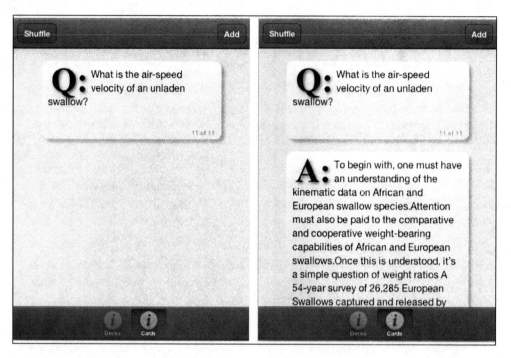

We will start off our application with the models and stores.

Creating the models and stores

The model for our deck is very simple and only needs two pieces of information. We will use an ID to link cards to a specific deck and a name for display purposes:

```
Ext.define('MyApp.model.Deck', {
    extend: 'Ext.data.Model',
    config: {
        fields: [
            {
                name: 'id'
            },
```

```
            {
                name: 'name'
            }
        ]
    }
});
```

The card model needs an ID of its own so that we can uniquely identify it and a deckID value so that we know which deck it's a part of. We will also need the question and answer for each card:

```
Ext.define('MyApp.model.Card', {
    extend: 'Ext.data.Model',
    config: {
        fields: [
            {
                name: 'id'
            },
            {
                name: 'deckID'
            },
            {
                name: 'question'
            },
            {
                name: 'answer'
            }
        ]
    }
});
```

For the two stores, we will initially use a local storage proxy as we have in previous chapters. This will let us test our application before we start using the Sencha.io service.

Our deck store looks like this:

```
Ext.define('MyApp.store.DeckStore', {
    extend: 'Ext.data.Store',
    requires: [
        'MyApp.model.Deck'
    ],
    config: {
        autoLoad: true,
        model: 'MyApp.model.Deck',
        storeId: 'DeckStore',
        proxy: {
```

```
            type: 'localstorage',
            id: 'Decks'
        },
        fields: [
            {
                name: 'id',
                type: 'int'
            },
            {
                name: 'name',
                type: 'string'
            }
        ]
    }
});
```

If you have worked your way through the first chapter, this basic setup should look pretty familiar to you. We extend the basic store, require our `model` file, and then set up our configuration. The configuration sets the store to load when it is created, tells it which model to use, sets up our local storage `proxy`, and tells it which `fields` to expect.

Our card store is almost an exact duplicate:

```
Ext.define('MyApp.store.CardStore', {
    extend: 'Ext.data.Store',
    requires: [
        'MyApp.model.Card'
    ],
    config: {
        autoLoad: true,
        model: 'MyApp.model.Card',
        storeId: 'CardStore',
        proxy: {
            type: 'localstorage',
            id: 'Cards'
        },
        fields: [
            {
                name: 'id',
                type: 'int'
            },
            {
                name: 'deckID',
                type: 'int'
            },
```

```
          {
              name: 'question',
              type: 'string'
          },
          {
              name: 'question',
              type: 'string'
          }
       ]
    }
});
```

Here we have just changed the name from `Deck` to `Card`, and specified our card fields in place of our deck fields.

> If you configure your store with a model, you don't actually have to specify the fields. We are doing so here just for the sake of completeness.

As mentioned before, we will be revisiting these stores once we get things set up with `Sencha.io`, but first we need to get our display together for our lists, cards, and editing.

Creating the views

For our main view, we will be using a tab panel with two containers, one for our decks and one for our cards. We will use sheets for editing and adding new decks and cards. Our initial `main.js` file looks like this:

```
Ext.define('MyApp.view.Main', {
    extend: 'Ext.tab.Panel',

    config: {
        id: 'mainView',
        items: [],
        tabBar: {
            docked: 'bottom'
        }
});
```

Remember to add this file into your `app.js` file and set the launch function to create a copy of the component when the application starts (if you are using Sencha Architect, then this should happen automatically). Your `app.js` file should look like this:

```
Ext.Loader.setConfig({
    enabled: true
});

Ext.application({
    models: [
        'Deck',
        'Card'
    ],
    stores: [
        'DeckStore',
        'CardStore'
    ],
    views: [
        'Main'
    ],
    name: 'MyApp',

    launch: function() {

        Ext.create('MyApp.view.Main', {fullscreen: true});
    }

});
```

Next we need to add the two containers to our `main.js` view. In the empty items section, add the following container:

```
{
    xtype: 'container',
    layout: {
        type: 'fit'
    },
    title: 'Decks',
    iconCls: 'info',
    items: [
        {
            xtype: 'list',
            itemTpl: [
                '<div>{name}</div>'
```

```
        ],
        store: 'DeckStore'
    },
    {

        xtype: 'titlebar',
        docked: 'top',
        title: 'Decks',
        items: [
            {
                xtype: 'button',
                itemId: 'mybutton',
                text: 'Add',
                align: 'right'
            }
        ]
    }
    ]
}
```

This will be the list for our decks. The overall container has a fit layout so the items will fill the entire width and height of the container. We have given the container a title and an iconCls value, which will be used to label the tab in our Main tab panel.

The container has a list view that uses our DeckStore store and a simple itemTpl template that displays the name of each deck in a separate div tag.

We have also added a title bar where we can display a button for adding new decks and a title to let the user know what they are looking at.

Our second container follows the same pattern as our first, but instead of a list, we have a separate container with a carousel layout, as shown in the following code:

```
{
    xtype: 'container',
    title: 'Cards',
    iconCls: 'info',
    items: [
        {
            xtype: 'titlebar',
            docked: 'top',
            items: [
                {
                    xtype: 'button',
                    itemId: 'mybutton1',
                    text: 'Add',
```

```
                    align: 'right'
                },
                {
                    xtype: 'button',
                    text: 'Shuffle'
                }
            ]
        },
        {
            xtype: 'carousel'
        }
    ]
}
```

This container has a `titlebar` control that will be set to display the name of the current deck at the top and pull the cards into our `carousel` layout. We also have a second button that will shuffle the current deck of cards.

Next we need to set up the two sheets for adding cards and decks. The deck sheet is a simple sheet with a `textfield` element for naming the deck, a `button` element for saving, and another `button` element for canceling:

```
Ext.define('MyApp.view.addDeckSheet', {
    extend: 'Ext.Sheet',
    alias: 'widget.addDeckSheet',

    config: {
        id: 'addDeckSheet',
        items: [
            {
                xtype: 'textfield',
                margin: '0 0 10 0',
                label: 'Name'
            },
            {
                xtype: 'button',
                ui: 'confirm',
                text: 'Save',
                itemID: 'saveDeckButton'
            },
            {
                xtype: 'button',
                itemId: 'cancelDeckButton',
                ui: 'decline',
                text: 'Cancel'
```

```
            }
        ],
        listeners: [
            {
                fn: 'hideDeckSheet',
                event: 'tap',
                delegate: '#cancelDeckButton'
            }
        ]
    },

    hideDeckSheet: function(button, e, options) {
        button.up('sheet').hide();
    }

});
```

We also add a listener for the `Cancel` button that will hide the sheet without saving the values. The listener delegates the `tap` event to our `cancelDeckButton` delegate and calls the `hideDeckSheet` function when the `tap` event occurs.

The `hideDeckSheet` function receives the `button` element as part of its arguments. We can then travel up the DOM structure from the button, find the sheet, and hide it.

A note about using up and down

The up and down functions in Sencha Touch are extremely useful when you have a component and you need to get to either a sub component or a parent component. However, it should be noted that both up and down only return the first component that matches. For example, if a `button` element is inside of a `container` element, which is itself inside another `container` element, then `button.up('container')` would return the first container and not the second, outer container.

Our card sheet is a duplicate of the deck sheet, but with text fields for `question` and `answer`:

```
Ext.define('MyApp.view.addCardSheet', {
    extend: 'Ext.Sheet',
    config: {
        id: 'addCardSheet',
        items: [
            {
                xtype: 'container',
                html: 'Deck Name Here',
```

```
                          style: 'color: #FFFFFF; text-align:center;'
            },
            {
                  xtype: 'textareafield',
                  id: 'cardQuestion',
                  margin: '0 0 10 0',
                  label: 'Question'
            },
            {
                  xtype: 'textareafield',
                  id: 'cardAnswer',
                  margin: '0 0 10 0',
                  label: 'Answer'
            },
            {
                  xtype: 'button',
                  ui: 'confirm',
                  itemId: 'saveCardButton',
                  text: 'Save'
            },
            {
                  xtype: 'button',
                  itemId: 'cancelCardButton',
                  ui: 'decline',
                  text: 'Cancel'
            }

        ],
        listeners: [
            {
                  fn: 'hideCardSheet',
                  event: 'tap',
                  delegate: '#cancelCardButton'
            }
        ]
    },
    hideCardSheet: function(button, e, options) {
        button.up('sheet').hide();
    }
});
```

As before, we have our **Save** and **Cancel** buttons, with the **Cancel** button hiding the sheet when tapped.

You should now be able to start the application and test the different views as shown:

Before we can get things working further in the application, we need to get set up with Sencha.io.

Getting started with Sencha.io

The Sencha.io service will allow us to store our data using Sencha's cloud service. We will need to register a new account, add our application and user groups using the Sencha.io dashboard, and then configure our application to use the service.

The sign-up process

To register a new account, go to `https://manage.sencha.io` and click on the **Register** link at the bottom of the page. Fill out the forms with your information and submit. Once your account is created, log in to the Sencha.io dashboard at the same address you used for registration, and you will see something similar to the following screenshot:

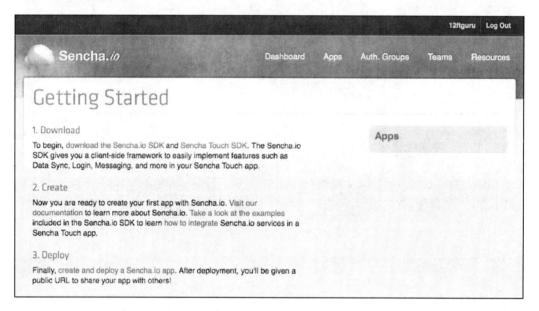

Downloading and installing the Sencha.io SDK

Now that you have an account you can download and install the Sencha.io SDK. There is a download link in the first part of the **Getting Started** page (which should be where you first start when you log in).

Download the SDK to your computer and unzip the file. Move it into your web directory (someplace where you can easily reference it from your application). Next we need to add these files to our application. You can begin by opening your main `app.html` file and adding the following lines in the `head` section of the file (with your other script includes):

```
<script type="text/javascript" src="lib/io/lib/socket.io.js"></script>
<script type="text/javascript" src="lib/io/sencha-io-debug.js"></script>
```

In this example, we have copied all of the Sencha.io files into a folder called `io` in the `lib` directory of our application. If your path is different, you will need to adjust the lines above to fit your setup.

Now that we have included the two main files we need for Sencha.io, we also need to set some options in `app.js` so that the autoloader picks up these files as well. At the top of the `app.js` file, add the following code:

```
Ext.Loader.setPath({
    'Ext.io': 'lib/io/src/io',
    'Ext.cf': 'lib/io/src/cf'
});
```

Once we have this information set, our application should be able to pick up all the files it needs to work with Sencha.io, but we still need to register our application before we can continue building.

Registering your application and Auth group

Registering your application and Auth group with Sencha.io provisions the application with its own data storage and an authorized user base. As with most API services, your application needs a way to uniquely identify itself to the remote system so that it will know where to store your data.

With Sencha.io, we will get two pieces of information when we register our application: an `appID` value and an `appSecret` value. These two pieces of information will be added to `app.js` to identify our application to the Sencha.io system.

Let's start by adding an Auth group. The Auth group sets up a group where users can register to use your application. If you have multiple applications, you can set up one Auth group for each application or set up a single Auth group to be shared across multiple applications.

From the **Dashboard** section of your Sencha.io account (`http://manage.sencha.io`), click on the **Auth Groups** link at the top of the page and choose **Create Auth Group**.

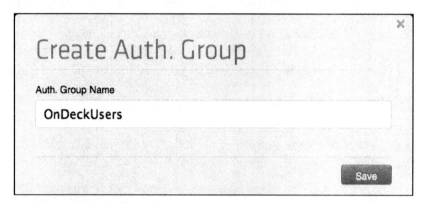

Enter a name for your Auth group and click on **Save**. The name is arbitrary, but if you are using the group for a single application, it's probably best to name it something like `myAppNameUsers` so that you can keep track of which application this is for.

The Auth group also controls how the users authenticate in your application. Once you have saved the Auth group, you can edit it and change the way users log in to your application.

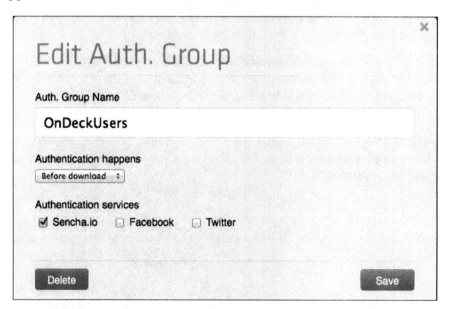

You can choose to have users authenticate before the application fully downloads or afterwards. You can also choose to let users log in with a valid Facebook, Twitter, or Sencha.io account.

If you choose the **Sencha.io** login option, then the SDK will automatically handle both user registration and authentication within your application, no extra coding required.

If you choose the **Facebook** or **Twitter** login option, Sencha.io will handle the authentication automatically. Users will have to be registered with either service before they can access the application.

Now that we have a set of users for the application, we need to register the application itself. From the Sencha.io dashboard, click on **Apps** and then click on **Create App**. As before, we only need to enter a name for the application. For this application we chose the name **OnDeck** as shown in the following screenshot:

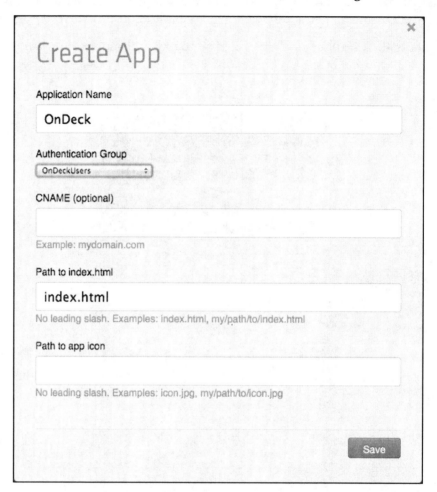

Next we need to select our **Authentication Group** name from the drop-down menu. This tells Sencha.io to authenticate and assign users from this group to our application. There is an optional **CNAME** field for setting the domain your application will reside on, as well as a field for the path to the index.html file. This should be set if you are using the app.html file instead of index.html, or if you have your application hosted inside a sub directory on your server.

We can also set an application icon here. This is the icon that will be used if the user saves our web application to their home screen. Click on **Save** when you are finished.

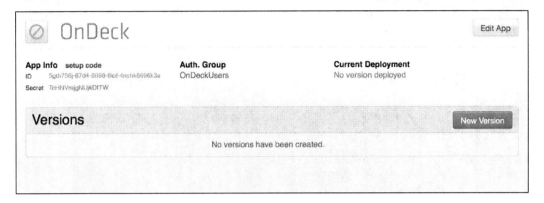

On the page application page, you should now see a listing for your application's ID (mentioned in the **ID** field) and secret (mentioned in the **Secret** field). Make note of these, as we will need to add them into app.js once we are finished with registration.

Please note that the **ID** and **Secret** values in the preceding example screenshot are example data only. You will need to generate your own information on the Sencha.io site to make your application work. You will also need to generate your own ID and secret to make the example code from the chapter work.

Once you have completed this part of the registration, you will need to add the ID and secret values into your app.js file. Open the file and add the following code at the top of the Ext.application({ section:

```
config: {
    io: {
    appId: 'YouAppIDHere',
    appSecret: 'YouAppSecretHere'
  }
}
```

Substitute your information for the appId and appSecret placeholders shown. Once you have added the information into app.js, we can get back to updating our stores and creating our controller.

Updating the application for Sencha.io

Now that our application is registered, we need to set up the stores to use Sencha.io. We will also set up our controller for the application and show you how to override the `Carousel` component to make it work with a data store.

Updating the stores

Our original stores were simple local storage for testing. We are going to edit these now to use Sencha.io to store our data. Most of these changes will be in the `proxy` section. For example, the `DeckStore` code should be updated to look like this:

```
Ext.define('MyApp.store.DeckStore', {
    extend: 'Ext.data.Store',
    requires: [
        'MyApp.model.Deck'
    ],

    config: {
        autoLoad: true,
        model: 'MyApp.model.Deck',
        storeId: 'DeckStore',
        proxy: {
            type: 'syncstorage',
            id: 'decks',
            owner: 'user',
            access: 'private'
        },
        autoLoad: true,
        autoSync: false
    }
});
```

Notice that we now use a new type of proxy called `syncstorage`. This is the special Sencha.io proxy that works much the same as a local store, but it stores the data remotely on the Sencha.io servers.

We also have new configurations for `owner` and `access`. The `owner` and `access` field must both be set for `syncstorage` to work correctly. As of this writing, the only `owner` option is `user`. This is the currently authenticated user.

The `access` configuration determines if the store is **private**, available only to the currently authenticated user, or **public**, available to all members of the group of users. This is the user group we set up in the Sencha.io dashboard.

Next, we added a configuration of `autoLoad: true`. This will load any local data if the connection is lost while the user is still logged in. We then set `autosync: false` to prevent the store from automatically syncing when the application starts. We should to wait until the user logs into the application before we load the store. We will do this manually as part of the application controller.

You can make the exact same changes to the `CardStore.js` file to get it working with Sencha.io, but it requires one additional setting for `remoteFilter: false`. We will be loading all of the user's cards when they log in, and filtering them by deck once a deck is selected.

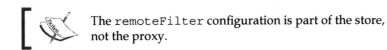

> The `remoteFilter` configuration is part of the store, not the proxy.

Now that we have our stores configured we can move on to the controller.

Creating the controller

Our controller has a few things it needs to handle for us:

- Setting up for Sencha.io
- Handling anything that needs to happen at login and logout
- Adding cards and decks
- Selecting a deck for display
- Syncing between the local application and Sencha.io

We will start by setting up our basic controller with the models, views, stores, and references:

```
Ext.define('MyApp.controller.MyController', {
    extend: 'Ext.app.Controller',
    config: {
        selectedDeck: false,
        models: [
          'Deck',
          'Card'
        ],
        stores: [
          'DeckStore',
          'CardStore'
        ],
        views: [
```

```
                'Main',
                'addCardSheet',
                'addDeckSheet',
                'CardView'
            ],
        refs: {
            addCardSheet: '#addCardSheet',
            addCardSaveButton: '#addCardSheet button[text="Save"]',
            addDeckSheet: '#addDeckSheet',
            addDeckSaveButton: '#addDeckSheet button[text="Save"]',
            deckList: '#deckList',
            mainView: '#mainView',
            shuffle: 'button[text="Shuffle"]'
        }
    }
});
```

The first section defines our controller and then lists the `models`, `stores`, and `views` values we previously created. We also add an empty configuration for `selectedDeck`. We will be using this as a placeholder for storing the record of the currently selected deck. This will allow us to easily get and set the value anywhere in our controller functions using `getSelectedDeck` and `setSelectedDeck`.

Getters and setters

Sencha Touch automatically creates `get` and `set` functions for configuration settings as well as references (see the following section). These functions take the form of `getWhateverYouCalledIt` and `setWhateverYouCalledIt`. It is important to remember that even if you lowercase the first letter of the `config` option or reference, the `get` and `set` functions will uppercase the first letter.

The `refs` section allows us to create a reference to a component either by `id` (such as `#addCardSheet`) or a component query, such as (`#addCardSheet button[text="Save"]`).

The preceding component query will look for a component with an `id` value of `addCardSheet` and then find the button within the component that has a `text` configuration of `"Save"`.

We can now reference anything in our `refs` list with `this.getReferenceName`.

Immediately after the `refs` section we need to add a `control` section. This section uses our references and defines a set of listeners and functions for some of our components:

```
control: {
    addCardSaveButton: {
  tap: "addCard"
    },
    addDeckSaveButton: {
  tap: "addDeck"
    },
    deckList: {
  select: "onDeckSelected"
    },
    addCardSheet: {
  show: "updateCardSheetDeckInfo"
    },
    shuffle: {
  tap: 'shuffleDeck'
    }
}
```

Each member of our `control` section has a reference, an event to listen for and a function to fire when the event occurs. We will create each of these functions later in the controller, but first we need to add our `init` function to set up Sencha.io and the other functions for authentication.

When our application first starts, it needs to listen to the Sencha.io controller for authentication and messaging. We handle this in our `init` function (this goes right after the `config` section):

```
init: function() {
  this.getApplication().sio.on({
    authorized: this.onAuth,
    logout: this.onLogout,
    usermessage: this.onUserMessage,
    scope: this
  });
}
```

This code tells our controller three events from the Sencha.io controller:

- `authorized`: The user has successfully logged in
- `logout`: The user has logged out of the system
- `usermessage`: The user has received a message

We have assigned a function to each one of these events and now we need to add them below our `init` function.

The first is our `onAuth` function, which syncs all of the user's stores once they have logged in:

```
onAuth: function(user) {
  Ext.getStore('DeckStore').sync();
  Ext.getStore('CardStore').sync();
  return true;
}
```

Our `onLogout` function does the reverse and clears out any locally stored data:

```
onLogout: function() {
    var deckStore = Ext.getStore('DeckStore');
    deckStore.getProxy().clear();
    deckStore.load();
    var cardStore = Ext.getStore('CardStore');
    cardStore.getProxy().clear();
    cardStore.load();
    return true;
}
```

Our message function is a bit more interesting.

Sencha.io allows an application to send messages to the user. These can be system messages (for example, the data in a store has updated) or even direct messages between users.

We have set up the following function to simply sync our stores when a message has been received (we will set up the function to send the message a bit later). This means if the user has the program open on one device and makes a change to the data, any other device that user has logged in will update and receive the change:

```
onUserMessage: function(sender, message) {
    var userId = sender.getUserId();
    console.log("user got a message!", arguments, userId);
    Ext.getStore('DeckStore').sync(function() {
        console.log("DeckStore sync callback", arguments);
    });
    Ext.getStore('CardStore').sync(function() {
        console.log("CardStore sync callback", arguments);
    });
    return true;
}
```

We have also added a number of console logs, which you can use to take a look at the messages being sent and the data that is potentially available to your application.

 Be sure to pull up your console when testing the application and examine the different message elements available to you. We will delve deeper into messaging in the final chapter, but you can also check out the *Overview Guide* available at `http://docs.sencha.io` for more information about messaging.

Next we need to add the functions that will save our new cards and decks. Both functions are tied to their respective save buttons. They need to grab the data from the sheet, add it to the store, and then sync the store:

```
addCard: function() {
 var cards = Ext.getStore('CardStore'),
 sheet = this.getAddCardSheet();
 cards.add({
  deckID: this.getSelectedDeck().get('id'),
  question: sheet.down('#cardQuestion').getValue(),
  answer: sheet.down('#cardAnswer').getValue()
 });
 cards.sync(Ext.bind(this.syncCallback, this));
 sheet.down('#cardQuestion').setValue("");
 sheet.down('#cardAnswer').setValue("");
 sheet.hide();
}
```

We use our references here to grab the `addCardSheet` value using `this.getAddCardSheet()` and then we add the data as a new record to our card store.

We then sync the store and *bind* a function called `syncCallback`. This is the function that will send out our message telling the application that data has been updated. The `syncCallback` function can go right below our `addCards` function:

```
syncCallback: function() {
    console.log("broadcast update", arguments);
    this.getApplication().sio.getUser(function(user, error) {
        if (user) {
            console.log("user", user);
            user.send({
                message: "updated"
            },
            function() {
```

```
                  console.log("send callback");
          }
          );


      }
    });
}
```

The console logs have been left in to provide an inside view of the data being passed inside the function. The first part of the code, `this.getApplication().sio.getUser`, grabs the currently authenticated user and runs a function. The function checks to see if we got back a user and, if so, we send the user a message that simply says, `updated`.

This message gets processed by our `onUserMessage` function, which causes our stores to update their data. You can change this message and use the console logs to see how the data is passed between the two functions.

Our `addDeck` function is a virtual duplicate of our `addCard` function:

```
addDeck: function() {
 var decks = Ext.getStore('DeckStore'),
 sheet = this.getAddDeckSheet();
 decks.add({
  name: sheet.down('textfield').getValue()
 });
 decks.sync(Ext.bind(this.syncCallback, this));
 sheet.down('textfield').setValue("");
 sheet.hide();
}
```

Here we only need to get one `textfield` value before we sync the store and do our `syncCallback` function. As before, we also clear the field values before hiding the sheet.

Next we will need to leave our controller for a bit and take a look at how our cards will be displayed.

Overriding the Carousel component

For a flash card application, `Carousel` seems like an ideal component to use because it allows the user to quickly flip from one card to the next. This would allow us to present a question and have the user swipe to get to the answer. The user can then swipe again to get to the next question and so on.

This problem is that `Carousel` is actually a collection of panels and what we really need is something that will pull records from our data store the way a list view does. In order to do this we need to override the `Carousel` component and add some additional behavior.

We will start with our basic component that extends `Carousel`:

```
Ext.define('MyApp.view.CardView', {
 extend: 'Ext.carousel.Carousel',
 alias: 'widget.flashcards',
 config: {
  store: null,
  indicator: false
 }
});
```

We start out setting our `store` configuration to `null` by default. We will set this when we declare the component in the `Main.js` file. In our `Main.js` file, locate the section that says:

```
xtype: 'carousel'
```

Replace that line with the following:

```
xtype: 'flashcards',
store: 'CardStore'
```

This sets the container to our new `flashcards` carousel and sets the `store` configuration to `CardStore`.

If we had hardcoded the store for the component in our `CardView.js` file, it would be more difficult to re-use. When you override a component to extend functionality, it is always a good idea to write it with an eye towards re-using it somewhere else, later on.

Back in `CardView.js`, we need to add a pair of strings to use as xTemplates for our question and answer cards. These go in the `config` section of our component:

```
questionTpl: '<div class="question qa"><span class="count">{number} of
{total}</span><span class="question">{question}</span></div>',
answerTpl: '<div class="question qa"><span class="count">{number}
of {total}</span><span class="question">{question}</span></div><div
class="answer qa"><span class="answer">{answer}</span></div>'
```

These will control how to display the question and answer cards. Since we will be using these same templates multiple times, it's a good idea to compile them in our `constructor` function. Otherwise, the xTemplate will be compiled and recompiled each time a new flashcard is created:

```
constructor: function(config) {
    this.callParent(arguments);
    this.getQuestionTpl().compile();
    this.getAnswerTpl().compile();
    this.setStore(Ext.getStore(this.getStore()));
    this.getStore().on({
        load: this.createCards,
        refresh: this.createCards,
        addrecords: this.createCards,
        scope: this
    });

}
```

Our `constructor` function also sets up the store we passed in `Main.js`. This one is a bit complex and requires a bit of explaining. Let's start from the inside and work our way out:

- `this.getStore()`: This grabs the string value we passed in `Main.js` (`store: 'CardStore'`)
- `Ext.getStore()`: This grabs the store with a `storeId` value of `'CardStore'`
- `this.setStore()`: This applies the store to our `CardView` component, replacing the original string value

When we call `this.getStore()` on the next line to set `listeners`, it now returns an actual store instead of the string value from before.

Then we assign a single function to the store events for `load`, `refresh`, and `addrecords`. We need to add that function next.

We have broken this function into two parts. The first part is the `createCards` function, which gets our store and removes any existing panels from our custom carousel. It then checks to see if we have any cards in the store:

```
createCards: function() {
    var store = this.getStore();
    this.removeAll(); // removes all the old panels
    if (store.getCount() > 0) {
        store.each(this.createFlashCard, this);
    } else {
```

```
        this.add({xtype: 'panel', html: 'No Cards Available for this
Deck.<br />Please click Add to add a card to this deck.'});
    }
    this.setActiveItem(0);
}
```

If not, we give the user a message that there are no cards in the deck and they can click on **Add** to create new cards.

This is where the second part of our function comes into play. If we have records, we pass each one along to a second function called `createFlashCard`:

```
createFlashCard: function(record, index, total) {
  var data = Ext.apply({ total: total, number: (index + 1) }, record.
data);
  this.add({ xtype: 'panel', html: this.getQuestionTpl().apply(data),
scrollable: 'vertical' });
  this.add({ xtype: 'panel', html: this.getAnswerTpl().apply(data),
scrollable: 'vertical' });
}
```

This function is run on each record in `CardStore`. The first line creates our initial data array and sets values for the `total` (the number of cards in the deck), `number` (the sequential number of the current card), and `data` records from the store (which contains both our question and answer for the card).

We then create a new `panel` component and set `html` to our compiled question template with the applied data.

We do the same thing for our answer template, so we end up with two new panels for each record in the store; a question panel, followed by an answer panel.

Since `CardStore` contains all of the records for every deck, we need to filter these down by deck before our `CardsView` carousel loads. We'll handle that back in the controller.

Back in the controller

Once the user selects a deck from our list, we need to filter `CardStore` so that only the cards for that deck are available. We do this in our `onDeckSelected` function:

```
onDeckSelected: function(list, record) {
 var cards = Ext.getStore('CardStore');
 this.setSelectedDeck(record);
 cards.clearFilter();
 cards.sort('id', 'ASC');
```

```
    cards.filter('deckID', record.get('id'));
    this.getMainView().down('#cardsPanel').enable();
    this.getMainView().setActiveItem(1);
}
```

This function is triggered by the select event in our `deckList` component and passes us the list and the record that was selected. Once we grab `CardStore`, we set the `selectedDeck` function to the record that was passed to us when the deck in the list was selected.

Next, we clear any existing filters on `CardStore` and sort it by its `id` value. We then filter the cards to only display the ones for the current deck. Finally, we enable `cardsPanel` and set it to be the active item.

We also have a `control` function that fires when `cardPanel` is shown. This function sets the title bar of the card panel to the name of the deck:

```
    updateCardSheetDeckInfo: function(sheet) {
    sheet.down('#deckName').setHtml(this.getSelectedDeck().get('name'));
    }
```

Since our initial load of the card store presents them in order by `id`, it might be a good idea to let the user shuffle the cards. We do this with our final controller function:

```
    shuffleDeck: function() {
     Ext.getStore('CardStore').sort({
      sorterFn: function() {
       return (Math.round(Math.random())-0.5);
      }
     });
    }
```

This function grabs `CardStore` and sorts it using JavaScript's `Math.random` function to assign a random sort order to each card.

 For a more complete understanding of how sorting works in JavaScript (and Sencha Touch), consult the excellent Mozilla Developer Network's JavaScript Reference for sorting at https://developer.mozilla.org/en/JavaScript/Reference/Global_Objects/Array/sort.

You should now be able to add decks and cards to the application. When you select a deck, the card stack will appear. You can advance from one card to the next by swiping from right to left as shown:

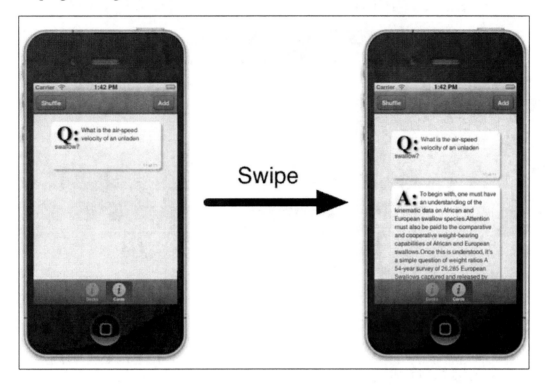

You can use the CSS files to style the answer and question to fit your own personal tastes.

Remember, you will need to register with the application before you can start creating decks and cards. Once you are registered, you can log in from any Sencha Touch Compatible browser and access the same information across multiple devices. Fortunately, since we are using Sencha.io, all of this is taken care of automatically.

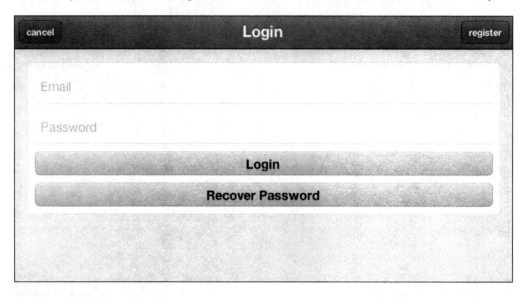

Sencha.io automatically creates these login and registration forms for our application. If the user clicks the **register** button, they will be offered the opportunity to register and use your application. Sencha.io handles all of the forms, data storage, and interactions, which include password recovery without the need for any additional code.

Deploying the application

Sencha.io also offers you the option of deploying your application to the Sencha.io cloud service.

From the Sencha.io dashboard, you can click on your application in the list on the right-hand side of the page. When the main page for the application appears, click on **New Version** and you will be able to upload a zipped file containing all of your code to the Sencha.io website.

When the upload completes, you will be presented with a public URL you can use to access the application. You can also specify if the release is for development or production.

You can also choose to deploy your application to your own web server if you prefer.

Homework

There are a few things that can be added to the application to make it more complete:

- Add the ability to edit/delete cards and decks
- Update the deck list template to show the number of cards in the deck
- Provide a more detailed layout and CSS styling for the questions and answers
- Switch the login method in the Sencha dashboard to allow login with Facebook
- Use the messaging system to present an alert to the user when new cards or decks are available

The opportunities offered by Sencha.io are huge. With its integrated messaging system, you have the potential to communicate with a single user or every user of the application. This opens up possibilities such as publishing and sharing decks between users.

For more information, take a look at the documentation available at `http://docs.sencha.io/0.3.3/index.html#!/guide/overview_introduction`.

Summary

In this chapter we used a simple Flash card application to explore some of the uses and possibilities of Sencha.io. We covered the following points:

- Building the basic application including the stores, models, and views
- Getting started with Sencha.io, signing up, downloading, installing, and configuring the basic application to communicating with the Sencha.io service
- Creating a controller for the application and updating the stores to connect to the Sencha.io service
- Overriding the carousel so that it can read from a data store
- Deploying the application to Sencha.io

In the next chapter we will explore creating your own API for use with Sencha Touch.

6
Catalog Application and API

In this chapter we are creating a simple catalog application that allows you to enter in items for sale and assign them to a category. From an interface and functionality aspect, this will be similar to the previous applications we have created. The difference here is that we are going to explore creating our own API to create, read, update, and delete data from your application.

In this chapter we will cover:

- What is an API?
- Creating the basic application
- Getting started with an API
- Using PHP to create an API
- Connecting the API and the application

What is an API?

An **API** is an **Application Programming Interface**, which is simply a way to make data stored in one place available to a remote application.

Remember our first problem with local storage? The data is stored on the device, which limits its usefulness in a number of ways. If we store the data separately from the device (on a server), we can allow multiple devices to access the data, we can limit and secure the data through authentication, and we can back up the entire data set for all our users.

When we store data separately from the application, we need a way to get to it and make changes. This is where the API comes in. In the last chapter, we used the Sencha.io API to store and retrieve data. In this chapter, we will explore how to create your own API.

The API is a set of code files written in a server-side language such as PHP, Ruby, ASP, or Perl. The JavaScript code sends data to these files as part of an HTTP request (GET, POST, PUT, or DELETE). In the case of Sencha Touch, this data is typically sent formatted either as JSON or XML. The server-side language will then parse the data and send it to the database as SQL statement. The database returns a result, which gets translated by the server-side language back into JSON and returned to the browser.

The entire process would look like this:

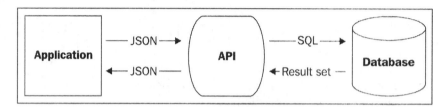

That's a lot of acronyms for a single paragraph, so let's break this down into smaller pieces. Let's assume that you want to add some new user data: a name, an email address, and a phone number. In its most basic form, we can use a browser URL to send this information as:

```
http://mydomain.com/myapifile.php?action=add&&name=john&&email=john@
mydomain.com&&phone=555-1212
```

This would allow our server-side language (we will use PHP for this example) to grab the data we sent and process it correctly. This might look something like this:

```php
<?php
$action = $_GET["action"];
$name = $_GET["name"];
$email = $_GET["email"];
$phone = $_GET["phone"];
?>
```

Please note this is only an example; you would almost certainly want to filter and sanity check any incoming data. Since we are not going to cover all of PHP here, we will only talk about the server-side code in very general terms. It is not intended for actual use, just as a general idea of how things work.

Now that the PHP has our variables it can convert them into something our server-side database can understand:

```
if($action == "add") {
 $sql = "INSERT INTO users VALUES($name, $email, $phone)";
 $results = $db->query($sql);
}
```

This would pass the data from PHP to a database (like MySQL). The database then returns a result, which we can then loop through to create a new array that matches the format we need. We can then format the results as JSON and echo it back:

```
foreach($results as $result) {
  $newArray[$result['key']] = $result['value'];
}
json_encode($newArray);

print $result;
```

As previously noted, this is a very raw general example and APIs can get very complex, very quickly. Fortunately for us, Sencha Touch handles some of this work automatically.

Using a remote API in Sencha Touch

When using Sencha Touch, the JavaScript side of an API becomes a lot easier to manage. We can accomplish most of what we need using the store and a model. Following our previous example, we would create a model that looks like this:

```
Ext.define('MyApp.model.User', {
    extend: 'Ext.data.Model',
    config: {
        idProperty: 'id',
        fields: [
            {name: 'id', type: 'int'},
            {name: 'name', type: 'string'},
            {name: 'email', type: 'string'},
            {name: 'phone', type: 'string'}
        ]
    }
});
```

This sets up our simple model with a unique `id`, `name`, `email`, and `phone` fields. However, we can also add a `proxy` setting and `api` definition to this (right after we finish declaring the fields):

```
proxy: {
  type: 'scripttag',
  url: 'api/Users.php',
  reader: {
    type: 'json',
    root: 'children'
  },
  api: {
    create: 'api/Users.php?action=create',
    read: 'api/ Users.php?action=read',
    update: 'api/ Users.php?action=update',
    destroy: 'api/ Users.php?action=destroy'
  }
}
```

In this example, we are using a `scripttag` proxy. Later on in the chapter we are going to use a different proxy, called a `rest` proxy for the actual application. You should get a feel for the various types of proxies provided by Sencha Touch, and use the one that best suits your application and needs.

The `scripttag` proxy allows us to communicate with another domain (if the PHP and Sencha Touch code are running on the same domain, an `ajax` proxy should be used instead).

> As we mentioned in *Chapter 2, A Feed Reader*, this is due to the same origin policy, which prevents cross-domain attacks in JavaScript. If you would like to learn more about this origin policy, this Wikipedia article is a good place to start:
>
> `http://en.wikipedia.org/wiki/Same_origin_policy`

The `url` property tells the model where to send information for creating, reading, updating, and destroying users (often referred to as **CRUD** functions).

The `reader` property tells the model where to look for the data when it gets back a JSON encoded list of users.

Finally, the `api` section tells the model which URLs to use for each of our CRUD functions. This API setup allows us to do things such as:

```
var user = Ext.create('User', {
    name : 'Stacy McClendon',
    email  : 'stacy@superhappyfuntimego.com',
```

```
      phone: '555-555-5555'
});

user.save();
```

We create a new user with all of our information and then call save. By calling save, the information is submitted to the create URL we set up previously in our model.

Notice that we didn't send an ID. When we create a new user, the database will actually set the unique ID. A properly written API should return this value along with the rest of the user information if the transaction is successful. The JSON that comes back to us should look something like this:

```
{
"totalCount":1,
"children":[
  {
      id:1,
      name : 'Stacy McClendon',
      email  : 'stacy@superhappyfuntimego.com',
      phone: '555-555-5555'
  }
 ]
}
```

We can then use this information for any post processing we require.

We can also save changes to an existing user, or delete the user by calling:

```
user.destroy();
```

We also use the same proxy when we set up a user store:

```
Ext.define('MyApp.store.UserStore', {
  extend: 'Ext.data.Store',
  model: ' MyApp.model.User',
  requires: [' MyApp.model.User'],
  storeID: 'UserStore',
  emptyText: 'No Users To List',
  proxy: {
    type: 'ajax',
    url: 'api/users.php',
    reader: {
      type: 'json',
      root: 'children'
    },
    api: {
      create: 'api/users.php?action=create',
```

```
         read: 'api/users.php?action=read',
         update: 'api/users.php?action=update',
         destroy: 'api/users.php?action=destroy'
       }
    }
});
```

This will let us create, read, update, and delete multiple users at once.

The `api` section will be called when we load or sync the store, as follows:

- Calling `load()` on the store will contact `users.php` which should return a list of users
- Adding new user records to the store and calling `sync()` will contact `users.php` and save the new users
- Updating existing user records in the store and calling `sync()` will contact `users.php`, and update the records for each user
- Removing users from the store and calling `sync()` will contact `users.php`, and destroy the specified user records in the database

 Defining a `proxy` setting on both the model and the store isn't strictly necessary. If your model has a `proxy` setting defined and your store does not, then the store will automatically use the model's `proxy`.

If you are using an API you didn't write, you would need to make sure that you are sending the data and requests in the correct format. Check the documentation for the API you are using to see if there are any additional requirements.

As you may have noticed, we have been a bit vague on what is happening at the API end of things. This is because each API is a little different in terms of the data they expect, and the data they return.

Most publicly accessible APIs are fairly well documented, but it is also helpful to have a general idea of what goes into making an API.

Creating your own API

At their most basic, APIs perform three core functions:

- Receive data from a remote source
- Connect to and modify a database (or other data source)
- Transmit data to the remote application

When you create your own API, you will need to account for each of these functions. You can create your API in any server-side language you want, as long as it can handle these three basic things. Let's take a high-level view at each of these functions.

Receiving data

When you receive data from an application, you need to figure out what the user is asking for and how they are expecting the answer to be returned.

When you use the standard Sencha Touch API requests for models and stores, the `create`, `read`, `update`, and `destroy` functions are triggered, causing requests to be transmitted to the URLs you specify in the proxy configuration, along with any relevant data for the transaction. You can also send additional data using the `params` configuration like so:

```
store.load({
  params:{paramName: paramValue}
});
```

Your API will need to be set up to receive and translate the data and any extra parameters, so that it can decide what actions to take and what data to return.

The first thing you will need to do is determine if the variables are being sent as part of a `GET` or `POST` request. The server-side language you choose should have methods for dealing with either of these two transmission types.

As mentioned before, PHP can collect this data using `$_GET["variableName"]` and `$_POST["variableName"]`. Your chosen language will have similar functions. This data will also be encoded as JSON, so you will need to decode it before you can get to the individual pieces.

Most server-side languages have functions for dealing with this. For example, PHP uses `json_decode($myJSONData)` to transform the JSON data into a PHP array.

Once the data is collected, it should be checked to make sure that it is something we expected. For example, if our API receives an `action` value as `read` and an `id` value as `DELETE * FROM users`, we might not want to send this on to our database. Most languages also have ways to validate data types and sanitize any potentially hostile values.

Additionally, a store can often combine multiple requests into an array of data. Your code will need to check and see if the data being passed is an array or a single item, and deal with each appropriately.

Communicating with the database

Once you have your variables and you understand what the user needs to accomplish, you will likely need to make a connection to your database to get or modify the data. For example, if you get an `action` value of `read` and an `id` value of `45`, you will likely want to query the database for any users with an `id` value of `45`.

Performing this action will require knowledge of how the server-side language you are using connects to a database, and how your database accepts queries for information. You will need to consult the reference guides for your language and database to determine how this is done.

Sending data back to the application

Once you have communicated with the database and you are ready to send information back to the application, you will need to encode it correctly in order for Sencha Touch to process it.

Something to keep in mind is that Sencha Touch expects to receive data encoded as JSON. Most server-side languages have functions for dealing with this. For example, PHP uses `json_encode($myArrayOfData)` to bundle up the information into a JSON format.

Once you have the JSON-encoded data, you can output it directly to the browser using something like PHP's `print` or `echo` functions.

More information on APIs

Now that you have some idea of how APIs function you can gather some specific data for the server-side language you want to use. For more specific information, take a look at:

`http://www.webresourcesdepot.com/how-to-create-an-api-10-tutorials/`

Building the basic application

For this chapter, we will not be going through the entire build process of the application. Instead, we will be focusing mainly on the models, stores, and the basic API. The application itself is composed of a tabbed layout with two tabs. Each of our two tabs is a panel with a Card Layout, one for Items and one for Categories. In turn, these two panels have their own subpanels for listing, showing details, and editing (a list, a panel, and a form panel respectively).

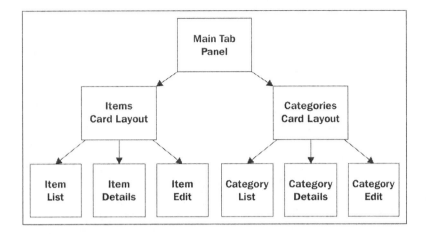

You can take a look at the application code to see how these components are laid out. The Main Tab Panel and the two Card Layout panels for Items and Categories are part of the `Main.js` file. The List, Details, and Edit panels are all separate views inside the `app/views` folder. We will come back to the views a bit later, but what we are really interested in for this chapter is the stores and models.

Creating the item model

The model is where most of the interesting stuff is going on. In the model we will be using two new options: a `rest` proxy and model relations.

```
Ext.define('CatHerder.model.Item', {
    extend: 'Ext.data.Model',
    uses: [
        'CatHerder.model.Category'
    ],
    config: {
        idProperty: 'itemID',
        fields: [
            {
                name: 'itemID',
                type: 'int'
            },
            {
                name: 'name'
            },
            {
                name: 'description'
            },
            {
```

```
                    name: 'price',
                    type: 'float'
            },
            {

                    name: 'photoURL'
            },
            {

                    name: 'categoryID',
                    type: 'int'
            }
        ],
        hasOne: {
         model: 'CatHerder.model.Category',
         name: 'category',
         primaryKey: 'categoryID'
            },
            proxy: {
              type: 'rest',
         url: '/api/item'
        }
    }
});
```

This starts out in the same manner as our previous models, but we have a new configuration option called uses. This option is set to our other model, CatHerder. model.Category, and tells us that we will have a relationship between our Item model and our Category model.

Below our fields, we have another new option called hasOne. This option tells us that each Item is related to a single Category.

> You can also use the option hasMany. This would allow you to set several categories on an item. For the sake of simplicity, we will be going with hasOne for this example. To see some examples of hasMany, take a look at http://docs.sencha.com/touch/2-0/#!/api/Ext.data.association.HasMany.

The hasOne option includes:

- The model we are relating to: CatHerder.model.Category

- The name property we will reference to get the related information: category

- The primaryKey property indicates the field that is part of our Item model, which we will use to match the id property set for our related model, categoryID

This configuration will let us use the fields in the `Category` model the same way as we would use any of the `Item` model's other attributes.

We also have a new type of proxy called a `rest` proxy. Unlike the `scripttag` proxy we covered earlier, the `rest` proxy uses different types of HTTP requests to denote if we are creating, reading, updating, or deleting data.

The different types of requests include:

- Creating a new record will be sent as a `POST` request
- Reading data will be sent as a `GET` request
- Updating an existing record will be sent as a `PUT` request
- Deleting records will be sent as a `DELETE` request

Each of these request types will be sent to `api/item` for processing. We have done a bit of trickery here with the URLs to make them look a bit cleaner to the user.

RewriteRule and .htaccess

Normally we would point our model at a particular file as we did in the earlier `scripttag` proxy example. In that case we would have done something like:

```
proxy: {
  type: 'rest',
  url: '/api/item.php'
}
```

When we want to view a particular item, the URL looks like:

```
http://myapp.com/api/item.php?item=143
```

However, with a little bit of configuration, we can change that so the URL would look like this:

```
http://myapp.com/api/item/143
```

This is shorter and much easier to read. It just requires a `RewriteRule` directive and a `.htaccess` file.

The .htaccess file is used by the Apache web server to determine a number of options and configurations for the server you are using. These options can be set by creating or editing the .htaccess file in the api directory of your application. In this case, we will create one with the following information:

```
RewriteEngine on
# Send item requests to item.php
RewriteRule ^item(/.*)?$ /api/item.php [L]

# Send category requests to category.php
RewriteRule ^category(/.*)?$ /api/category.php [L]
```

The first line turns on the ability to rewrite a URL. This means that while the user's address bar shows one thing, we direct the request to a different file. As the previous comments state, the next block sends any requests for item to item.php and the next block sends requests for category to category.php. The [L] directive says that if a rule matches the currently requested URL, no more rules should be checked, as this is the last rule to match against. This is a very simple change that gives a more professional and friendly feel to an application.

 If you would like to learn more about .htaccess and Apache, a good place to start is at http://www.addedbytes.com/for-beginners/url-rewriting-for-beginners/.

Save the file and close it. Now all of our different HTTP requests will be sent to api/item and api/category.

Our API will need to be able to distinguish the different HTTP request types in order to understand what to do with the data. We will get to how that works in a second, but first let's take a quick look at the store.

The item store

The item store is extremely simple for this one:

```
Ext.define('CatHerder.store.itemStore', {
    extend: 'Ext.data.Store',
    requires: [
        'CatHerder.model.Item'
    ],
    config: {
        model: 'CatHerder.model.Item',
        storeId: 'itemStore',
        autoLoad: true
    }
});
```

Since we don't declare a proxy, the store will automatically use the one we set on our model. Other than that, we simply require our model to give the store a `storeId` value and set `autoLoad` to `true`.

Creating the category model and store

Our category model and store are just variations of our item model and store. The model uses `hasMany` instead of `hasOne`:

```
Ext.define('CatHerder.model.Category', {
    extend:'Ext.data.Model',
    config:{
        idProperty:'categoryID',
        fields:[
            {
                name:'categoryID',
                type:'int'
            },
            {
                name:'name'
            }
        ],
        hasMany:{
            model:'CatHerder.model.Item',
            name:'items',
            autoLoad:false
        },
        proxy:{
            type:'rest',
            url:'/api/category'
        }
    }
});
```

We use `hasMany` because we are going to have multiple items in a single category. Other than that, the basic structure of the model is the same as our item model, using the `rest` proxy and contacting our PHP API at `/api/category`.

Our `categoryStore` is also a virtual duplicate of the `itemStore`:

```
Ext.define('CatHerder.store.categoryStore', {
    extend: 'Ext.data.Store',
    requires: [
        'CatHerder.model.Category'
    ],
```

```
config: {
    model: 'CatHerder.model.Category',
    storeId: 'categoryStore',
    autoLoad: true
}
});
```

As before we just extend the basic store component, declare which model we are using (`'CatHerder.model.Category'`), and give the store an ID we can reference later.

Once we have these two pieces in place, it's time for a bit of testing.

Testing the store and the model

When creating an API for your application, it's usually a good idea to begin with just a flat text file. This will let you test the read abilities of the store and help you better understand how the data will need to be formatted for your API.

For this test file, we are going to create a couple of very basic PHP files. These files will simply create a static array of data, encode it as JSON, and echo it back to the application.

 You can use any server-side language you would like; Sencha Touch doesn't care as long as it can accept and return JSON. If you'd like to use PHP for your server code, but need a place to get started, try http://phpmaster.com/. PHP Master has lots of tutorials for all levels of PHP programmers.

We will start with the item.php file:

```php
<?PHP

$test = array(
  array(
    'itemID' => 1,
    'name' => 'Test Item 1',
    'description' => 'Lorem Ipsum',
    'price' => 1.00,
    'photoURL' => 'http://placekitten.com/200/300',
    'categoryID' => 1,
    'category' => array(
      'categoryID' => 1, 'name' => 'Category 1', 'itemID' => 1
    )
  ),
  array(
```

```
      'itemID' => 2,
      'name' => 'Test Item 2',
      'description' => 'Lorem Ipsum',
      'price' => 2.00,
      'photoURL' => 'http://placekitten.com/400/300',
      'categoryID' => 2,
      'category' => array(
        'categoryID' => 2, 'name' => 'Category 2', 'itemID' => 2
      )
    ),
    array(
      'itemID' => 3,
      'name' => 'Test Item 3',
      'description' => 'Lorem Ipsum',
      'price' => 3.50,
      'photoURL' => 'http://placekitten.com/200/200',
      'categoryID' => 1,
      'category' => array(
        'categoryID' => 1, 'name' => 'Category 1', 'itemID' => 3
      )
    )
);

echo json_encode($test);
?>
```

This file creates an array called $test. The $test array has three arrays nested inside of it, one for each of our items. These arrays each contain various fields such as itemID, name, description, price, photoURL, and categoryID. They also contain the category data as part of an additional nested array. We include the category data as part of the item data so that our stores can access it via the hasOne relationship without requiring an extra AJAX call per item to the server to load the category data.

When you write the final PHP code for your application, it will query a database to get this information for both the items and the categories. The PHP will then need to format it in just this fashion.

 PHP formats an array in a similar fashion to Sencha Touch, where Sencha Touch uses key: value, and PHP uses 'key' => value.

The last line of the PHP file takes our array and encodes it as JSON. We then use echo to send the data back to our application.

We do the exact same thing for our categories array in `category.php`:

```php
<?PHP

$test = array(
  array(
    'categoryID' => 1,
    'name' => 'Category 1',
    'items' => array(
      array(
        'itemID' => 1,
        'name' => 'Test Item 1',
        'description' => 'Lorem Ipsum',
        'price' => 1.00,
        'photoURL' => 'http://placekitten.com/200/300',
        'categoryID' => 1
      ),
      array(
        'itemID' => 3,
        'name' => 'Test Item 3',
        'description' => 'Lorem Ipsum',
        'price' => 3.50,
        'photoURL' => 'http://placekitten.com/200/200',
        'categoryID' => 1
      )
    )
  ),
  array(
    'categoryID' => 2,
    'name' => 'Category 2',
    'items' => array(
      array(
        'itemID' => 2,
        'name' => 'Test Item 2',
        'description' => 'Lorem Ipsum',
        'price' => 2.00,
        'photoURL' => 'http://placekitten.com/400/300',
        'categoryID' => 2
      )
    )
  )
);

echo json_encode($test);
?>
```

Notice that in this case, we only have two categories, but we also include the items associated with each category. This lets us do a lot more with the data later on (such as showing the number of items in a category).

While these may look like large and messy arrays, the final PHP code is going to do most of the work for you. This is simply for testing and making sure you have the initial data formatting correct.

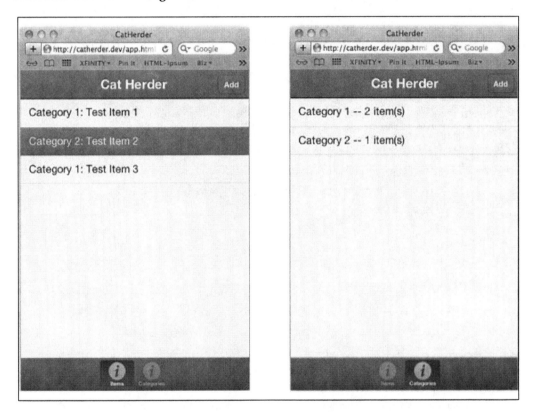

When you load the application you can now see the two lists with our flat data. Let's take a quick look at the XTemplates we are using for this data.

Creating the XTemplates

Now that we have seen how the data is being sent to the application, we need to understand how we can use it in our XTemplates. In our list view, the `itemTpl` looks like this:

```
itemTpl: [
  '{category.name}: {name}',
  '<p class="delete hidden" style="position: absolute; right: 10px;
top: 12px;">',
    '<img src="resources/images/delete.png" alt="delete" />',
    '</p>'
]
```

Both our category and our item include field values for name. Since the item is our main piece of data here, we can refer to the item's name value as `{name}`. Since category is related to item (and our PHP passes back as a nested array within each item), we refer to the category name value as `category.name`.

Our category list XTemplate uses a similar format to provide us with the category name, but it uses a slightly different method to get the number of items in each category:

```
itemTpl:[
    '<div>{name} -- {[values.items.length]} item(s)</div>'
]
```

Since the category is our main piece of data here, name refers to the category name. We can get to any of the item properties by doing `item.propertyName`, but what we really want to know is the number of items in the category.

Remember in our PHP flat file we included the individual items as part of a nested array in our category. This nested array was called `items`. We can print the name of the first item by using `items[0].name` or the second item by using `items[1].name` and so on for each of the various items and properties. We can also use the JavaScript `length` property to find out how many individual items are in our `items` array.

In order to do this we need to use JavaScript code inline in our template. That's why we use both curly braces and brackets: `{[function goes here]}`. When you're using inline code in your template, you have to access the template variables via the `values` array rather than by name.

In this case, `values.items.length` returns the number of elements in the `items` array.

Now that we can see how the values are formatted by PHP and displayed in the XTemplate, let's take a look at how we work within a database to store and retrieve this data.

The API and the database

To begin with, we need to replace our flat PHP file with some new code. This code will have three basic tasks:

- Decide what kind of request is coming in
- Contact the database and make the appropriate request
- Format the data to be returned to the Sencha Touch application

 Please note that from this point on, we are looking at PHP code. While some of it looks similar to JavaScript, this code is completely separate from both JavaScript and Sencha Touch.

These three basic functions will hold true no matter what language your API is written in, though the implementation will vary. In PHP our first task would look something like this:

```php
include_once 'dbSetup.inc';

switch ($_SERVER['REQUEST_METHOD']) {
case "GET":
    doGet();
    break;
case "POST":
    doPost();
    break;
case "PUT":
    doPut();
    break;
case "DELETE":
    doDelete();
    break;
default:
    doGet();
}
```

Here we include our database setup file, which handles the basics of our connection between the database and our code. Next we use a special variable `$_SERVER['REQUEST_METHOD']`, which tells us whether the request was sent via GET, POST, PUT, or DELETE.

GET, POST, PUT, and DELETE are known as **HTTP methods**, or **verbs**, and are used to represent a user's interactions with the web server. To learn more about HTTP verbs, check out the RFC at `http://www.w3.org/Protocols/rfc2616/rfc2616-sec9.html`.

We use a `switch` statement (just like the one in JavaScript) to send the different requests out to different functions. Each function will contact the database and perform the request.

We are not going to go too deeply into the details of the PHP code to do this, but we will take a look at the basic operations for our different requests.

The GET request

The GET request is used to read from the database and it has two basic uses in the API: get a single item or get a list of items. First we need to figure out if the request is for a single item or all the items.

In a REST API, a request for a single item would look like this:

```
http://mydomain.com/api/items/123
```

In this case, we want to send back a single item with an ID of 123. However, if we get a request that looks like:

```
http://mydomain.com/api/items/
```

We just send back all the items in the database.

So, the first thing our `doGet()` function needs to do is check the URL and see if we have some extra numbers at the end of our request URL:

```php
function doGet() {
    $db = dbSetup();

    if (preg_match('/item\/(\d+)[\/]*$/', $_SERVER['REQUEST_URI'],
$matches)) {
        /* We've got a single item to grab. */
        $itemID = array($matches[1]); // execute() expects an array.
        $stmt = $db->prepare("select * from `items` where itemID =
?");
        if (is_object($stmt) && $stmt->execute($itemID)) {
            /* We only asked for one. */
            $row = $stmt->fetch();
```

```
                $row['category'] = getCategory($row['categoryID'], $db);
                doJson($row);
            } else {
                doJson(array(), false, $stmt->errorInfo());
            }
        }
    }
```

The first line sets up our database so we can make requests.

> We have included setup files for the database in with the sample
> code for this chapter. For this application we are assuming
> a MySQL database, which is freely available. There is a
> dbSetup.inc file to handle the basic setup and configuration
> of the database, and a setup.sql file that can be imported
> into MySQL to set up the initial tables for the application. More
> information can be found at http://dev.mysql.com/doc/.

The next part of the PHP code uses regular expression matching to check the URL
that we received as part of our request ($_SERVER['REQUEST_URI']).

> Regular Expressions are an extremely powerful tool for
> matching strings, numbers, and characters. You can use
> it to find not just words or letters, but patterns within any
> string. For more information, go to:
>
> http://www.regular-expressions.info/.

If we get a match, it means that we are looking for a single item. We then take
our single item and use it to send a request to MySQL for the relevant data. We
grab the row data that gets returned from MySQL. We use the categoryID value
in the row data to attach category data to row data using another function called
getCategory(). The whole thing then gets passed to a function called doJson()
for final formatting.

This doJson() function will be used in multiple places in our code. It simply takes
an array, an option success value, and an optional message, and turns them into the
JSON encoded format that Sencha Touch can process:

```
function doJson($data, $success = true, $message = '') {
    $output = array('success' => $success, 'data' => $data);
    if ($message != '') {
        $output['message'] = $message;
    }
    echo json_encode($output);
}
```

Back in our doGet() function, we have taken care of the request for single item, and now we need to handle the request for all items. This means that in addition to our original if statement (that handled our request for one item) we need an else statement:

```
} else {
        $data = array();
        $categories = array();
        $filters = json_decode($_GET['filter'], TRUE);
        $start = intval($_GET['start']);
        $limit = intval($_GET['limit']);
        /* For simplicity, just use one filter */
        $filterColumn = $filters[0]['property'];
        $filterValue = $filters[0]['value'];
        $sql = "select * from `items`";
        if (!is_null($filterValue) && $filterValue != 'null' &&
$filterValue != "") {
                $sql .= " where `$filterColumn` = '$filterValue'";
        }
        if ($limit > 0) {
                $sql .= " limit $start,$limit";
        }
        foreach ($db->query($sql) as $row) {
                /* Only fetch categories once. */
                if (!isset($categories[$row['categoryID']])) {
                        $categories[$row['categoryID']] =
getCategory($row['categoryID'], $db);
                }
                $row['category'] = $categories[$row['categoryID']];

                $data[] = $row;
        }

        echo json_encode($data);
        exit;
}
```

This one works a bit differently because we are getting back multiple results. This means we need to loop through our results (using foreach), and get them into a single array we can process using json_encode(). We also have to use our getCategory() function on each round of the loop to grab the category data and add it to each of our items.

Once we have everything, we echo back the encoded array and exit. This will send the JSON back to our application for display in our XTemplate.

We have also included a few optional pieces that we can use later on: filters and start/limit. This will let us pass values for filters (as an array), and for start and limit as individual values. We can then pass these to MySQL and control the number of results we get back or filter the results by a particular column. It's always a good idea to build this kind of flexibility into an API. It can really save you some time when you start adding new features to your application.

The POST request

The POST request is where we will need to handle the creation of new items. The variables get passed to us as a POST request this time instead of as part of the URL (like our previous GET method).

Using zero when sending a POST for new items

In our item model, we have set the itemID as our id property. This is the unique id for our data record. There is an old programming habit of setting the id to 0 when you want to create a new data record. However, if you set an id of 0 on your model, Sencha Touch sees that as a valid ID and determines that you are updating a record, which sends your request as a PUT, not a POST request.

Our doPost() function needs to grab the data sent by the request and decode the JSON sent by Sencha Touch. Since we need to do this for our doPut() and doDelete() functions, we will create a separate function to do our decoding:

```
function getJsonPayload() {
    return json_decode(file_get_contents('php://input'), true);
}
```

In PHP, we can grab the raw data stream of the request with file_get_contents('php://input'). We can then decode this stream from JSON to an associative array ('key' => 'val') using json_decode(). We simply return the associative array whenever the function gets called.

This new function gets called right at the top of our doPost() function:

```
function doPost() {
    $data = getJsonPayload();
    $sql = "insert into `items` (`itemID`, `name`, `description`,
`price`, `photoURL`, `categoryID`) values (NULL, :name, :description,
:price, :photoURL, :categoryID)";

    $db = dbSetup();
```

```
        /* Prepare our data. Here is where you should add filtering, etc.
*/
        $insert = array();
        foreach ($data as $key => $val) {
            if ($key != "category_id") {
                $insert[':'.$key] = $val;
            }
        }

        $stmt = $db->prepare($sql);
        $stmt->execute($insert);
        $data['itemID'] = $db->lastInsertId();
        $data['category'] = getCategory($data['categoryID'],$db);
        doJson($data);
}
```

Next we create the SQL statement that we will use to place the data into our database. Then we need to format our data so that it will correctly fit with our MySQL statement.

We do this by looping through our data and creating a modified array that will work with the `execute()` command to combine the data with the `sql` statement and `insert` our new data record.

We then grab the unique ID for the new data row with `$db->lastInsertId()` and add it to our data array so we can pass it back to the Sencha Touch application. We do this with our `doJson()` function.

Our PUT request follows a very similar format.

The PUT request

The PUT request is executed when we save an object in Sencha Touch that has a valid `id` property, in this case, an `itemID` value. When Sencha Touch sends a `save` request for this type of pre-existing object, it uses the PUT request.

Our API function `doPut()` does the same basic thing as our `doPost()` function:

```
function doPut() {
    $data = getJsonPayload();
    $sql = "update `items` set `itemID` = :itemID, `name` = :name,
`description` = :description, `price` = :price, `photoURL` =
:photoURL, `categoryID` = :categoryID where `itemID` = :itemID";

    $db = dbSetup();

    /* Prepare our data. Here is where you should add filtering, etc.
*/
```

```
    $insert = array();
    foreach ($data as $key => $val) {
        if ($key != "category_id") {
            $insert[':'.$key] = $val;
        }
    }

    $stmt = $db->prepare($sql);
    $stmt->execute($insert);
    $data['category'] = getCategory($data['categoryID'],$db);
    doJson($data);
}
```

Since we already have the unique `itemID` we don't need to grab it from the database after we update the row. Other than that, the basic structure is the same. We simply type an `update` command instead of `insert` in MySQL.

The DELETE request

A `DELETE` request is sent when we call `erase()` on our model record in Sencha Touch. In this case, our API only cares about the unique `itemID`, so we don't need to create a new array to use with our `execute()` statement. We still use `getJsonPayload()` to grab the data and after we execute, we echo the JSON encoded data.

```
function doDelete() {
    $db = dbSetup();
    $data = getJsonPayload();
    $itemID = array($data['itemID']);
    $sql = 'delete from items where itemID = ?';
    $stmt = $db->prepare($sql);
    $stmt->execute($itemID);
    echo json_encode($data);
}
```

Back on the Sencha Touch side of things, you will need to reload the store in order to see the record removed from the list.

The rest of the API

The Category side of the API works in exactly the same way as the Item part we just covered. You can look things over in the sample code for this chapter, but the logic is all the same. There is a `switch` statement at the top, which determines how the request was received. We then have the same basic functions set to respond to each type of request.

This simple repeatable structure can be used to generate a basic API for use with any application.

If you need additional functionality in your API beyond the basic CRUD functions you can also use AJAX stores to send requests to an API file, where it can be processed appropriately. The API would need to perform the same basic functions:

- Determine the type of request either from the variables that are sent or the type of request being made
- Process the request through the database
- Encode the necessary request into JSON and send it back to the Sencha Touch application
- A message should also be sent in the event of failure to help with debugging or offer the user some information to help fix the problem

Summary

In this chapter we used a simple catalog application in order to build our own API. In addition we covered:

- How to set up Sencha Model associations
- Tricks using `.htaccess` and `mod_rewrite` to make prettier URLs for our API
- Using `Ext.data.proxy.Rest` to communicate with an API via basic CRUD interactions

In the next chapter we will use the data from several third party APIs to enhance our application.

7

The Decider: External APIs

One of the key aspects of mobile technology is the ability to tie different systems together into a meaningful application. More and more companies are allowing access to their programs and data through an **Application Programming Interface** or **API**. These APIs include things such as:

- Maps via Google, Yahoo, and other providers
- Music applications such as Rdio and Spotify
- Location aware data providers such as Foursquare
- Social networks such as Facebook and Google Plus
- Photo services such as Flickr and Picassa

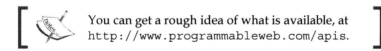 You can get a rough idea of what is available, at http://www.programmableweb.com/apis.

This is just a small sampling of the data available to make your application more useful. The trick is how to get the data and how to use it. In this chapter we will be using the Foursquare API to explore the use of these types of APIs and how to get started. We will talk about:

- An overview of external APIs
- Getting started with the Foursquare API
- Building the basic application
- Loading a data store with information from Foursquare
- Displaying the data to the user

We will start with a general look at how external APIs generally work and what you need to get started with one.

Using an external API

APIs are provided as a service from many different companies. This is not an entirely altruistic move on the part of the company. The expectation is that by providing the information and access to the company's data, the company gets more usage for their service and more customers.

With this in mind, most (if not all) companies will require you to have an account on their system in order to access their API. This allows you to access their systems and information from within your application, but more importantly from the company's perspective, it allows them to maintain control over how their data can be used. If you violate the company's usage policies, they can shut off your application's access to the data, so play nice.

The API key

Most APIs require a key in order to use them. An API key is a long string of text that gets sent as an extra parameter on any request you send to the API. The key is often composed of two separate pieces and it uniquely identifies your application to the system much like a username and a password would for a regular user account. As such it's also a good idea to keep this key hidden in your application so that your users can't easily get it.

While each company is different, an API key is typically a matter of filling out a web form and getting the key. Most companies do not charge for this service. However, some do limit the usage available to outside applications, so it's a good idea to look at any restrictions the company sets on their service.

Once you have an API key you should take a look at the available functions for the API.

API functions

API functions typically come in two types – public and protected:

- The public functions can simply be requested with the API key
- The protected functions will also require that a user be logged into the system in order to make the request

If the API function is protected, your application will also need to know how to log in correctly with the remote system. The login functions will usually be a part of the API or a web standard such as Facebook and Google's OAuth.

> It should be noted that while OAuth is a standard, its implementation will vary depending on the service. You will need to consult the documentation for the service you are using to make sure that the features and functions you need are supported.

Be sure to read through the service's API documentation to understand which functions you will need and if they require a login.

Another thing to understand about APIs is that they don't always do exactly what you need them to do. You may find that you need to do a little more work than you expect to get the data you need. In this case, it's always good to do a little bit of testing.

Many APIs offer a console interface where you can type commands directly into the system and examine the results:

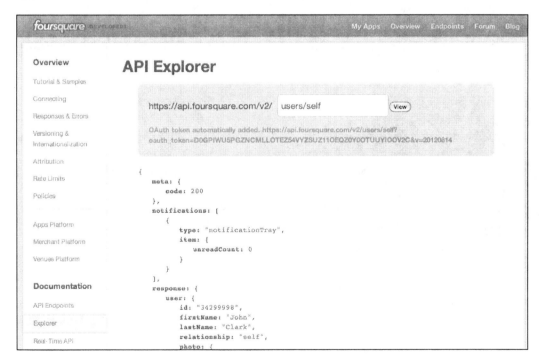

This can be really helpful for digging into the data, but consoles are not always available for every API service. Another option is to send the commands in your application (along with your API credentials) and examine the data returned in the Safari console.

The drawback of this method is that the data is often returned as a single-line string that is very difficult to read as shown in the screenshot:

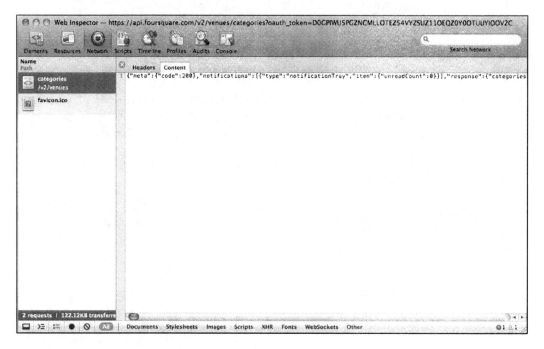

This is where a tool like JSONLint comes in handy. You can copy and paste the single-line string from your Safari console into the page at `http://jsonlint.com` and have the string formatted so that it is much easier to read and validate the string as JSON at the same time:

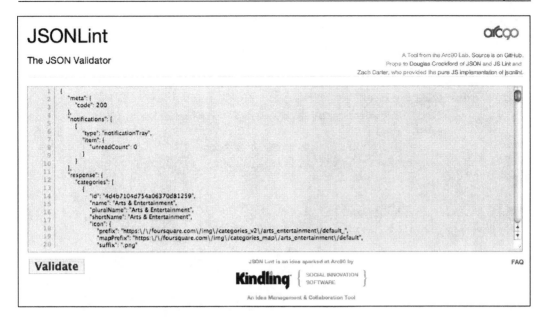

Once you get a hold of what data is being sent and received, you will need to set it all up in Sencha Touch.

External APIs and Sencha Touch

As we have talked about earlier in the book, you cannot use a standard AJAX request to get data from another domain. You will need to use a JSONP proxy and store to request data from an external API.

Using the API or the Safari console, you can get a good idea of the data that is coming back to you and use it to set up your model. For this example, let's use a simple model called `Category`.

```
Ext.define('MyApp.model.Category', {
    extend: 'Ext.data.Model',
    config: {
        fields: ['id', 'name', 'icon']
    }
});
```

We can then set up a store to load data from the API:

```
var store = Ext.create('Ext.data.Store', {
    model: 'Category',
    proxy: {
        type: 'jsonp',
        url : 'http://foursquare.com/vendors/categories' ,
        extraParams: {
          apiKey: 'XXXXXXXXXXXXXXXXXXXXXXXXX',
          appSecret: 'XXXXXXXXXXXXXXXXXXXXXXXXXXXXX'
        },
        reader: {
            type: 'json',
            rootProperty: 'categories'
        }
    }
});
```

This will set up a store with our Category model and call the url property for our external API. Remember that we have to send our credentials along with the request so we set these as extraParams on the proxy section.

 The apiKey and appSecret properties shown here are examples. You will need your own API key information to use an API.

We also need to set a property called rootProperty in the reader section. Most API's send back a ton of detailed information along with the request and the store needs some idea of where to start loading in the category records.

We can also add additional parameters later by calling the setExtraParam() function on our store proxy. This will let us add additional parameters to be sent to our external API URL.

 Please note that setExtraParam() will add an additional parameter but setExtraParams() will replace all of our extraParams with the new values.

Let's take a look at our application for this chapter to see how this all fits together.

The basic application

The Decider application is designed to use a combination of local storage, Google's Map API, and the Foursquare API. The application will take a list of people and their food preferences, and then use Foursquare and Google Maps to find nearby places to eat that will match everyone's food preferences.

This screenshot provides a pictorial representation of the preceding explanation:

Our contacts and categories will be stored using local storage. External APIs from Google and Foursquare will generate our maps and restaurant listings respectively. We will start with a quick overview of the basic application structure and forms, before diving into the store setup and API integration.

Our main container is a simple card layout:

```
Ext.define('MyApp.view.ViewPortContainer', {
    extend: 'Ext.Container',

    config: {
        id: 'viewport',
        layout: {
            type: 'card'
        },
        items: [ ]
    }

});
```

In this viewport we will add two cards: a navigation view and a form panel. Our navigationvew will serve as our main window for display. We will add additional containers to it via our controller:

```
{
    xtype: 'navigationview',
    id: 'mainView',
    navigationBar: {
        items: [
            {
                xtype: 'button',
                handler: function(button, event) {
                    Ext.getCmp('viewport').setActiveItem(1);
                },
                id: 'addContactButton',
                ui: 'action',
                iconCls: 'add',
                iconMask: true,
                align: 'right'
            }
        ]
    },
    items: [
        {
            xtype: 'container',
            id: 'homeScreen',
            layout: {
                type: 'hbox'
            },
            items: [
                {
                    xtype: 'button',
                    action: 'go',
                    margin: 75,
                    text: 'Get Started!',
                    flex: 1
                }
            ]
        }
    ]
}
```

This `mainView` contains our `navigationBar` and our `homeScreen` container with the big `Get Started` button. This button will add new containers to the navigation view (we will look at this later in the controller).

 Remember that Sencha Touch automatically creates a back button for each container that is added to the navigation view. This means that we don't have to write an extra code for it.

The second item that is added to our viewport is our form panel. This will contain text fields for first and last name, as well as a selectable list for our different food categories:

```
{
    xtype: 'formpanel',
    id: 'editContact',
    layout: {
        type: 'vbox'
    },
    items: [
        {
            xtype: 'textfield',
            label: 'First Name',
            labelWidth: '40%',
            name: 'firstname'
        },
        {
            xtype: 'textfield',
            label: 'Last Name',
            labelWidth: '40%',
            name: 'lastname'
        },
        {
            xtype: 'label',
            html: 'Choose what kind of food they like:'
        },
        {
            xtype: 'list',
            id: 'categoryList',
            itemTpl: [
                '<div><span class="icon"><img src="{imgURL}" /></span>
{shortName}</div>'
            ],
```

```
                store: 'Categories',
                mode: 'MULTI',
                flex: 1
            },
            {
                xtype: 'segmentedbutton',
                margin: '0 0 10 0',
                layout: {
                    pack: 'center',
                    type: 'hbox'
                },
                items: [
                    {
                        xtype: 'button',
                        text: 'Cancel'
                    },
                    {
                        xtype: 'button',
                        text: 'Save'
                    }
                ]
            },
            {
                xtype: 'titlebar',
                docked: 'top',
                title: 'Add Contact'
            }
        ]
    }
```

We close out the form with a `segmentedbutton` property, which has options for `Save` and `Cancel`. We will add the handler functions for these buttons later on in our controller.

We also include a title bar at the top of the form to give the user some idea of what they are doing.

One of the key pieces of this form is the categories list, so let's take a closer look at how it works.

Creating the categories list

Since we will be getting our list of potential restaurants from the Foursquare API, we need to use their categories as well so that we can match things up with some degree of accuracy.

> The Foursquare API can be found at `https://developer.foursquare.com/`. As mentioned before, you will need a Foursquare account to access the API. You will also need an API key in order to integrate Foursquare with your application.

We can use the Foursquare's API to get a list of categories, however the API returns a list of a few hundred categories including Airports, Trains, Taxis, Museums, and Restaurants. Additionally, each of these has its own subcategories. All we really want is the subcategories for Restaurants.

To make things more complicated, Foursquare's API also returns the data like this:

```
categories: [
  {category 1},
  {category 2},
  {category 3},
  {category 4}...

]
```

This means we can only get at a specific category by its order in the array of categories. For example, if Restaurants is the twenty-third category in the array, we can get to it as: `categories[23]`, but we cannot get to it by calling `categories['Restaurants']`. Unfortunately, if we use `categories[23]` and Foursquare adds a new category or changes the order, our application will break.

This is a situation where it pays to be adaptable. Foursquare's API includes a console where we can try out our API requests. We can use this console to request the data for all of our categories and then pull the data we need into a flat file for our application. Check this URL to see the output:

`https://developer.foursquare.com/docs/explore#req=venues/categories`

We can copy just the Restaurant information that we need from categories and save this as a file called `categories.json` and call it from our store.

> A better solution to this conundrum would be to write some server code that would request the full category list from Foursquare and then pull out just the information we are interested in. But for the sake of brevity, we will just use a flat `json` file.

Each of our categories are laid out like this:

```
{
    id: "4bf58dd8d48988d107941735",
    name: "Argentinian Restaurant",
    pluralName: "Argentinian Restaurants",
    shortName: "Argentinian",
    icon: {
        prefix: "https://foursquare.com/img/categories_v2/food/
argentinian_",
        mapPrefix: "https://foursquare.com/img/categories_map/food/
argentinian",
        suffix: ".png",
    },
    categories: [ ]
}
```

The main pieces we care about are the `id`, `name`, `shortname` and `icon` values. This gives us a data model that looks like this:

```
Ext.define('MyApp.model.Category', {
    extend: 'Ext.data.Model',
    config: {
        fields: [
            {
                name: 'id'
            },
            {
                name: 'name'
            },
            {
                name: 'shortName'
            },
            {
                name: 'icon'
            },
            {
                convert: function(v, rec) {
                    return rec.data.icon.prefix+ '32' + rec.data.icon.
suffix;
                },
                name: 'imgURL'
            }
        ],
        proxy: {
```

```
                type: 'ajax',
                url: '/categories.json',
                reader: {
                    type: 'json',
                    rootProperty: 'categories'
                }
            }
        }
    });
```

Notice that we also add a function to create an image URL for the icons we need. We do this with the `convert` configuration, which lets us assemble the data for image URL based on the other data in the record:

```
{
 convert: function(v, rec) {
  return rec.data.icon.prefix+ '32' + rec.data.icon.suffix;
 },
 name: 'imgURL'
}
```

The `convert` function is automatically passed both the data value (v), which we ignore in this case, and the record (rec), which lets us create a valid Foursquare URL by combining the `icon.prefix` value, a number, and the `icon.suffix` value in our record. If you take a look at our previous category data example, this would yield a URL of:

```
https://foursquare.com/img/categories_v2/food/argentinian_32.png
```

By changing the number we can control the size of the icon (this is part of the Foursquare API as well).

We combine this with our XTemplate:

```
'<div><span class="icon"><img src="{imgURL}" /></span> {shortName}</
div>'
```

This gives us a very attractive list for choosing our categories:

Next we need to take a look at the controller for the contact form.

Creating the contact controller

The contact controller handles saving the contact and canceling the action. We start out the controller by declaring our references and controls:

```
Ext.define('MyApp.controller.Contact', {
    extend: 'Ext.app.Controller',
    config: {
        refs: {
            contactEditor: '#editContact',
            categoryList: '#editContact list',
            cancelButton: '#editContact button[text="Cancel"]',
            saveButton: '#editContact button[text="Save"]',
```

```
                viewContainer: '#viewport'
            },
        control: {
            cancelButton: {
                tap: 'doCancel'
            },
            saveButton: {
                tap: 'doSave'
            }
        }
    }
});
```

Remember that our refs (references) provide a handy shortcut we can use anywhere in the controller to get to the pieces we need. Our control section attaches tap listeners to our cancel and save buttons.

Next we need to add our two functions after the controls section. The doCancel function is really simple:

```
doCancel: function() {
    this.getContactEditor().reset();
    this.getCategoryList().deselectAll();
    this.getViewContainer().setActiveItem(0);
}
```

We just use our references to clear the contact editor, deselect all the items in our category list, and switch back to our main view.

The save function is a little more complex, but similar to the functions we have covered elsewhere in this book:

```
doSave: function() {

    var contact = Ext.create('MyApp.model.Contact', this.
getContactEditor().getValues());
    var categories = this.getCategoryList().getSelection();
    var categoryIDs = [];
    Ext.each(categories, function(category) {
        categoryIDs.push(category.get('id'));
    });
    contact.set('categories', categoryIDs.join(','));

    contact.save(function() {
        console.log('Contact: ',contact);
    });

    this.doCancel();
}
```

As with our previous save functions, we create a new `MyApp.model.Contact` and add the values from our form. However, since our list isn't really a standard form component we need to grab its selections separately and add them to the contact data as a comma-separated list.

We do this by creating an empty array and using `Ext.each()` to loop through and run a function on all our categories. We then use `join` to implode the array into a comma-separated list.

Finally, we save the contact and run our `doCancel` function to clean up and return to our main view.

Now that we can add contacts we need to create a controller to handle our requests to the Foursquare and Google APIs, and get the data back to our users.

Integrating with Google Maps and Foursquare

Our application still has a couple of tasks to accomplish. It needs to:

- Handle the click of the **Get Started** button
- Add our maps panel and offer to adjust the current location via Google Maps API
- Display a list of friends to include in our search
- Display the search results in a list
- Display the details for a selected result

We will start out with the basic skeleton of the controller, create the views and stores, and then finish up the controller to complete the application.

Starting the mainView.js controller

We will start the `mainView.js` controller file with some placeholders for the stores. We will add views later on and some references for those components.

 Keep in mind that when working with placeholders in this fashion the application will not be testable until all the files are actually in place.

We create the `mainView.js` file in our `controllers` folder:

```
Ext.define('MyApp.controller.mainView', {
    extend: 'Ext.app.Controller',
    requires: 'Ext.DateExtras',
    config: {
        views: [ 'confirmLocation', 'restaurantList',
'ViewPortContainer', 'friendChooser', 'restaurantDetails'],
        stores: [ 'ContactStore', 'RestaurantStore'],
        refs: {
            viewContainer: '#viewport',
            mainView: '#mainView',
            startButton: '#homeScreen button[action="go"]',
            cancelButton: 'button[action="cancel"]',
            finishButton: 'button[action="finish"]',
            locationButton: 'button[action="newlocation"]',
            nextButton: 'button[action="choosefriends"]',
            map: 'confirmlocation map',
            restaurantList: 'restaurantlist',
            friendList: 'friendchooser list'
        }
    }
});
```

At the top of this configuration we require `Ext.DateExtras`. This file provides us with formatting options for date objects. If this file is not included, only the `now()` method for date objects will be available in your application.

In our `views` section we have added placeholders for `confirmLocation`, `restaurantList`, `friendChooser`,and `restaurantDetails`. We will add these files later on, along with the `RestaurantStore` file listed in our `stores` section.

We also have a number of references for these views, stores, and some of their sub-components. We will need to create these views before getting to the rest of our controller. We will take these views in the order the user will see them, starting with the `confirmLocation` view.

Creating the confirmLocation view

The `confirmLocation` view first appears when the user clicks on the **Get Started** button. This view will present the user with a map showing their current location and offer an option to switch to a different location if the user desires.

The following screenshot gives a pictorial representation of the preceding code:

In order to give ourselves a bit more flexibility, we will be using the Google Maps Tracker plugin as part of this view. You can find this plugin in your Sencha Touch 2 folder in `examples/map/lib/plugin/google/Tracker.js`. Copy the file into a `lib/google` folder in your main application folder and be sure to add it into the `requires` section of your `app.js` file:

```
requires: [
  'Ext.plugin.google.Tracker'
]
```

You should also set the path that corresponds to the `Ext.plugin` namespace, just above where you enable `Ext.Loader` in `app.js` file:

```
Ext.Loader.setPath({
    'Ext.plugin': 'lib/plugin'
});
```

This plugin will let us easily drop markers on the map.

Once the Google Tracker plugin file is included in the application, we can set up our `confirmLocation.js` view like so:

```
Ext.define('MyApp.view.confirmLocation', {
 extend: 'Ext.Container',
 alias: 'widget.confirmlocation',
 config: {
  layout: {
   type: 'vbox'
  },
  items: [
   {
    xtype: 'container',
    height: 25,
    html: 'Please confirm your location:'
   },
   {
    xtype: 'map',
    useCurrentLocation: true,
    flex: 1,
    plugins: [
     new Ext.plugin.google.Tracker({
      trackSuspended: false,    //suspend tracking initially
      allowHighAccuracy: false,
      marker: new google.maps.Marker({
      position: new google.maps.LatLng(37.44885, -122.158592),
      title: 'My Current Location',
      animation: google.maps.Animation.DROP
      })
     })
    ]
   }
  ]
 }
});
```

The view itself is a simple container with some HTML at the top asking the user to confirm their location. Next we have a map container that uses our Google Tracker plugin to configure the map and animate the location marker to drop from the top of the screen to the current location of the user. The position configuration is a default location, which is used when the user denies the application access to their current location. This one is set to the Sencha Headquarters.

Next we need a few options for the user to choose from: **Cancel, New Location,** and **Next**. We will add these as a segmented button under our map container. We add the code to the end of our items container (after the map container):

```
{
 xtype: 'segmentedbutton',
 height: 40,
 margin: '10 0 10 0',
 layout: {
  pack: 'center',
  type: 'hbox'
 },
 items: [
   {
    xtype: 'button',
    text: 'Cancel',
    action: 'cancel'
   },
   {
    xtype: 'button',
    text: 'New Location',
    action: 'newlocation'
   },
   {
    xtype: 'button',
    text: 'Next',
    action: 'choosefriends'
   }
 ]
}
```

Each of our buttons has an associated action. This allows us to assign functions to each button within the mainView.js controller. By creating buttons in this fashion, we maintain separation between the display of the application and the functionality of the application. This is really helpful when you want to re-use a view component.

The next view the user encounters is the Friends Chooser.

Creating the Friends Chooser view

The `friendsChooser.js` file uses a similar list to our previous category chooser. This lets our users select multiple people to include in the restaurant search:

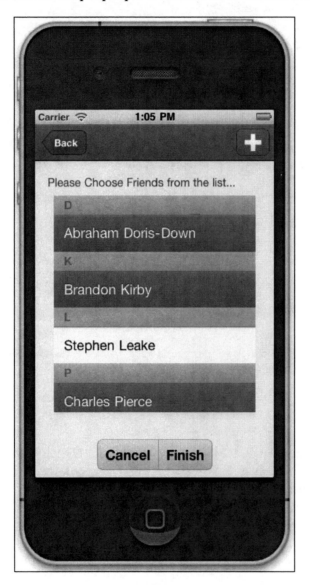

Our `friendChooser` extends the `Ext.Container` component and allows the user to select from a list of friends:

```
Ext.define('MyApp.view.friendChooser', {
 extend: 'Ext.Container',
 alias: 'widget.friendchooser',
 config: {
  id: 'friendChooser',
  layout: {
   type: 'vbox'
  },
  items: [
   {
    xtype: 'container',
    height: 20,
    html: 'Please Choose Friends from the list...',
    styleHtmlContent: true
   },
   {
    xtype: 'list',
    margin: 25,
    store: 'Contacts',
    itemTpl: [
     '<div>{firstname} {lastname}</div>'
    ],
    mode: 'MULTI',
    flex: 1,
    grouped: true,
    emptyText: 'No Contacts to display.<br />Please add some by
clicking the plus icon.'
   }
  ]
 }
});
```

As with our previous panel, we have a container with HTML at the top to provide some instructions to the user. Below that is our `list` container, which, like our category list, allows for selection of multiple items via the `mode: 'MULTI'` configuration. We also set `grouped` to `true`. This allows our store to group the contacts together by last name.

If you take a look at the `ContactStore.js` file, you can see where we do:

```
grouper: {
 groupFn: function(record) {
  return record.get('lastname')[0];
 }
}
```

This configuration returns the first letter of the last name for grouping.

The last thing we need to do with our `friendChooser.js` file is add the buttons at the bottom to **Cancel** or **Finish** the search. The buttons go out in the `items` section, just below the list:

```
{
  xtype: 'segmentedbutton',
  height: 40,
  margin: '10 0 10 0',
  layout: {
   pack: 'center',
   type: 'hbox'
  },
  items: [
   {
    xtype: 'button',
    text: 'Cancel',
    action: 'cancel'
   },
   {
    xtype: 'button',
    text: 'Finish',
    action: 'finish'
   }
  ]
}
```

As in our previous view, we use a `segmentedbutton` property with actions assigned to each of our individual buttons.

Once the user clicks on **Finish**, we will need to return a list of restaurants they can select from.

Creating the restaurant list, store, and details

Our restaurant list will use a store and the Foursquare API to return a list of restaurants based on the shared preferences of everyone the user selected.

The following screenshot exemplifies the preceding explanation:

This component is pretty basic:

```
Ext.define('MyApp.view.restaurantList', {
    extend: 'Ext.dataview.List',
    alias: 'widget.restaurantlist',
    config: {
        store: 'Restaurants',
        itemTpl: [
            '<div>{name}</div>'
        ],
        onItemDisclosure: true,
        grouped: true
    }
});
```

This component uses a simple list with a configuration option for `onItemDisclosure: true`. This places an arrow next to the restaurant name in the list. The user will be able to click on the arrow and see the details for that restaurant (which we will create after the store).

We also set `grouped` to `true`, only this time our store will use a function to calculate and sort by distance.

Creating the restaurant store and model

The restaurant store is where we set up our request to the Foursquare API:

```
Ext.define('MyApp.store.RestaurantStore', {
  extend: 'Ext.data.Store',
  requires: [
   'MyApp.model.Restaurant'
  ],
  config: {
   model: 'MyApp.model.Restaurant',
   storeId: 'Restaurants',
   proxy: {
    type: 'jsonp',
    url: 'https://api.foursquare.com/v2/venues/search',
    reader: {
     type: 'json',
     rootProperty: 'response.venues'
    }
   },
   grouper: {
    groupFn: function(record) {
     var distM = record.raw.location.distance;
     var distMiles = Math.round(distM * 0.000621371); //give or take.
     return (distMiles == 1)?"1 Mile":distMiles+' Miles';
    }
   },
   sorters: [
    { property: 'name', direction: 'ASC' }
   ]
  }
});
```

The `RestaurantStore.js` file sets a `model` and `storeId` field for our store and then defines our proxy. The `proxy` section is where we set up our request to Foursquare.

As we mentioned at the start of the chapter, this needs to be a jsonp request since it is going to another domain. We make our request to https://api.foursquare. com/v2/venues/search and we are looking for the responses.venues section of the JSON array that gets returned.

You will note that this store currently has no other parameters to send to Foursquare. We will add these later on in the controller before we load the store.

For the model, we can consult the Foursquare API documentation to see the information that is returned for a restaurant (called a venue in Foursquare terms) at https://developer.foursquare.com/docs/responses/venue

You can include any of the fields listed on the page. For this app, we have chosen to include the following code in our model:

```
Ext.define('MyApp.model.Restaurant', {
    extend: 'Ext.data.Model',
    config: {
        fields: [
            {
                name: 'id'
            },
            {
                name: 'name'
            },
            {
                name: 'categories'
            },
            {
                name: 'location'
            },
            {
                name: 'contact'
            },
            {
                name: 'menu'
            },
            {
                name: 'specials'
            }
        ]
    }
});
```

You can add more fields if you want to display more information in the details view.

Creating the details view

The details view is a simple panel and XTemplate combination. Using our controller, the panel will receive the data record when a user clicks on a restaurant in the list:

```
Ext.define('MyApp.view.restaurantDetails', {
 extend: 'Ext.Panel',
 alias: 'widget.restaurantdetails',
 title: 'Details',
 config: {
  tpl: [
   '<div class="restaurant"><span class="name">{name}</span>',
   '<tpl for="contact">',
    '<span class="phone">- {formattedPhone}</span>',
   '</tpl>',
   '<div class="icons"><tpl for="categories">',
    '<span><img src="{icon.prefix}32{icon.suffix}" /></span>',
   '</tpl></div>',
   '<div class="address">Address:<br />',
   '<tpl for="location">',
    '{address}<br />',
    '{city}, {state} {postalCode}',
   '</tpl></div>',
   '<tpl for="menu">',
    '<a class="menu" href="{mobileUrl}">Menu</a>',
   '</tpl>',
   '<tpl for="specials">',
    '<tpl if="count &gt; 0">',
     '<div class="specials">Specials:<dl><tpl for="items">',
       '<dt>{title}</dt>',
       '<dd>{description}<br>{message}</dd>',
     '</tpl></dl></div>',
    '</tpl>',
   '</tpl>',
   '</div>'
  ]
 }
});
```

Since the `tpl` tag is basically HTML, you can use any CSS styling you like here. Keep in mind that certain fields such as `contact`, `location`, and `categories` can have more than one entry. You will need to use `<tpl for="fieldname">` to loop through these values.

Now that the views are complete, we need to head back to our controller and add the functions to put everything together.

Finishing the main view controller

When we started out with our main controller, we added all of our views, stores, and references. Now it's time to add the functionality for the application. We start by adding a `control` section to the end of our `config`:

```
control: {
 startButton: {
    tap: 'doStart'
 },
 cancelButton: {
    tap: 'doCancel'
 },
 locationButton: {
    tap: 'doNewLocation'
 },
 nextButton: {
    tap: 'doChooseFriends'
 },
 finishButton: {
    tap: 'doShowRestaurants'
 },
 restaurantList: {
    disclose: 'doShowRestaurantDetails'
 }
}
```

The controls are based on the references in the controller and they add functions to specific listeners on the component. These are each in the format of:

```
reference: {
 eventName: 'functionName'
}
```

Once these controls are in place, we can add our functions after the `config` section of our controller.

Our first function is `doStart`. This function loads our `Contacts` store and checks to see if we have any existing contacts. If not, we alert the user and offer to let them add some. If they have contacts we create a new instance of our `confirmLocation` container and `push` it onto the main navigation view:

```
doStart: function() {
 var contactStore = Ext.getStore('Contacts');
 contactStore.load();
 if(contactStore.getCount() > 0) {
```

```
        this.getMainView().push({ xtype: 'confirmlocation' });
   } else {
      Ext.Msg.confirm('No Contacts', 'You will need to add some
contacts before we can search for restaurants. Would you like to add
contacts now?', function(btn){
      if(btn == 'yes') {
         Ext.getCmp('viewport').setActiveItem(1);
      }
   }, this);
  }
}
```

Remember that since the `mainView` is a navigation view, a **Back** button will automatically be created in the top toolbar. This function will show the user our initial map panel with the users current location.

This panel needs four functions: one to cancel the request, one to pop up a new location window, one to set the new location, and one to move on to the next step:

```
doCancel: function() {
 var count = this.getMainView().items.length - 1;
 this.getMainView().pop(count);
}
```

We actually want to be able to use the `doCancel` function from anywhere in the process. As we add new panels to our `mainView` navigation, these panels simply pile up in a stack. This means we need to get the number of panels currently on the `mainView` stack. We use `length-1` to always leave the initial panel (the one with our big **Get Started** button) on the stack. We use `pop` to remove all but the first panel from the stack. This way the **Cancel** button will take us all the way back to the beginning of our stack, while the **Back** button will take us back just to the previous step.

The next function is `doNewLocation()`, which uses `Ext.Msg.prompt` to ask the user to enter a new location:

```
doNewLocation: function() {
 Ext.Msg.prompt(
     '',
     'Please enter the address you want to search from:',
     this.setNewLocation,
     this,
     100
 );
}
```

If the user enters a new location, we call `setNewLocation` to process the text the user entered in the prompt textbox:

```
setNewLocation: function(buttonID, address) {
 var geocoder = new google.maps.Geocoder();
 var map = this.getMap();
 geocoder.geocode({'address': address}, function(results, status) {
  if (status == google.maps.GeocoderStatus.OK) {
   map.getGeo().suspendUpdates();
   map.getMap().setCenter(results[0].geometry.location);
   var marker = new google.maps.Marker({
    map: map.getMap(),
    position: results[0].geometry.location,
    title: 'My Current Location',
    animation: google.maps.Animation.DROP
   });
   map.getGeo().setLatitude(results[0].geometry.location.lat());
   map.getGeo().setLongitude(results[0].geometry.location.lng());
  } else {
   Ext.Msg.alert('Error', 'Unable to find address.');
  }
 });
}
```

This code gets our map and encodes the text the user passed us as a geocode location. If Google returns a valid address, we center the map on the location and drop a marker to show the exact location. We also set the latitude and longitude so that we can reference them later.

If we fail to get a valid address, we alert the user so they can fix it and try again.

Once the user is happy with the location they can click on the **Next** button, which fires our `doChooseFriends` function:

```
doChooseFriends: function() {
 this.getMainView().push({ xtype: 'friendchooser' });
}
```

This function pushes our `friendchooser` view onto the stack for display. The `friendchooser` view allows the user to select multiple friends and click on **Cancel** or **Finish**.

Since we have already taken care of our **Cancel** button with our `doCancel` function, we just need to write the `doShowRestaurants` function.

This function starts by looping through the selected friends. For the first one in the list, we grab the restaurant categories we have stored for the friend and convert it from a comma-separated list (which is how we stored it) into an array.

This lets us grab every subsequent selection and run `Ext.Array.intersect()` to find the common categories between all of the selected friends:

```
doShowRestaurants: function() {
  var location = this.getMap().getGeo();
  var friends = this.getFriendList().getSelection();
  var store = Ext.getStore('Restaurants');
  var categories = [];
  var dt = new Date();
  var first = true;
  Ext.each(friends, function(friend) {
    if (first) {
      categories = friend.get('categories').split(',');
      first = false;
    } else {
      categories = Ext.Array.intersect(categories, friend.
get('categories').split(','));
    }
  });
  store.load({
    params: {
      ll: location.getLatitude()+','+location.getLongitude(),
      client_id: FourSquare.clientID,
      client_secret: FourSquare.clientSecret,
      radius: 2000,
      categoryId: categories.join(','),
      v: Ext.Date.format(dt, 'Ymd')
    }
  });
  this.getMainView().push({xtype: 'restaurantlist', store: store});
}
```

Next, we load the store based on the common categories by `categoryID`, the location data we have stored in our map, `client_id`, and `client_secret` that comprise our API key for Foursquare and a `radius` value (in meters).

We also send a required field called `v` that is set to the current date.

Finally, we push our restaurant list component onto the stack of containers. This will display our list of results and allow the user to click on for details.

This brings us to our doShowRestaurantDetails function:

```
doShowRestaurantDetails: function(list, record) {
  this.getMainView().push({xtype: 'restaurantdetails', data: record.
data});
}
```

When the user taps one of the disclosure icons in our list of restaurants, we push a restaurantdetails view onto the stack of containers and set its data to the record that was tapped. This displays the details for the restaurant in our details XTemplate.

Homework

There are a number of additional features that can be added to this type of application, including:

- Editing for contacts (or automatically pulling friends from Facebook)
- Setting up a live feed for the categories menu
- Adding additional venues other than restaurants
- Combining the application with additional APIs such as Yelp for reviews

Just remember the key requirements of using additional APIs: the API key(s), studying the API documentation, and using the JSONP store for grabbing the data.

Summary

In this chapter we talked about using external APIs to enhance your Sencha Touch applications. This included:

- An overview of API basics
- Putting together the basic application
- Interaction with Google Maps and Foursquare
- Building the views, models, and stores
- Building the application controller

In the next chapter we will talk about the use of progressive enhancement to target sites to a specific device or screen size.

8

Evolver: Using Profiles

With the growing popularity of mobile devices, web designers have had to deal with a wide variety of screen sizes. This is even tougher on web application developers who also need to allow for different functionality between devices. Sencha Touch offers an easy way of dealing with multiple devices, called profiles.

Since the Sencha Touch framework is aware of which device it is running on, we can set up individual profiles for each device we want to support. Sencha Touch will then swap out components and functionality based on the device.

In this chapter we will look at:

- An overview of profiles
- Setting up profiles
- Testing profiles
- Loading custom CSS by device

We will create an application that reads pages and posts from a WordPress website and translates them into a custom application for mobile devices. We call this application, Evolver.

Evolver will use separate profiles to create a view for iPhone and a different view for iPad. These views will have their own functionality and can be customized to suit the needs of the user and the device.

However, before we get too far ahead of ourselves, we should probably talk a little bit about what profiles do and when to use them.

An overview of profiles

Profiles in Sencha Touch act much like a director, or a traffic cop. When the application loads, the profiles determine what kind of device they are being run on and load a different set of controllers and views based on the device (the stores and models typically do not change).

As you may have guessed, this means that each profile (device) needs its own set of controllers and views. While they can, and do share elements such as stores and models, most of the display logic is unique to the device. This can seem like a lot of extra work, which leads to the question: when and why should you use profiles?

Profile basics

As a general rule, it is usually a good idea to design an application specifically for a device or screen size. A smaller screen requires bigger fonts in order to be readable, but it also has less space for information. This means that it usually relies on multiple screens to get the information across to the user. A similar interface on a tablet device would be clunky and frustrating in most cases.

However, with a few simple applications, a change in CSS stylesheets will accomplish the necessary changes to the interface. A profile is not needed in this case and the stylesheet can simply be loaded based on the device being used. This method allows us to use the classes and IDs of our individual elements to control the overall appearance of our application.

For most professional applications, a combination of profiles and stylesheet changes will better serve the end user. We can demonstrate this using some drawings of our Evolver application. Let's start with our tablet version:

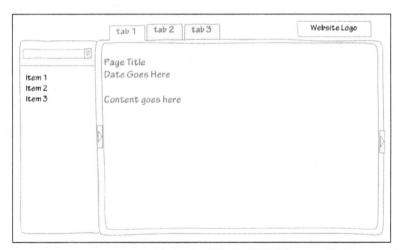

Here we have a lot of screen real estate we can put to use. We can easily show our list of pages and posts, and still show the content of the selected item at the same time. We have room for multiple tabs and even a website logo.

If we were to view this kind of layout on a phone-sized screen, it would be far too small to effectively use or even read. As we noted before, a phone-sized screen needs larger fonts and multiple screens to display the data the user needs:

In this case we have two screens. The first is for our list of pages or posts. Our tabs at the bottom will determine which list the user sees. When the user selects an item from the list, we will use a second screen to display the content for the page or post. We will also provide a back button to allow the user to return to the mail list.

Sketches or Wireframes

Sketches like these are often called **wireframes**. It is a really good idea to draw out these types of ideas before you begin coding the application. They don't have to be fancy, they just need to make you think about how the application will be organized and how the user will get from one screen to the next. Wireframes can quickly highlight any issues you hadn't thought of yet, and they will save you a huge amount of time later on when you begin coding. It's also a good idea to show these wireframes to potential users. Non-technical people can often reveal areas of confusion for a user, and their questions and feedback will make your application more useful.

From looking at the two sketches, we can determine the views that we need and the different functions we will need in our controllers. For example, clicking on an item in the phone version will need to add a panel to a navigation view, while in the tablet version, clicking on an item will just replace the content in our main panel.

Now that we have some idea of the different views and functions we want, we can take a look at how the profiles actually work.

Using profiles

The first part of our profile setup takes place in app.js. This file is typically where we load our initial stores and models, as well as set up a launch function to start the application.

With profiles, things work a bit differently. We start by declaring the profiles we wish to use like so:

```
Ext.application({
  name: 'Evolver',
  profiles: ['Phone', 'Tablet'] …
```

The names for our two profiles are arbitrary and we can have as many as we like. They can be specific to an OS as well as device type. When we use profiles such as these, we typically do not use a launch function inside our app.js file. Since the profiles will have different starting screens, we place the launch function inside the individual profiles.

The profiles should be placed in a directory called profile, inside the app directory of your application. They should be named the way you named them in your app.js file (in our case this would be Phone.js and Tablet.js).

 If it helps, you can think of the profile files as a way to have multiple app.js files, one per device.

These individual profiles will load our views and controllers, and they will launch our initial screen. However, the first thing we need to do is figure out which profile is active. We do this by creating an isActive function in our Phone.js file like so:

```
Ext.define('Evolver.profile.Phone', {
    extend: 'Ext.app.Profile',
    config: {
        name: 'Phone'
```

```
    },
    isActive: function() {
        return Ext.os.is.Phone;
    }
});
```

This `isActive` function will return true if the application is running on a phone. We use a similar function in our `Tablet.js` profile:

```
Ext.define('Evolver.profile.Tablet, {
    extend: 'Ext.app.Profile',
    config: {
        name: 'Tablet'
    },
    isActive: function() {
        return Ext.os.is.Tablet;
    }
});
```

Our `app.js` file will load one of these profiles, if the `isActive` function returns true. Only one of these profiles should ever return true.

 You can find more information about the `Ext.os.is` function in the Sencha Touch developer documentation located at `http://docs.sencha.com/touch/2-1/#!/api/Ext.env.OS-method-is`.

Each profile will also contain its own views and controllers, as well as its own launch function. However, it is important to note that the `Ext.loader` function will automatically look for these items in a subfolder named after the profile.

For example, our tablet profile has a controller called `Main.js`. We include this in our profile the same way we normally would in `app.js`:

```
controllers: ['Main']
```

However, since this controller is inside a profile, the `Ext.loader` function will look for the file as `app/controllers/tablet/Main.js`. Conversely, in our phone profile, we still include the controller as `controllers: ['Main']`, but the loader will automatically look for the file as `app/controllers/phone/Main.js`.

You can override this behavior in a profile by using the full name of the controller like this:

```
controllers: ['MyApp.controller.Main']
```

This would look for the Main.js file in the app/controller folder. This works the same for views, models, and stores as well.

You will also find that some files are common to both profiles. Rather than including them in our individual profiles, we can include these common files in app.js. For example, in our Evolver application, we will have models and stores for pages and posts. These will be common to both profiles, so we can add them as normal in app.js:

```
models: ['Page', 'Post'],
stores: ['pageStore', 'postStore']
```

Since these load from app.js (and not from one of our profiles), the loader will look for them in the app/model and app/store folders respectively.

As we noted before, the profiles also have individual launch functions in addition to the optional launch function in app.js. In a profile-based application, the app.js launch function is typically ignored since the profiles will likely launch different components to create the main screen. However, if the application requires it, you can use the app.js launch function as well, to perform clean up or load stores if desired.

The order works something like this (when the application starts):

1. The active profile is determined.
2. Any controllers in the profile or in app.js are instantiated (meaning the init function is fired).
3. The launch function in the profile fires.
4. The launch function in app.js fires.

It should be noted that both the profile and app.js launch functions are optional and will only be called if they are defined.

Now that we have the profile basics out of the way, let's get a little more specific about our application.

Creating the Evolver application

The Evolver application takes an RSS feed from a WordPress website and translates the feed into data in a Sencha Touch store. We did something similar in our previous Feedback application with the RSS feed. However, we are going to need a bit of extra help to get all of the information we need out of WordPress.

About WordPress

For those of you who don't know about WordPress, it is a content management system that was initially designed for blogging. WordPress allows a user to easily create posts and pages using simple web-based forms. Posts tend to be shorter, time-sensitive items, while pages contain longer, more general information.

When WordPress began to gain popularity, users quickly began to use it for all kinds of websites from personal, to business and shopping. Current estimates are that the WordPress site numbers somewhere north of 55 million, comprising an estimated 15 to 20 percent of the active websites on the Internet.

With the ease of installation and massive amounts of customization, WordPress has become a darling of the small business community. The one drawback is that the design complexity of a typical WordPress website doesn't always lend itself to a mobile-sized screen and platform. The following screenshot is an example of a standard WordPress style website:

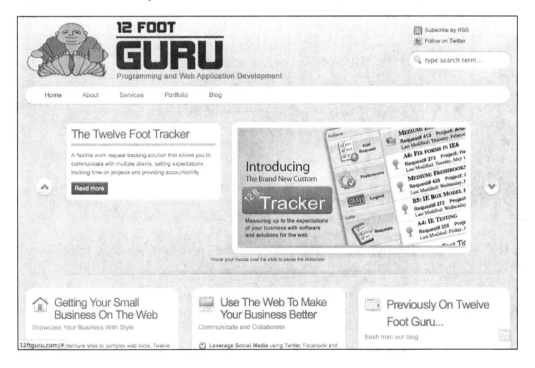

While this kind of layout appears fine on a desktop or laptop screen, it's not a great use of space for a tablet, and way too much information for a phone-sized screen. We need a mobile-friendly version of the site that makes effective use of the advantages and limitations of tablet and phone platforms. The following screenshot is an example of the approach we want to take:

Since the data behind the WordPress website already lives in a MySQL database, we just need a way to get it into a data store so we can use it in Sencha Touch.

The posts from WordPress are available in RSS format, but the pages are not. We are going to need to use a plugin for WordPress in order to get the pages we want as well. You will need to use your own WordPress website to make this work.

Using the plugin

WordPress plugins allow you to extend the basic functions and features of WordPress. In most cases this process is as simple as searching and clicking on the install button. In this case, we will be installing Dan Phiffer's JSON API plugin. This plugin will allow us to make standard API calls into our WordPress site.

Let's install the plugin and then we can see how it works with a bit of testing:

1. From your WordPress admin page, select **Plugins** from the menu.

2. On the **Plugins** page, click on the **Add New** button.

3. Enter JSON API in the **Search** field and click on **Search Plugins**.

4. Click on **Install** next to the **JSON API** plugin (it should be the first one in the list).

You can test to see if the plugin has been installed correctly by checking the following URL in your web browser(replace yourwordpressdomain.com with the address of your WordPress installation):

```
http://yourwordpressdomain.com/api/get_page_index/
```

You should get back a JSON response string with the pages for your site. Note that this string comes back as shown here:

```
{"status":"ok",
 "pages":[
   {page 1 data},
   {page 2 data},
   {page 3 data},
   {etc...}
 ]
}
```

We need to keep in mind that the pages array actually contains the data we are looking for. This will get set as rootProperty of the store's reader component when we create our store.

Setting up the profiles and app.js

We will start with a basic Sencha Touch application, set up from our command-line SDK tools (as we did in some of our earlier chapters). This creates our application shell and our view, model, store, and controller folders.

In our `app.js` file, we will add lines for our profiles. We also have some common elements in both profiles, specifically, the models and stores for pages and profiles. Since these will need to load for both profiles, we can add them in our `Ext.application` declaration, rather than adding them twice, once in each profile file:

```
profiles: ['Phone', 'Tablet']
models: ['Page', 'Post'],
stores: ['pageStore', 'postStore']
```

Now that we have our `app.js` file set up, we need to create a `profile` folder in our app directory. This is where our two profiles will go.

Our `Phone.js` profile looks like this:

```
Ext.define('Evolver.profile.Phone', {
    extend: 'Ext.app.Profile',
    config: {
        name: 'Phone',
        controllers: ['Main'],
        views: ['Main', 'Evolver.view.PostList', 'Evolver.view.
PageList', 'PageDetails', 'PostDetails']
    },
    isActive: function() {
        return Ext.os.is.Phone;
    },
    launch: function() {
        Ext.fly('appLoadingIndicator').destroy();
        Ext.create('Evolver.view.phone.Main', {fullscreen: true});
    }
});
```

We have three pieces here: the `config` section, our `isActive` function, and our `launch` function.

Our `config` section has the profile `name`, `controllers` and `views` values. Remember that since we are in the profile, the loader will be looking for these files in `app/controller/phone` and `app/view/phone` respectively.

Notice that we also have two of our views listed with the full names: `Evolver.view.PostList` and `Evolver.view.PageList`. These views will actually be shared by both profiles, so we put them in the `app/views` folder. We could also just put them in `app.js` and it would accomplish the same thing. We included them here to demonstrate that the file location can be overridden if required.

Our `isActive` function will return true if we are running on a phone.

isActive, device types, and Safari

If you are testing on Safari with a desktop or laptop, you will run into some issues using this function. Despite the ability to set the user agent in Safari to iPad or iPod, the browser does not correctly report the device type to Sencha Touch.

When you are testing, you will need to comment out the `return Ext.os.is.Phone` or `return Ext.os.is.Tablet` lines in the `isActive` function. Then you can set the `isActive` function in the profile you want to test to `return true;` and the other one to `return false;`. Just remember to uncomment the correct functions before moving to production.

If you are testing with the iOS or Android simulators, this is not an issue.

The `launch` function removes our loading indicator and creates an instance of our `Evolver.view.phone.Main` view at full screen size.

Our `Tablet.js` profile follows the same pattern as our phone profile:

```
Ext.define('Evolver.profile.Tablet', {
    extend: 'Ext.app.Profile',
    config: {
        name: 'Tablet',
        controllers: ['Main'],
        views: ['Main', 'Evolver.view.PostList', 'Evolver.view.
PageList', 'PageDetails', 'PostDetails']
    },
    isActive: function() {
      return Ext.os.is.Tablet;
    },
    launch: function() {
        Ext.fly('appLoadingIndicator').destroy();
        Ext.create('Evolver.view.tablet.Main', {fullscreen: true});
    }
});
```

Much like the phone profile, the controllers and views will be loaded from a `tablet` folder in our `app/controllers` and `app/views` folders.

We are going to take a very brief look at the stores, models, and views for the application as there isn't much new here. Then, we will finish up with the controllers, where the action really happens.

Setting up the models and stores

Our models are very basic, and they are taken from the data that is sent back from the RSS feed for posts and the JSON API plugin for pages. We are only using some of that data, but you can easily look through the values that are returned from `yoursite/feeds/rss/` (posts) and `yoursite/api/get_page_index/` (pages) to see if there is any other interesting data you might want to use.

Our post model looks like this:

```
Ext.define('Evolver.model.Post', {
    extend: 'Ext.data.Model',
    config: {
    idProperty: 'guid',
        fields: [
            {
                name: 'guid',
                type: 'string'
            },
            {
                dateFormat: 'D, d M Y H:i:s Z',
                name: 'pubDate',
                type: 'date'
            },
            {
                name: 'title',
                type: 'string'
            },
            {
                name: 'author',
                mapping: 'creator',
                type: 'string'
            },
            {
                name: 'content',
                mapping: 'encoded',
                type: 'string'
            },
```

```
            {
                name: 'category',
                type: 'string'
            },
            {
                name: 'link',
                type: 'string'
            }
        ]
    }
});
```

The only thing new here is the use of mapping to indicate that, while we will refer to the strings as author and content, the data is actually received as creator and encoded respectively. This is often helpful to keep values consistent across the application, avoid naming conflicts, or simply preserve a coder's sanity.

The postStore attribute for this model is configured to run from the same server as the WordPress website you are using. This means we can use an ajax store instead of a jsonp store. If you want to use this from a different server, you will need to change the proxy to jsonp and use the JSON API to grab the posts instead of the standard WordPress RSS feed (which is in XML):

```
Ext.define('Evolver.store.postStore', {
    extend: 'Ext.data.Store',
    requires: [
        'Evolver.model.Post'
    ],
    config: {
        storeId: 'postStore',
        autoLoad: true,
        model: 'Evolver.model.Post',
        proxy: {
            type: 'ajax',
            url: '/feed/rss/',
            reader: {
                type: 'xml',
                record: 'item'
            }
        }
    }
});
```

The `record: 'item'` configuration tells the reader to look in the XML for a collection of items to be used as the data for its records.

WordPress RSS feeds

By default, RSS feeds in WordPress are set to only show a partial text of the post. You can change this in the **Admin** control panel of your WordPress site. In the **Admin** menu select **Settings | Reading** and change the feed settings from **Summary** to **Full Text**.

Since this store is not a JSONP store, it has to be run on the same server as the WordPress site it is pulling from. There is not an equivalent XMLP store, so testing on a local machine will require a bit of a workaround. During testing, you can download the RSS feed from your WordPress site to your local machine and read from the local XML file. Later, when you move to production, you can change the URL to the live link.

Our `pageStore` is designed to use the JSON API plugin, so we will be taking in JSON instead of XML:

```
Ext.define('Evolver.store.pageStore', {
    extend: 'Ext.data.Store',
    requires: [
        'Evolver.model.Page'
    ],
    config: {
        model: 'Evolver.model.Page',
        autoLoad: true,
        storeId: 'pageStore',
        proxy: {
            type: 'jsonp',
            url: 'http://yourWordPressSite.com/api/get_page_index/',
            reader: {
                type: 'json',
                rootProperty: 'pages'
            }
        }
    }
});
```

With this store we are reading JSON from our API. The `get_page_index` function will return a hierarchical list of the pages for the website.

The JSON API plugin for WordPress has a number of helpful functions you can use to read and write data to your WordPress website. A full list of functions can be found here at `http://wordpress.org/ extend/plugins/json-api/other_notes/`.

Our data model for the pages is using a limited set of the data supplied by the JSON API plugin:

```
Ext.define('Evolver.model.Page', {
    extend: 'Ext.data.Model',
    config: {
        fields: [
            {
                name: 'id',
                type: 'int'
            },
            {
                name: 'title',
                type: 'string'
            },
            {
                name: 'content',
                type: 'string'
            },
            {
                dateFormat: 'Y-m-d H:i:s',
                name: 'modified',
                type: 'date'
            }
        ]
    }
});
```

You can see a full list of all the data available by going to the API URL for your WordPress site (`http://yourWordPressSite.com/api/get_page_index/?dev=1`). The `dev1` argument will format the JSON response and make it more readable.

Now that we have our stores and models, we can work on our views for displaying the data.

Creating the views

Since we will be sharing the list views for our post and pages between our two profiles, let's start there. We will be using a data view instead of a list view, as this provides us with a few more display options than a simple list.

Our `PostList.js` file looks like this:

```
Ext.define('Evolver.view.PostList', {
    extend: 'Ext.dataview.DataView',
    alias: 'widget.postlist',
    title: 'Posts',
    id: 'postList',
    config: {
        store: 'postStore',
        itemTpl: [
            '<div class="postItem">',
            '    <div class="postTitle">{title}</div>',
            '    <div class="postMeta"><span
class="postAuthor">{author}</span> - <span class="postDate">{[Ext.
util.Format.date(values.pubDate, "m/d/Y")]}</span></div>',
            '</div>'
        ]
    }
});
```

Much like our standard list, `DataView` takes a data store and displays the items in order from the store. However, `DataView` is more flexible from a styling point of view, allowing the creation of tiled lists and other more interesting layouts.

This view reads from `postStore` and uses `itemTpl` to display the title, author, and date from each post. Each of our data items is styled with a particular class, which means we can display them in different ways depending on which stylesheet we load, or even turn them off completely. We will talk about these kinds of conditional stylesheets towards the end of the chapter.

Our `PageList` view follows a similar structure:

```
Ext.define('Evolver.view.PageList', {
    extend: 'Ext.dataview.DataView',
    alias: 'widget.pagelist',
    title: 'Pages',
    config: {
        store: 'pageStore',
```

```
        itemTpl: [
            '<div class="pageItem">',
            '    <div class="pageTitle">{title}</div>',
            '    <div class="pageMeta">Updated <span
class="pageDate">{[Ext.util.Format.date(values.modified, "m/d/Y")]}</
span></div>',
            '</div>'
        ]
    }

});
```

This shared view reads from our `pageStore` and displays just the title and date.
As noted, you can add any of the other data generated by the WordPress JSON API,
and then use a conditional stylesheet to show it or hide it, based on the device the
user is viewing from.

Our other views will be unique to either the phone or tablet profile. For the purposes of
this chapter, each of the views are similar, each is a simple container with a template to
format the record for display. Let's start with our phone details container.

Creating the phone details view

Since this details container is part of our phone profile, it is named `Evolver.view.`
`phone.PageDetails` and it will be in the `app/view/phone/` folder.

```
Ext.define('Evolver.view.phone.PageDetails', {
    extend: 'Ext.Container',
    alias: 'widget.pagedetails',
    config: {
    layout: 'fit',
    scrollable: {direction: 'vertical', directionLock: true},
    tpl: [
      '<div class="pageDetails">',
      '    <div class="pageTitle">{title}</div>',
      '    <div class="pageMeta"><span class="pageAuthor">{author}</
span> <span class="pageDate">{updated}</span></div>',
      '    <div class="pageContent">{content}</div>',
      '</div>'
      ]
    }
});
```

We also set a configuration for scrollable in this view. Since we are in a navigation view, which can be triggered with a swipe, we set the direction and direction lock to keep the swipe from triggering a page change.

Creating the tablet details view

The tablet version of our PageDetails.js view looks like this:

```
Ext.define('Evolver.view.tablet.PageDetails', {
 extend: 'Ext.Container',
 alias: 'widget.pagedetails',
 config: {
  tpl: [
   '<div class="pageDetails">',
   '<div class="pageTitle">{title}</div>',
   '<div class="pageMeta"><span class="pageAuthor">{author}</span>
<span class="pageDate">{updated}</span></div>',
   '<div class="pageContent">{content}</div>',
   '<div class="pageContent"><a href="{url}">View Original Page</a></
div>',
   '</div>'
  ]
 }
});
```

The only differences between the two are the name (Evolver.view.tablet. PageDetails) and the URL for the page which we include at the bottom of tpl. While a **View Original Page** link is common in most tablet-based apps, it's not really needed for a phone app since we are trying to avoid the original site in the first place.

We will be handling the scrolling differently in the tablet version, so we do not include a scrollable configuration here.

As previously noted, you could make these two containers as different as you want. You could make one of them a panel and the other a container if you prefer. Since only one of them will actually be included, we can even keep the same value for our alias attribute of widget.pageDetails. There will not be an xtype conflict because only the phone version or the tablet version will ever be active at one time.

Our postDetails object for phone and tablet follow the same format, so we won't bother covering them here. You can see them in the sample code for the chapter. Just remember that the phone versions go in app/view/phone and the tablet versions go in app/view/tablet. Also, the view naming conventions will follow the format of Evolver.view.phone.viewName and Evolver.view.tablet.viewName.

Now, we need to put the individual pieces together into a main container for each of our profiles.

The main views

From our original sketches, we have two different interfaces. The first one we will look at is the phone interface:

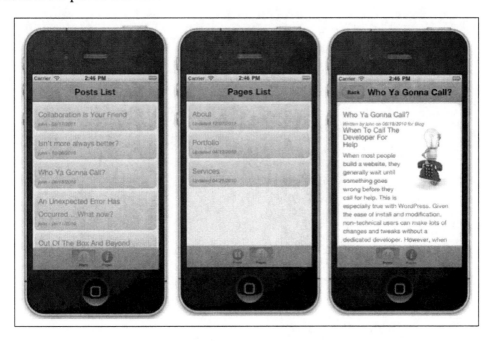

Since a phone screen has limited size, we need to create a more compact and layered interface. This will allow us to display all of our data, while still providing the user with readable text.

Creating the phone main view

The phone `Main.js` interface will consist of a tab view with two DataViews (one for pages and one for posts). Each DataView is inside a navigation view. When we click an item in the DataView, the controller will pop our details container onto the navigation view, creating a back button automatically:

```
Ext.define('Evolver.view.phone.Main', {
    extend: 'Ext.tab.Panel',
```

```
        alias: 'widget.phonemain',
        id: 'mainView',
        config: {
            tabBar: {
                docked: 'bottom'
            },
            items: [
                {
                    xtype: 'navigationview',
                    iconCls: 'quote_black2',
                    iconMask: true,
                    title: 'Posts',
                    items: [
                        {xtype: 'postlist', title: 'Posts List'}
                    ]
                },
                {
                    xtype: 'navigationview',
                    title: 'Pages',
                    iconCls: 'info',
                    iconMask: true,
                    items: [
                        {xtype: 'pagelist', title: 'Pages List'}
                    ]
                }
            ]
        }

    });
```

We give this view an `id` value of `mainView` to make it easy to address within our controller. You will notice that the navigation views have a `title` configuration, and the DataView inside each navigation view has its own `title` configuration as well.

The two navigation views are direct children of the overall tab panel. This means that the title on the tabs at the bottom of our main tab panel will use this title. The DataViews inside the navigation views each have a title bar component, which will display the title for each DataView at the top.

By using a two-list strategy with the navigation view for popping on the details, we make the best use of our limited phone screen area. With our tablet profile, we have a bit more room to work with, so we can take a different approach.

Creating the tablet main view

Since we have additional room available on a tablet-sized screen, we can use a different view to take advantage of the extra space:

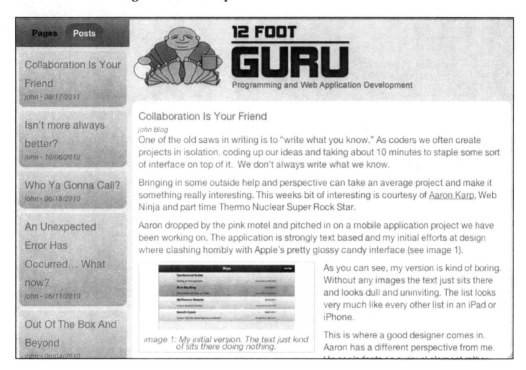

Our tablet `Main.js` view has the two DataViews in a tab panel much like our phone profile version. However, the tablet version keeps a visible main content area where we can display the currently selected item. We also include an area above the content where we can place the website logo using the following code:

```
Ext.define('Evolver.view.tablet.Main', {
  extend: 'Ext.Panel',
  id: 'mainView',
  config: {
    layout: 'fit',
    items: [
      {
        xtype: 'tabpanel',
        width: 200,
        docked: 'left',
```

```
        items: [
          {
           xtype: 'pagelist',
           title: 'Pages'
          },
          {
           xtype: 'postlist',
           title: 'Posts'
          }
         ]
        },
        {
        xtype: 'container',
        layout: 'vbox',
        scrollable: true,
        items: [
          {
           xtype: 'container',
           layout: 'fit',
           id: 'banner',
           height: 140,
           html: '<img src="http://12ftguru.com/wp-content/themes/small-
business/images/sb_logo.png">'
          },
          {
           xtype: 'pagedetails'
          },
          {
           xtype: 'postdetails',
           hidden: true
          }
         ]
        }
       ]
      }
    });
```

We start by extending the basic Ext.Panel component and giving it a fit layout. Inside this panel are a tab panel and two containers.

The tabpanel component contains our two DataViews (pages and posts), just as we had them in the phone version of the application. We set this up to have a width value of 200.

The content container is set to a vbox layout with three child containers. The top container for our logo will have a `height` value of `140` and an HTML link to the logo from our WordPress site. The vbox layout means that our other containers, with our content for posts and pages, will automatically resize to fit the rest of the available space.

Notice that our `postdetails` container is hidden by default and the page details are visible. We will swap these two containers based on which DataView is selected in our controller.

Creating the controllers

The Evolver application uses a pair of DataViews (one for posts and one for pages), which are shared between both the phone and tablet profiles. In the case of the phone profile, the DataView needs to listen for the tap event and add a new details component to the navigation container. In the case of the tablet profile, the DataView is still listening for the tap event, but it needs to swap the two details containers based on which the DataView is selected.

By isolating the functionality from the display logic, we can make a single DataView perform two different actions (one in the phone version and another in the tablet version). We start this out in both our `phone.js` and `main.js` controllers, and our `tablet.js` and `main.js` controllers like so:

```
Ext.define('Evolver.controller.phone.Main', {
  extend: 'Ext.app.Controller',
  config: {
   refs: {
    postList: '#postList',
    pageList: '#pageList',
    mainView: '#mainView'
   },

   control: {
    postList: {
     itemtap: 'onListItemTap'
    },
    pageList: {
     itemtap: 'onListItemTap'
    }
   }
  }
});
```

The phone profile version is shown here, but at this point the tablet version is actually the same, just named `Evolver.controller.tablet.Main`.

Our references set up our short hand pointers to our components. Since `postList` and `pageList` are the same for both applications, and we consistently named our main container for both profiles, the references are the same in both controllers.

We also use the same code for our `control` configurations, where both lists need to listen for the `itemTap` event to trigger our function. To make our lives easier, we also make the DataViews trigger the same function called `onListItemTap`. We can decide what needs to happen based on which list got tapped.

Here is where our two controllers diverge. Let's start with the phone version of the `onListItemTap` function:

```
onListItemTap: function(dataview, index, target, record) {
 var original = record.get('content');
 var converted = original.replace(/src=\"/g, 'src=\"http://src.sencha.
io/120/');
 var final = converted.replace(/((width|height)\s*=\s*"*\d+"*)/g, '');
 record.set('content', final);
 if(dataview.id == 'postList') {
  var details = Ext.create(
    'Evolver.view.phone.PostDetails', {
     title: record.get('title'),
     data: record.data
   });
 } else {
  var details = Ext.create(
    'Evolver.view.phone.PageDetails', {
     title: record.get('title'),
     data: record.data
   });
 }
 this.getMainView().getActiveItem().push(details);
}
```

We do some interesting manipulations with the first part of this function to modify our content to display better on a phone-sized screen. Since the content coming back to us has full-sized images, it will often take up a huge amount of space on a phone-sized screen, making the layout kind of crummy.

To solve this problem, we first grab the content out of the record with this:

```
var original = record.get('content');
```

Next, we make two passes through the content to find and replace some of the image information so that we can manipulate the sizes the way we want. The first pass looks like this:

```
var converted = original.replace(/src=\"/g, 'src=\"http://src.sencha.
io/120/');
```

This will take an image tag with a `src` link that looks like `http://mydomain.com/images/image15.png` and turn it into `http://src.sencha.io/120/http://mydomain.com/images/image15.png`.

This format will grab the image and run it through `src.sencha.io` for processing before it is displayed. The value of 120 indicates that the image will be automatically resized to a maximum width of 120 pixels or about half the size of a typical phone screen.

> **src.sencha.io**
>
> src.sencha.io can be used to resize any image on the fly. There are a number of useful features to this service and more information can be found here at `http://docs.sencha.io/current/index.html#!/guide/src`.

The third and final transformation removes the original height and width configurations from the `<img>` tags using a regular expression to match and remove the values. By default, WordPress will insert `height` and `width` tags when an image is included as part of a post or a page:

```
var final = converted.replace(/((width|height)\s*=\s*"*\d+"*)/g, '');
```

If we just used our first bit of code to resize the actual image without removing the height and width configurations, the image will actually appear at the original size, just pixelated and ugly looking.

> **Regular expressions**
>
> Regular Expressions, or **Regexes**, are an incredibly valuable tool for matching patterns in strings. You can find out more information on Regexes at `http://www.rexv.org/`.

Once, we have done all of our conversions, we set the content value of our record to our new and improved value:

```
record.set('content', final);
```

With the conversion out of the way, we need to figure out which details container we need. Fortunately, we are passed the view that was clicked as part of our itemTap handler. We can use this to check to see which DataView is active:

```
if(dataview.id == 'postList') {
  var details = Ext.create(
   'Evolver.view.phone.PostDetails', {
    title: record.get('title'),
    data: record.data
  });
} else {
  var details = Ext.create(
   'Evolver.view.phone.PageDetails', {
    title: record.get('title'),
    data: record.data
  });
}
```

If we have postList, we need to create a new post details container, and if not, we want to create a new page details container. Once we have the new container, we push it onto the active item with this code:

```
this.getMainView().getActiveItem().push(details);
```

We use this.getMainView() to grab our main view using the reference we created earlier. By using getActiveItem(), we are assured of getting the DataView the user is looking at and pushing the container onto the correct navigation view.

That's all there is to the phone profile's Main.js controller file. The tablet version of the Main.js controller is exactly the same except for the onListItemTap() function, which looks like this:

```
onListItemTap: function(dataview, index, target, record, e, options) {
  var original = record.get('content');
  var converted = original.replace(/src=\"/g, 'src=\"http://src.sencha.
io/240/');
  var final = converted.replace(/((width|height)\s*=\s*"*\d+"*)/g, '');
  record.set('content', final);
  var pageDetails = this.getMainView().down('pagedetails');
```

```
var postDetails = this.getMainView().down('postdetails');
if(dataview.id == 'pageList') {
  postDetails.hide();
  pageDetails.setRecord(record)
  pageDetails.show();
} else {
  pageDetails.hide();
  postDetails.setRecord(record)
  postDetails.show();
}
}
```

In this function we do our conversion the way we did before in the phone version. This time we increase the maximum width to 240 pixels.

Next, we grab our two details containers with the following:

```
var pageDetails = this.getMainView().down('pagedetails');
var postDetails = this.getMainView().down('postdetails');
```

Once we have those, we use the `dataview id` just as we did before to get the currently active DataView. We then hide one and show the other after adding our record to it for display.

As you can see from the two controllers, we can completely dictate the functions in the application, regardless of whether or not the view itself is shared between profiles. Combined with the ability to include different views based on a particular profile, we can easily target the application to a particular platform's strengths and overcome any potential weaknesses.

However, as powerful as this is, there is still one other trick we can use to further customize our application based on platform or device, that is, conditional styling.

Conditional styling

You should be familiar with the use of CSS stylesheets to control the look of elements of your web page based on `id` or `class`. Since these can be applied to Sencha components and within xTemplates, we can use these classes and IDs to control the look of our application as well. We do this by checking the device's width using a media query.

Media queries

Media queries are actually a part of the CSS standards and not a direct part of Sencha Touch. However, since Sencha Touch uses CSS, we can inherit this tool and use it as an easy way to make decisions based on the environment that the web page is being displayed in. While this functionality has been around for quite some time, it was not standard across all web browsers until recently. Fortunately for us, Sencha Touch is only supported on modern web browsers, so the late adoption of the standard does not affect us.

If you have used a lot of CSS in the past few years, you may have noticed the use of media in stylesheet links like this:

```
<link rel="stylesheet" type="text/css" href="main.css" media="screen"
/>
<link rel="stylesheet" type="text/css" href="print.css" media="print"
/>
```

This setup would use `main.css` for displaying in the browser and `print.css` when printing the page out to a printer. This was typically used to remove navigation and extraneous page elements during printing.

However, these same media queries can be used to include stylesheets based on the screen size like so:

```
<link rel="stylesheet" type="text/css" media="screen and (max-device-
width: 480px)" href="iPhone.css" />
```

This media query will load the stylesheet if the device is using a web browser (screen) with a maximum screen width of 480px (like an iPhone 3G).

We can even take this a step further and change the stylesheet based on the orientation:

```
<link rel="stylesheet" type="text/css" media="screen and (max-device-
width: 480px) and (orientation:portrait" href="iPhonePortrait.css" />
<link rel="stylesheet" type="text/css" media="screen and (max-device-
width: 480px) and (orientation:landscape" href="iPhoneLandscape.css"
/>
```

These two links will include `iPhonePortrait.css` when the iPhone is held in portrait orientation and `iPhoneLandscape.css` when held in landscape orientation.

Combining these CSS media queries with Sencha Touch's profiles allows us to target a particular device at a very granular level.

Summary

When designing applications for a mobile environment, it is extremely important to take advantage of any special features of the device and avoid any potential shortfalls the device may have. By tailoring an application directly to the device, you provide a better overall user experience. In this chapter, we showed you how to make the most of this ability by covering the following points:

- The basics and usage of profiles
- Setting up WordPress to work with Sencha Touch
- Creating the basic Evolver application
- Setting up the controllers to manage functionality on both phone and tablet devices
- Using media queries to further style your applications for a particular device

In the next chapter we will take a look how to access some of the hardware capabilities of your device, specifically the camera. We also show you how to compile your application to take advantage of more of your device's features.

9

Workbook: Using the Camera

By far, the most common feature of mobile devices today is the camera. It is difficult to imagine a mobile device without one. A quality application needs to be able to take advantage of this feature and in this chapter, we will show you how it's done.

In this chapter we will build a basic workbook application where you can:

- Create notebooks
- Add notes to each notebook
- Add an image to each note

We will also use a tiled layout data view to spice up the appearance of the application, and talk about ways to send an image to another application such as WordPress or the Sencha.io storage system.

Designing the basic application

For this application we will have "books" that contain "notes", which means we will only see a note when the user clicks on a specific book. In this case, a tabbed interface probably doesn't make much sense, so we will use a navigation view to move between our list of books and the list of notes for a particular book.

We also want to move beyond the traditional list and use a tiled view with some icons. This will give us something like this:

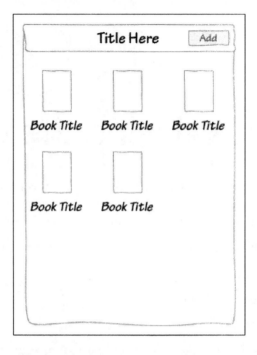

When the user taps on one of the books, they will get a similar screen with the notes for that particular book. We will have an **Add** button for new books and an **Add** button for new notes. Since the navigation view uses the same title bar for both views, we will need to swap between the two **Add** buttons based on which view we are looking at.

We will also need forms for our books and notes. The notes form will also need a button that allows us to either take a picture with the device camera, or select a photo from the device's photo library.

In terms of data, we need a title and an ID for our books. Our notes will also have a title and an ID, and we will need fields for our notes, an image, and a book ID to tell us which book the note belongs to.

Since we have a good idea of what data we need, let's start by setting up our models and stores.

Creating the models and stores

Our book is by far the simpler of the two pieces we need to deal with, so let's start there. Our book model looks like this:

```
Ext.define('Workbook.model.Book', {
    extend: 'Ext.data.Model',
    config: {
        fields: [
            {
                name: 'id',
                type: 'int'
            },
            {
                name: 'title',
                type: 'string'
            }
        ]
    }
});
```

Our `bookstore.js` file is equally simple and uses a local storage proxy for storing our data. Since the list of books is the first thing the user will see, we also want this store to automatically load. So, in that case we will use the following code:

```
Ext.define('Workbook.store.BookStore', {
    extend: 'Ext.data.Store',
    requires: [
        'Workbook.model.Book'
    ],
    config: {
        model: 'Workbook.model.Book',
        autoLoad: true,
        storeId: 'BookStore',
        proxy: {
            type: 'localstorage',
            id  : 'books'
        }
    }
});
```

Our notes need to be related to our books, so they will have an associated `bookID` as well as their own unique ID property:

```
Ext.define('Workbook.model.Note', {
    extend: 'Ext.data.Model',
    config: {
        fields: [
            {
                name: 'id',
                type: 'int'
            },
            {
                name: 'bookID',
                type: 'int'
            },
            {
                name: 'title',
                type: 'string'
            },
            {
                name: 'dateModified',
                type: 'date'
            },
            {
                name: 'notes',
                type: 'string'
            },
            {
                name: 'image',
                type: 'string'
            }
        ]
    }
});
```

We also have fields for our title, `dateModified`, `notes`, and `image`. We will set `dateModified` to the current date when a new note is created and when an existing note is updated and saved.

Our `noteStore.js` file looks much the same as our book store, except we don't want this one to load automatically so we set `autoLoad` to `false`:

```
Ext.define('Workbook.store.NoteStore', {
    extend: 'Ext.data.Store',
    requires: [
        'Workbook.model.Note'
    ],
    config: {
        model: 'Workbook.model.Note',
        storeId: 'NoteStore',
        autoLoad: false,
        proxy: {
            type: 'localstorage',
            id  : 'notes'
        }
    }
});
```

Now that we know what kind of data we are dealing with, we need to think about how things will be displayed.

The views

For our application views, we will need a list and edit views for our books. When the user clicks on a book, they will get the list of notes. We will also need a form for editing notes and a details view for the notes.

Let's start with the book views.

Creating the book views

The first book view is our list of books. Rather than going with the simple list, we will use a DataView and icons to give our list a bit more visual appeal:

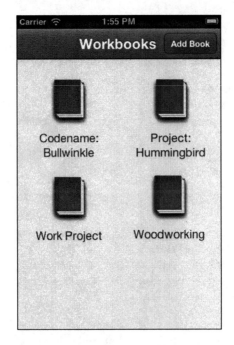

This layout will be created using the xTemplate (`tpl`) and CSS styles:

```
Ext.define('Workbook.view.bookList', {
    extend: 'Ext.dataview.DataView',
    alias: 'widget.booklist',
    config: {
        title: 'Workbooks',
        styleHtmlContent: true,
        scrollable: {
         direction: 'vertical',
         directionLock: true
        },
        emptyText: 'You don\'t have any Workbooks. Click the Add
button at the top of your screen to add a new Workbook',
        store: 'BookStore',
        id: 'bookList',
```

```
        itemTpl: '<img src="resources/icons/book.png" /><h4>{title}</
h4>',
        itemCls: 'bookItem'
    }
});
```

We start our `booklist.js` file by extending the standard `Ext.dataview.DataView` and adding our configuration options. We set a title and allow for styled HTML content in the panel. We also set up scrolling and give it providing `directionLock` so it only scrolls in one direction.

Next, we add some empty text that instructs the user how to add a book and finish up with our `itemTpl` and an `itemCls`. `itemTpl` and `itemCls` will be used to position each of our books within the view.

By default, when the DataView is rendered as HTML, each item in our DataView is wrapped in a `div` tag with a CSS class of `.x-dataview-item`. It looks something like this:

```
<div class="x-dataview-item">Our Book Item</div>
```

Potentially, we could just set styles on `.x-dataview-item`, but this would change the style for every DataView we use. By setting `itemCls`, the `div` tag now looks like this:

```
<div class="x-dataview-item bookItem">Our Book Item</div>
```

This means we can now style the `bookItem` class without affecting the rest of our data views. We style the `bookItem` class by placing the following into our CSS file:

```
.bookItem {
  width: 140px;
  display: inline-block;
  clear: none;
  margin: 10px;
  text-align: center;
  vertical-align: top;
}
.bookItem img {
    margin-left: auto;
    margin-right: auto;
  }
  .bookItem h4 {
    margin-bottom: 0px;
  }
```

This style data determines our width for each item and tiles them across the screen from left to right. It also sets our margins and centers the text and our icon.

Next, we need to create a view for adding our books using a `form` component:

```
Ext.define('Workbook.view.bookEdit', {
    extend: 'Ext.form.Panel',
    alias: 'widget.bookedit',
    config: {
        items: [
            {
                xtype: 'container',
                html: 'Please enter a book name below:',
                id: 'bookEditText',
                margin: 8,
                style: 'text-align:center;'
            },
            {
                xtype: 'textfield',
                id: 'bookName',
                name: 'title',
                label: 'Title'
            },
            {
                xtype: 'hiddenfield',
                id: 'bookID',
                name: 'id'
            }
        ]
    }
});
```

This form has a container for instructions, a text field for the user to enter a name for the book, and a `hiddenfield` component where we will add the book's `id` value when we are editing an existing book.

We are also going to add two buttons to the form; a **Save** button and a **Cancel** button. In this example, we will set handlers for each button inside the view itself. This code could also be moved into the controller if you prefer, and we will show you how to do it that way a bit later. For now, let's add the **Save** button first:

```
{
  xtype: 'button',
  margin: 8,
```

```
   id: 'saveBookButton',
   ui: 'confirm',
   text: 'Save Book',
   handler: function() {
    var form = this.up('formpanel');
    var store = Ext.getStore('BookStore');
    var values = form.getValues();
    if(values.id > 0) {
     var index = store.find('id', values.id);
     var record = store.getAt(index);
     record.set(values);
    } else {
     var record = Ext.ModelMgr.create(values, 'Workbook.model.Book');
    store.add(record);
    }
    store.sync();
    var main = this.up('navigationview');
    main.pop(form);
   }
  }
```

The basic setup for the button element should be pretty familiar to you now.
The handler component will automatically fire when the button is tapped.

This function grabs our store and form, values, and the value from the values
variable. We then check to see if the id value is a number greater than zero.
The only way this will occur is if we have loaded an existing book record into
our form for editing.

If the id value is greater than zero (we have an existing book), we grab the
current record value from the store and replace its values with the new values
from our form.

If the id value is null (it's a new book), we create a new record using our book
model, insert the form's values variable and add the record to the store.

We then sync the store to save our changes and pop the book form off of our
main navigationview.

Lastly, we add a **Cancel** button after our **Save** button. This one just needs to
pop the form off of our navigationview:

```
  {
   xtype: 'button',
   margin: 8,
```

```
  ui: 'decline',
  text: 'Cancel',
  handler: function() {
   var form = this.up('formpanel');
   var main = this.up('navigationview');
   main.pop(form);
  }
 }
}
```

Now that we have the views for adding and displaying books in our application, we need to create our main.js view that will launch when the application is started.

Adding the book list to the main view

Our main view needs to display the list of books and it needs a button to show our add book form. As we noted previously, we will be using navigationview for this main component:

```
Ext.define("Workbook.view.Main", {
 extend: 'Ext.NavigationView',
 requires: ['Ext.TitleBar','Ext.dataview.DataView'],
 config: {
  id: 'mainView',
  fullscreen: true,
  navigationBar : {
   docked : 'top',
   items : [
     {
      text : 'Add Book',
      align : 'right',
      id: 'addBookButton'
     }
    ]
   },
   items: [
    { xtype: 'booklist'}
   ]
  }
});
```

This view is defined in `app.js` as the one that will be added to the viewport when the application launches. You will notice that we have required the `TitleBar` and `DataView` components in our `Main` component. This is to prevent compiling errors later on when we build our native application. The main `navigationview` component also includes our booklist component and an add button to show our form.

> **Code in the controller versus the view**
>
> Unlike our previous book's `form` view, we will place the function code for our "Add Book" button inside the controller. Placing the functionality of a view in the controller is generally considered a "best practice", but it is important to understand that this can be done in a number of different ways.

Now that we have our main view created, let's jump over to the `Book.js` controller and set things up to test what we have so far.

Starting the book controller

The book controller will start with our views, models, and stores that we have created. It will also set up our references, our initial controls, and two functions:

```
Ext.define('Workbook.controller.Book', {
    extend: 'Ext.app.Controller',
    config: {
        stores: ['BookStore'],
        models: ['Book'],
        views: ['bookEdit', 'bookList'],
        refs: {
            bookList: '#bookList',
            addBookButton: '#addBookButton',
            main: '#mainView'
        },

        control: {
            addBookButton: {
                tap: 'onAddBookButtonTap'
            },
```

```
            bookList: {
                select: 'onBookSelect'
            }
        }
    },
    onAddBookButtonTap: function(button, event, options) {
        var bookForm = Ext.create('Workbook.view.bookEdit');
        this.getMain().push(bookForm);
    },
    onBookSelect: function(dataview, record, options) {
        console.log(dataview, record, options);
    }
});
```

Our `book.js` controller file needs to push our `bookEdit` form onto the `Main` navigation view. We do this by creating a reference (`refs`) for the `addBookButton` component using its `id` property. We then assign a function to the button's `tap` event in our `controls` section.

The `onAddBookButtonTap` function creates a new instance of our `bookEdit` form and pushes it onto our `Main` navigation view. This will make the form appear and add a back button at the top of the page.

We also added `refs` and `controls` for the `bookList` form, including an `onBookSelect` function. However, we don't have any of our other views so we can't display a list of notes for the book. Instead, we have added a console log that will show the DataView, record, and options that are passed when a book in the list is tapped. Once we add a book, we should be able to tap on it and see the information displayed in the Safari Error console.

 The `console.log()` function is a great way to test your application in the early stages of development. It can help you detect problems early on and deal with them before you build up the entire project.

If you test the project now, you should get the initial empty book screen and be able to add new books:

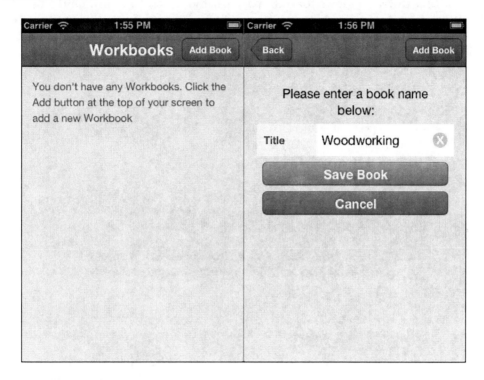

If you add a book and then tap it in the book list, you should see something like the following screenshot in the Safari Error console:

```
▶ Object    ▶ Object    ▶ Object                          Book.js:42
```

From left to right, these objects are the DataView (our book list), the record (which book was tapped), and the options (the object that was passed to the listener—serious nerd stuff).

We will use the information in the record object later on to tell us which notes to display. Now we need to create the views for our notes.

Creating the note views

We need three different views for our notes: a list view, an edit view, and a details view. We will start with our list view since it is similar to the one we use for books:

```
Ext.define('Workbook.view.noteList', {
    extend: 'Ext.dataview.DataView',
    config: {
        id: 'noteList',
        itemId: 'noteList',
        styleHtmlContent: true,
        scrollable: {
            direction: 'vertical',
            directionLock: true
        },
        itemTpl: '<img src="resources/icons/note.png" /><h4>{title}</
h4><h5>{dateModified:date("m/d/Y, g:i a")}</h5>',
        store: 'NoteStore',
        emptyText: 'You don't have any Notes in this Workbook. Click
the Add button at the top of your screen to add a new Note to the
Workbook',
        title: 'Notes For'
    }
});
```

We override the DataView, set up our IDs and our scrolling, just as we did with our book list. In the `itemTpl` configuration, we added the date the note was modified, using the `date()` function to change it to a shorter format than the default. We also set our empty text and a default title. Our book controller will update the title and display the book name for the current note.

We will be using the same basic styles as our book container to make the note list tile across the screen like our book list.

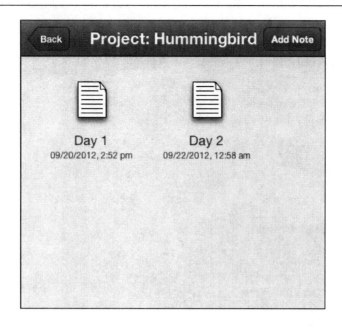

When the user taps a note in the list, we need to display the note details with the text and the image for the note. Our `noteDetails.js` view is a simple panel with an xTemplate:

```
Ext.define('Workbook.view.noteDetails', {
    extend: 'Ext.Container',
    alias: 'widget.notedetails',
    config: {
        layout: 'fit',
        scrollable: {direction: 'vertical', directionLock: true},
        tpl: '<h1>{title}</h1><img src="data:image/png;base64,{image}"
/><h5>{date}</h5><div class="notes">{notes}</div>'
    }
});
```

Don't worry too much about the `data:image/png;base64` section of this code. We will cover the base64 image format in the *Getting started with images* section of the chapter.

The edit view for our note will have fields for a title and note text. There will also be hidden fields such as bookID, image, and the note's id field (the value of these will be set by our controller).

```
Ext.define('Workbook.view.noteEdit', {
 extend: 'Ext.form.Panel',
 alias: 'widget.noteedit',
 config: {
  items: [
    {
     xtype: 'container',
     html: 'Please enter a note title, notes and select an image
below:',
     id: 'noteEditText',
     margin: 8,
     style: 'text-align:center;'
    }, {
     xtype: 'button',
     text: 'Select Image',
     id: 'imageSelectButton',
     width: 220,
     style: 'margin-top: 10px; margin-right:auto; margin-left:auto;
margin-bottom: 15px;'
    }, {
     xtype: 'container',
     id: 'imageView',
     width: 200,
     height: 200
    },
    {
     xtype: 'hiddenfield',
     id: 'imageField',
     name: 'image',
     value: ''
    },
    {
     xtype: 'textfield',
     id: 'noteTitle',
     name: 'title',
     label: 'Title'
    },
    {
     xtype: 'hiddenfield',
```

```
    id: 'bookID',
    name: 'bookID',
    value: 0
   },
   {
    xtype: 'hiddenfield',
    id: 'noteID',
    name: 'id',
    value: 0
   },
   {
    xtype: 'textareafield',
    id: 'notesArea',
    name: 'notes',
    label: 'Notes',
    value: ''
   }
  ]
 }
});
```

We will also have a button for selecting an image and a container for displaying the selected image. When the button is tapped, we will select an image from the device that will be returned to us as a base64 string. This string will be set as the value for our hidden image field.

We will also have two buttons just like our book edit form, one for for the purpose of saving and one for canceling. The **Cancel** button is exactly the same as the previous one for the book edit and it just pops the form off of the navigation view.

The **Save** button is a little different in that it needs to set a value for date modified whenever a note is saved:

```
{
 xtype: 'button',
 margin: 8,
 ui: 'confirm',
 text: 'Save',
 id: 'saveNoteButton',
 handler: function() {
  var form = this.up('formpanel');
  var store = Ext.getStore('NoteStore');
  var values = form.getValues();
```

```
  if(values.id > 0) {
   var index = store.find('id', values.id);
   var record = store.getAt(index);
   record.set(values);
   var date = new Date();
   record.set('dateModified', date);
  } else {
   var record = Ext.ModelMgr.create(values, 'Workbook.model.Note');
   var date = new Date();
   record.set('dateModified', date);
  }
  store.add(record);
  store.sync();
  var main = this.up('navigationview');
  main.pop(form);
  }
 }
```

Other than that, the button is mostly the same as our book save button. We grab the store and the form values, we check to see if we are dealing with a new note or an existing note, and we save the note accordingly.

With these basic views set up, it's time to get back into our controller and hook everything together.

Creating the controller

The first thing we need to do in our controller is update our `config` section to add the new views, stores, and models for our application. We also need to add some new references and controls for these new components.

```
config: {
  stores: ['BookStore', 'NoteStore'],
  models: ['Book', 'Note'],
  views: ['bookEdit', 'noteEdit', 'noteList', 'bookList'],
  refs: {
   bookList: '#bookList',
   noteList: '#noteList',
   addBookButton: '#addBookButton',
   addNoteButton: '#addNoteButton',
   imageSelectButton: '#imageSelectButton',
   main: '#mainView'
```

```
    },
    control: {
     addBookButton: {
      tap: 'onAddBookButtonTap'
     },
     addNoteButton: {
      tap: 'onAddNoteButtonTap'
     },
     imageSelectButton: {
      tap: 'onImageSelectButtonTap'
     },
     bookList: {
      select: 'onBookSelect'
     },
     noteList: {
      select: 'onNoteSelect'
     },
     main: {
      back: 'onBackClicked'
     }
    }
   }
```

The `refs` section will set up our shortcuts for the new note components we created and the controls will add new functions for the following actions:

- Tapping a note in the list
- Tapping the button to add an image
- Selecting a book in the list
- Selecting a note in the list
- Clicking the back button from anywhere in the application

Now that we have `refs` and `control` in place, let's start creating the functions we will need for the application.

The `onBookSelect` function is linked to the `select` event for the book list (in the `controls` section). The `select` event will automatically pass along the record that was selected as part of its arguments. We will use the book title from that record to set the `title` property of our new note list view. We will also use the `id` property from this record to limit the note's `store` to just the notes for that book:

```
onBookSelect: function(dataview, record, options) {
    console.log(dataview, record, options);
```

```
    var noteList = Ext.create('Workbook.view.noteList', {title: record.
get('title')});
    var bookID = record.get('id');
    this.getMain().push(noteList);
    this.getAddNoteButton().show();
    this.getAddBookButton().hide();
    var noteStore = noteList.getStore();
    noteStore.filter("bookID", bookID);
    noteStore.load();
    noteList.bookID = bookID;
}
```

Notice that we pass the title value as a configuration option when we create the new instance of the note list. This is often a handy way to set additional parameters when creating a new object.

Next, we push our new noteList object onto the Main navigation view, and swap our AddBook button with the AddNote button using show/hide functions.

We then use the bookID value to filter the store, limiting the notes to just the ones for our current book and load the store.

We also add bookID as a configuration option on noteList. This will let us easily grab bookID when we add new notes.

The next thing we need to take care of is the **Back** button. This button is created automatically by the navigation view and it will automatically pop the current view off of the navigation view stack, returning us to the previous page.

However, there are three problems with this:

- When we switch back to the previous view, we need to hide the **Add Note** button and show our **Add Book** button.

- When we switch back to the book list, we still have a filter on the notes store. This will mess things up if we select a different book.

- When we switch back to the book list, the book we originally selected will still be selected. This means that if you click on the same book again, the select event will not fire. This is also true for our notes list.

This means we need to tie into the back event on our navigation view and fix these issues:

```
onBackClicked: function(button, options) {
  var store = Ext.getStore('NoteStore');
```

```
  var activeItem = this.getMain().getActiveItem();
  if(activeItem.id == 'bookList') {
    this.getAddNoteButton().hide();
    this.getAddBookButton().show();
    this.getBookList().deselectAll();
    store.clearFilter();
  } else if(activeItem.id == 'noteList') {
    this.getAddNoteButton().show();
    this.getAddBookButton().hide();
    this.getNoteList().deselectAll();
  }
}
```

The first thing we have to determine is which item is active after the `back` event is fired.

If it is the book list, we hide the `AddNote` button, show the `AddBook` button, deselect all in `bookList`, and clear the filter on the store.

If `noteList` is active then the user is coming back from the note details. We still need to deselect all in `noteList` and show the correct buttons, but we keep the filters on the store.

The next function will be used to create a `noteEdit` form and add some initial values to it:

```
onAddNoteButtonTap: function(button, event, options) {
  var noteForm = Ext.create('Workbook.view.noteEdit');
  this.getMain().push(noteForm);
  var record = Ext.create(
  'Workbook.model.Note', {
    title: '',
    note: '',
    bookID: this.getNoteList().bookID
  });
  noteForm.setRecord(record);
}
```

In the `onAddNoteButtonTap` function we create a new instance of the `noteEdit` form and push it onto the `Main` navigation view. We also create a new record based on our `Note` model and set the `bookID` value. Lastly, we load the record into the form using `setRecord()`.

Next, we need a short function to push the details panel for a note onto our main navigation. This is accomplished by our `onNoteSelect` function:

```
onNoteSelect: function(dataview, record, options) {
 var noteDetails = Ext.create('Workbook.view.noteDetails');
 this.getMain().push(noteDetails);
 noteDetails.setRecord(record);
}
```

Now that we are done with the basic functions, we can finally move on to getting images into our application.

Getting started with images

There are a couple of important things to note about using images in an application. The first is that the application must be a compiled application in order for this feature to work. You will also need to add `Ext.device.Camera` to your `requires` section in `app.js`. Since this functionality is only used in compiled applications, the file is not included by default.

 Since we have covered compiling applications in *Chapter 3, Going Command Line*, for our TimeCop application, we will not cover it again here.

For security reasons, JavaScript has no access to the filesystem on a mobile device. Only by compiling the application can we bypass this limitation and use the camera or access existing photos on the device. This means that actual testing of the application can be somewhat limited before you compile it.

When you are testing in a web browser, Sencha Touch will return a placeholder image link for the purposes of testing. However, there are two different formats an image can be returned in.

The first is a `file` or URI format. This is basically a link to the existing file and the implementation can vary across devices. The second format is `data`, which is a base64-encoded string.

The `file` format can typically be used in an image link as `src`. For example:

```
<img src="file_URI_here" />
```

However, the base64 `data` needs a slightly different format, which you might recall from our `noteDetails.js` file:

```
<img src="data:image/png;base64,{image}" />
```

This base64 `data` format allows us to control the image format on the fly and store the value as a string in the database.

 Base64 data is a format that allows you to transmit files as a string of text. This lets us include things such as images as part of our JSON data. It also lets us store the string as part of the data in our database.

If we use the file URI and the user deletes the image from the device, the URI will also disappear from our application. While this may be the desired behavior in some instances, more often it is not.

We also need to consider where the source image is coming from. Is it coming from the camera itself, the stored photos, or a particular photo album?

All of these options and more are handled within the `capture` function.

Capturing an image

Let's take a look at how the image `capture()` function works in our `onImageSelectButtonTap` function works in our `Book.js` controller:

```
onImageSelectButtonTap: function(button, event, options) {
  var imageView = Ext.getCmp('imageView');
  var imageField = Ext.getCmp('imageField');
  Ext.device.Camera.capture({
    success: function(image) {
      imageView.setHtml('<img src="data:image/png;base64,'+image+'"
width=200px height=200px />');
      imageField.setValue(image);
    },
    quality: 100,
    destination: 'data'
  });
}
```

We start out by grabbing our `imageView` variable (where we will place a copy of the image after it is selected) and our `imageField` variable (the hidden field that will store the data for our image for saving). You can see our completed form in the following screenshot. This shows our button, our selected image, and the two form fields:

The `Ext.device.Camera.capture` function has an internal `success` function to which the image is passed. The format of the image is set in the `destination` config and can be either `data` (base64) or `file` (URI) format.

The `success` function is where we process the image information we receive. In this case we set the HTML of our `imageView` container to the image, scaled to 200 by 200 pixels. This provides the user with a preview of their selection before saving.

We also set the value of our hidden `imageField` component to the base64-encoded string so that it will save with our other form values.

However, before we save there are a number of options we can set on the image:

- `quality`: This specifies the image quality to be anything from 1 – 100.
- `source`: Where should the image come from? The options are `camera`, `library`, or `album`.
- `encoding`: The available encodings are `png` and `jpg`.
- `height`: This specifies the height of the image in pixels.
- `width`: This specifies the width of the image in pixels.

Any of these options can be set within the capture function, but it is good to keep in mind that `quality`, `height`, and `width` will be applied to the image before it can potentially be stored. Limiting these values can subsequently limit the usefulness of the image later on. It's always easier to make a big image smaller than it is to make a small image bigger.

Storing the image

In our `onImageSelectButtonTap` function, we set the value of our hidden field to the base64-encoded `data` string. If we had chosen `destination: file` instead of `destination: data`, we could still do much the same thing. The image is saved as part of our save button handler in `noteEdit.js` we built earlier in the chapter.

However, the `file` option would only store a reference to the image file. As we noted previously, if the user deletes the image from their device using their photo manager, it disappears from our application as well.

The `data` option gives us the actual data for the image itself. This means if the user deletes the image from their device using their photo manager, it doesn't affect the image stored in our application.

Displaying the image

Once you have the stored image, you can use it in your xTemplates as we described previously.

The `file` format can typically be used in an image link as `src` like this:

```
<img src="file_URI_here" />
```

The base64 `data` format is used like this:

```
<img src="data:image/png;base64,{image}" />
```

As we also noted, when you are testing in a web browser, Sencha Touch will return a test image link (http://www.sencha.com/img/sencha-large.png).

While the test image returned when testing in the browser will work fine, if you are using the file destination format, it will display a missing image if you are using the data destination format. In the compiled application, the image will display correctly.

Another thing to keep in mind with these images is that you can use the standard img height and width tags to shrink the image to a particular screen size. For example:

```
var imageWidth = Ext.Viewport.getWindowWidth();
var imageString = '<img src="data:image/png;base64,{image}"
width='+imageWidth' />';
```

This will give you a great deal of flexibility if you store the full size image and use it in different ways.

Sending images

If your application needs to transmit images, either to another user or an external API, you will need to use the data destination format. As noted previously, the file destination format is just a reference and it is relative to the device the application is running on.

Since the data format is base64, it can be transmitted just like any other string data. Unfortunately, there is currently no way to natively upload a file to a remote server without building your own custom API to accept the base64 data string and convert it to an image file.

However, if you compile your application using the PhoneGap compiler instead of the native Sencha Touch compiler, you can use their fileTransfer object to send files as a standard HTTP POST. You can find more information on PhoneGap and the fileTransfer object at http://docs.phonegap.com/en/1.0.0/phonegap_file_file.md.html#FileTransfer.

PhoneGap provides an online compiling service that can create native applications from the Sencha Touch code much like the Sencha Touch Command tools we covered in a previous chapter.

More information on PhoneGap can be found at http://www.phonegap.com/.

Summary

In this chapter we talked about setting up your application to take advantage of the camera on your mobile device. With this we covered the following points:

- How to use DataViews to create a different looking UI
- The difference between the `data` and `file` image formats
- Using Sencha Touch to interact with the device's camera and local photo storage

In the next chapter we will use DataViews to an even greater extent to create the board for a multiplayer game.

10
Game On

A quick browse through any of the online app stores quickly shows that the largest segment of the mobile applications market belongs to gaming. While most programmers would not think of JavaScript when it comes to developing games, it is actually well suited for a wide variety of games, including turn-based strategy games.

These games require only limited animation and can easily be built using the Sencha Touch Framework and the Sencha.io platform for communication. For turn-based strategy games, we only need to do a few basic things such as:

- Build a game board
- Build the individual pieces
- Handle moves
- Handle the outcomes when one piece attacks another
- Handle communication of the moves between players at the end of a turn
- Define the end of the game

While this might seem a trivial style of game, it covers everything from tic-tac-toe to chess, poker, Go, Risk, and the incredibly complex tabletop strategy games of the pre-Internet era, such as Axis and Allies.

 If you really want an idea of how complex some of these games can get, take a look at http://boardgamegeek.com/ and check out the strategy section.

Since we don't have an entire book to dedicate to this single topic, we are going to start with a relatively simple game of checkers. We will also explore some of the possible ways to take this simple game and build on it to create more complex games.

Building the basic board

With any type of turn-based strategy game, it all starts with the board. The board determines where the pieces are placed and where they are allowed to move.

A board for checkers or chess consists of an 8 by 8 grid of squares. The squares alternate in color between light and dark (typically red and black for a dedicated checkers board).

Additionally, only the dark squares can be used by the pieces in checkers.

You could use a number of different Sencha Touch components to create such a board, but for these purposes a DataView is probably the most appropriate. A DataView will allow us to tap and select the piece we want to move as well as the place we want to move it to. These selection methods are already built into the DataView. We can also apply styles based on these selections to let the user know which moves are valid.

Creating the square model

Our DataView will be fed by a store with a model we call `Square`. It looks like this:

```
Ext.define('Checkers.model.Square', {
    extend: 'Ext.data.Model',
    config: {
        fields: [
            {name: 'squareID', type: 'string'},
            {name: 'occupiedBy', type: 'string'},
            {name: 'pieceType', type: 'string'},
            {name: 'decoration', type: 'string'},
            {name: 'background', type: 'string'}
        ],
        idProperty: 'squareID'
    }
});
```

This model carries five key pieces of information:

*   `squareID` tells us exactly where the square is located on our board.
*   The value for `occupiedBy` tells us if the square is currently occupied by a red piece, a black piece, or if it is unoccupied (none).
*   `pieceType` will tell us if we are dealing with a regular piece or a king.

- The `decoration` setting will allow us to indicate the current movement path for the pieces and if a particular piece has been jumped.

- The `background` setting controls the background color of the piece. We will use this to set a style in our xTemplate for the DataView.

Our initial load in of data would look something like this:

```
{squareID: 'A1', occupiedBy: 'none', pieceType: 'none', decoration:
'', background: 'light'},
{squareID: 'B1', occupiedBy: 'black', pieceType: 'Piece', decoration:
'', background: 'dark'},
{squareID: 'C1', occupiedBy: 'none', pieceType: 'none', decoration:
'', background: 'light'},
{squareID: 'D1', occupiedBy: 'black', pieceType: 'Piece', decoration:
'', background: 'dark'},
{squareID: 'E1', occupiedBy: 'none', pieceType: 'none', decoration:
'', background: 'light'},
{squareID: 'F1', occupiedBy: 'black', pieceType: 'Piece', decoration:
'', background: 'dark'},
{squareID: 'G1', occupiedBy: 'none', pieceType: 'none', decoration:
'', background: 'light'},
{squareID: 'H1', occupiedBy: 'black', pieceType: 'Piece', decoration:
'', background: 'dark'},
{squareID: 'A2', occupiedBy: 'black', pieceType: 'Piece', decoration:
'', background: 'dark'},
{squareID: 'B2', occupiedBy: 'none', pieceType: 'none', decoration:
'', background: 'light'},
{squareID: 'C2', occupiedBy: 'black', pieceType: 'Piece', decoration:
'', background: 'dark'},
{squareID: 'D2', occupiedBy: 'none', pieceType: 'none', decoration:
'', background: 'light'},
{squareID: 'E2', occupiedBy: 'black', pieceType: 'Piece', decoration:
'', background: 'dark'},
{squareID: 'F2', occupiedBy: 'none', pieceType: 'none', decoration:
'', background: 'light'},
{squareID: 'G2', occupiedBy: 'black', pieceType: 'Piece', decoration:
'', background: 'dark'},
{squareID: 'H2', occupiedBy: 'none', pieceType: 'none', decoration:
'', background: 'light'}...
```

This would continue on to give us eight rows of eight squares per row. Squares are designated A through H and rows are numbered 1 through 8. This data will also lay out our initial pieces in the standard layout for the start of a checkers game.

You will also notice that when we alternate the backgrounds, we keep the last item of the row and the first item of the next row as the same color (H1 and A2 are both dark). This gives us our checkerboard pattern.

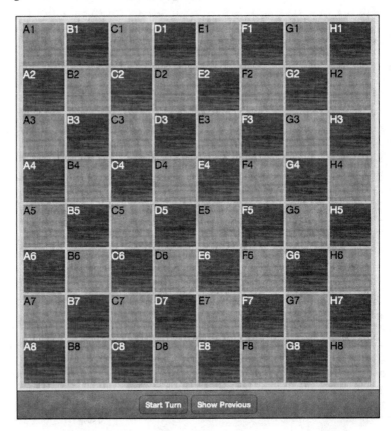

The actual board image itself is a single background image. We have arranged our DataView to fit over the board and align with the individual squares. This will let us place elements on any square we choose using CSS. The `dataview` code is included as one of the items in our `view/Main.js` file:

```
{
    xtype: 'dataview',
    itemTpl: ['<div class="gameSquare {background}
{decoration}">{squareID}',
            "<tpl if='occupiedBy != \"none\" && pieceType !=
\"none\"'><img src=\"resources/images/{occupiedBy}{pieceType}.png\"
height=\"72\" width=\"72\" /></tpl>",
```

```
               '</div>'],
        store: 'BoardStore',
        height: 619,
        width: 619,
        scrollable: false,
        cls: 'board',
        margin: 5,
        padding: 5,
        mode: 'MULTI'
    }
```

This DataView has a `cls` value of `board` so we can set the background image to the big checkerboard image in our `resources/css/app.css` file.

Exploring itemTpl

We also make extensive use of classes in the `itemTpl` config. Let's take a look at the template line by line:

```
'<div class="gameSquare {background} {decoration}">{squareID}'
```

The first line sets up a `div` element with a `class` value of `gameSquare`. Each `gameSquare` is set in the `app.css` file to:

```
.gameSquare {
  height: 72px;
  width: 72px;
  margin: 2px;
  float: left;
  position: relative;
}
```

This sets the individual items in our DataView to line up with our game board. By setting `position: relative`, we can also position items absolutely within `gameSquare`.

We also add a class for `{background}`. This value will be pulled from our data store and it will be either light or dark. We add this class so we can change the font color for our dark tiles to white. In the CSS, this looks like:

```
.gameSquare.dark {
    color: white;
}
```

The next class we set is decoration. The decoration class will be used to show arrows for movement and a negation symbol when a piece will be jumped as part of a move as shown in the following screenshot:

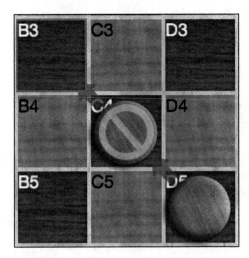

These images can be inserted into a style using the before CSS selector. This selector will insert content before our div element. In this case, we will insert a green arrow to indicate the direction the piece is moving.

For example, a piece moving up and to the left will have its decoration value set to up_left and the following style is applied in our app.css file:

```
.up_left:before {
    content: '';
    background: url("../images/up_left.png");
    height: 32px;
    width: 32px;
    margin: 0;
    padding: 0;
    position: absolute;
    top: -16px;
    left: -16px;
    z-index: 1000;
}
```

By using `position: absolute`, we can set the `top` and `left` position of our image to any value we like including a negative number. The negative number places it up and to the left of the actual square (overlapping the square to the upper-left corner). The high `z-index` value insures that the image appears on top of the other images and text.

We have similar CSS styles created for `.up_right`, `.down_left`, and `.down_right`. This gives us indicators for four diagonal directions of movement.

 All of our images have been saved in the `resources/images` directory. If you change the location of the images, you will need to adjust the CSS file to match your setup.

We also have a decoration class called `removed`. This class uses the CSS selector `after` to insert content after the `div` element and display our negation symbol over a piece that will be jumped during the current move. The CSS looks like this:

```
.removed:after {
    content: '';
    background: url("../images/removed.png");
    height: 72px;
    width: 72px;
    position:absolute;
    top: 0;
    left: 0;
    z-index: 1001;
}
```

It is similar to our styles for our arrows, except we need this symbol to show up over the top of our piece. We set its `top` and `left` attribute to `0` and because the image is the same size as our square, it floats over the top of the image of our piece. The higher z-index assures that it is the top element.

The next line of `itemTpl` is what controls the piece that occupies the square:

```
<tpl if='occupiedBy != \"none\" && pieceType != \"none\"'><img
src=\"resources/images/{occupiedBy}{pieceType}.png\" height=\"72\"
width=\"72\" /></tpl>
```

We use a `tpl if` statement here to check and see if the square is occupied and if so, by what kind of piece. We use two of our data values to determine this value.

The first is `occupiedBy`, which can be `red`, `black`, or `none`.

The second is `pieceType`, which can be `regular`, `king`, or `none`.

If both data values are set to `none`, we do not place a piece in the square. If we have a piece in the square, we use the combination of `occupiedBy` and `pieceType` to determine our image.

| Black King | Black Regular | Red King | Red Regular |

These CSS values along with the individual squares from our DataView allow us to set the appearance of every square on the board by using the values stores in our data store.

Our individual moves can be created using the `select` event in our DataView. By setting the `mode` attribute to `MULTI`, the user can tap the piece they want to move and then the square they wish to move to. They can continue to tap squares if they are in a position to jump multiple pieces. We can also use the DataView's built-in `x-item-selected` class to highlight the squares the user has tapped.

We just add the highlighted styles to our stylesheet:

```
.x-item-selected .gameSquare {
    outline: 3px solid rgba(0,175,0,0.75);
    color: rgb(0,175,0);
}
.x-item-selected .gameSquare.dark {
    color: rgb(0,255,0);
}
```

This gives us a green border to match our arrows and changes the text color as well. We also set a slightly different text color in our dark squares for readability.

Now that we have all of our different display possibilities mapped out, we need to set up the logic for the game.

Creating the game controller

The game controller is where the logic for our game will go. Here we will follow the basic rules for checkers:

- Pieces are initially arranged on the opposite sides of the board in three rows, only on the black squares
- Pieces can move diagonally
- Pieces can only move to an empty square
- Regular pieces can only move forward
- Pieces can only move one square, unless jumping over an adjacent piece
- Pieces can only jump one piece at a time
- Jumped pieces are removed from the board
- King pieces can move forward and backwards
- A regular piece that reaches the opposite side of the board is changed to a king piece, ending their current turn
- The game is finished when all the pieces from one side have been jumped and removed

Our controller will check each move to see if it follows these rules and remove the pieces that have been jumped. For the purposes of this chapter, we will only be creating a local game. This is one in which two players would play by passing back and forth a single device. However, this game could easily be modified to allow for networked play using Sencha.io or an external API.

Before we dive into the code for the controller, we need to add some things to our main view. We need a way for each user to start and finish a turn. We will also need a way to show a previous turn so that a user can see what occurred during the last move.

To do this, we will add a toolbar with two buttons to the bottom of our main view:

```
{
    xtype : 'toolbar',
    docked: 'bottom',
    items: [
        {
            xtype: 'spacer'
        },
```

```
            { text: 'Start Turn', action: 'mainButton' },
            { text: 'Show Previous', action: 'altButton' },
            {
            xtype: 'spacer'
            }
        ]
    }
```

We will expand the functionality of these two buttons in our controller, so that they will also allow us to finish a turn or clear a currently selected move if we change our mind before finishing.

Now let's see how this all fits together in the controller.

As always, we start out by setting up our controller with the `control` and `refs` sections:

```
Ext.define('Checkers.controller.Game', {
  extend: 'Ext.app.Controller',
  config: {
   control: {
    board: {
     select: 'doSelect',
     deselect: 'doDeselect'
    },
    mainBtn: {
     tap: 'doMainBtn'
    },
    altBtn: {
     tap: 'doAltBtn'
    }
   },
   refs: {
    board: 'main dataview',
    mainBtn: 'button[action="mainButton"]',
    altBtn: 'button[action="altButton"]'
   }
  }
});
```

We create references for our board and our two buttons. In the `control` section, we add `select` and `deselect` functions for our board, and `tap` functions for our two buttons. The `mainBtn` function will start a turn and execute the finished move. The `altBtn` function will show the previous turn or clear the current set of moves. We will swap the text and functionality appropriately as part of the `tap` functions.

In order to track the turns, we are going to add two custom variables to our controller. These go down below our `refs` section (inside the `config` section):

```
previousTurn: {
  player: null,
  piece: null,
  moves: [],
  removedPieces: []
},
currentTurn: {
  player: 'black',
  piece: null,
  moves: [],
  removedPieces: [],
  endOfTurn: false,
  hasJumped: false,
  started: false,
  kingable: false
}
```

The `previousTurn` variable will store red or black for `player`, `piece` (piece that was moved), `moves` (moves that were made — as an array), and `removedPieces` (pieces removed — as an array). This will let us highlight the squares from the previous turn when the user clicks on the **Show Previous Turn** button.

The `currentTurn` variable stores the same information as `previousTurn`, but it also adds `Boolean` data for:

- `endOfTurn`: Has the user confirmed and completed the current move?
- `hasJumped`: Has the user jumped a piece as part of their turn?
- `started`: Has the user pressed the **Start Turn** button?
- `kingable`: Has the user reached the opposite end of the board as part of the current move?

We also set the value for player to `black` by default, as black traditionally moves first in checkers.

By declaring these `previousTurn` and `currentTurn` variables as part of `config`, we automatically create getters and setters for both. This means we can do things like `this.getPreviousTurn()` and `this.setCurrentTurn()` inside any of our controller functions. We will be using these functions extensively throughout the controller.

Understanding basic controller functions

Another thing that we will be using extensively in this controller is the concept of **subordinate functions**. These are functions that are called by other functions. While it might seem counter intuitive at first, splitting larger functions apart into smaller sub functions makes the logic easier to follow.

This is especially true in the case of game logic, where the rules for the game can quickly spiral into a series of incomprehensible "if...then" statements. By splitting the logic into smaller functions, the logic is much easier to check. You can simply use `console.log()` to output the value you start with and the value you finish with in each of the smaller functions. This makes it much easier to tell which pieces are functioning as expected.

For this application, we have some smaller functions that help us with our game logic. We won't go into great detail about these smaller functions but they can be found in the `controller/Game.js` file. These functions include:

- `nextLetter` and `previousLetter`: Given a letter and a distance, these two functions return the next or previous letter in the sequence. For example, `nextLetter('c', 2)` would return e when called. These will help us determine positioning on the board.

- `getIntermediateSquare`: Given a *from location* and a *to location*, this function will return the square located between the two squares. This is used when a piece is jumped, so we can determine if a move is valid and apply the correct decorations to the square (arrows and negation symbol for jumped pieces).

- `isKingable`: Given the location the piece is moving to, is it eligible to be kinged?

- `clearTurn`: Clears out any old data from the current term and deselects any selected squares in the DataView.

- `clearDecorations`: Clears any decorations from the data store (clearing this data also removes it from the display).

Aside from these smaller functions, the main logic for the board is handled in the `select` event. This event needs to check and see if we have a valid move, and then add the appropriate decorations to the board. These decorations will show the selected piece, the direction of the move, and any affected squares or pieces.

The game board logic

The game logic will function as follows:

1. A player clicks on the **Start Turn** button.

2. The game responds with an alert telling the player it is black's or red's turn.

3. The player taps a piece.

4. The game checks that a valid piece was tapped and stores the information in the `currentMove` variable.

5. The player taps a destination square.

6. The game checks if the destination is valid and stores the information in the `currentMove` variable.

7. The player can then tap **Finish Turn!** to complete the turn or tap additional squares if jumping multiple pieces (finally tapping **Finish Turn!** when all moves for the turn are complete).

8. Once the player taps **Finish Turn!**, the system removes any jumped pieces, removes all decorations for the move, and stores the move in the `previousMove` variable.

We will begin our trip through the game logic at the most logical place, the function that fires when the user clicks on the **Start Turn** button.

Starting a turn

Our **Start Turn** button actually has two functions that it handles, starting and finishing the turn. This means that we will switch functionality based on the current status (text) of the button. In the controller, this button is referred to as `mainBtn` and the tap function looks like this:

```
doMainBtn: function(btn) {
 var turn = this.getCurrentTurn();
 if (btn.getText() == 'Start Turn') {
  btn.setText('Finish Turn!');
  this.getAltBtn().setText('Clear Moves');
  turn.started = true;
  this.setCurrentTurn(turn);
  this.clearTurn();
  Ext.Msg.alert("Ready to play!", "It is "+turn.player[0].
toUpperCase() + turn.player.slice(1)+"'s turn!");
```

```
    } else {
     if (turn.moves.length > 1) {
     this.commitTurn(turn);
     turn.player = (turn.player == 'red')?'black':'red';
     this.setCurrentTurn(turn);
     this.clearTurn();
     btn.setText('Start Turn');
     this.getAltBtn().setText('Show Previous');
       }
     }
   }
```

We start by grabbing our currentTurn variable using this.getCurrentTurn().
If the game has just started, the turn belongs to black. The rest of our values will
be empty or false at this point.

We then check to see what the text value of the button is, so that we can determine
what to do next. If the text is Start Turn, we need to change the text of the button
to Finish Turn!.

Our other button (altBtn) also changes its text based on the status of the current
turn. If we are starting a new turn, altBtn will be set to Clear Move. This will
allow the player to clear the move if they change their mind before finishing.

Next, we update our turn value for started to true. This lets us know that the
current move has begun. We use the function called clearTurn() to clear out
any old turn data and remove any previous selections from the board. We then
inform the current player that it is their turn.

If the text of the button is set to Finish Turn!, the button will commit the selected
move(s) for the current turn using another sub function called commitTurn(). We
then change the current player, clear out the turn data, and reset the text for our two
buttons. We'll come back to finishing a turn a bit later, but first we need to see what
happens once the turn begins.

Checking the turn

Once the turn has started, the user taps on the DataView to move a piece. We then
need to make sure that each selection they make is valid. We do this by listening to
the DataView's select event with a function called doSelect().

The first thing we want to make sure of is that the user has selected a valid piece,
so the first thing we do is get the current turn:

```
doSelect: function (view, record) {
  var turn = this.getCurrentTurn();
```

Next, we have a few moves we know are illegal, in which case we can return false to prevent the player from selecting this moves:

```
if (turn.endOfTurn || !turn.started) {
  return false;
}
```

This prevents the user from moving before the turn starts or after it has ended. We also don't want the user to select any or the light squares on the board:

```
if (record.get('background') == 'light') {
  return false;
}
```

With the obvious illegal moves out of the way, we start checking for allowed moves, starting with this one:

```
if (turn.moves.length == 0 && record.get('occupiedBy') != turn.player)
{
 return false;
}
```

This checks that we are at the beginning of a turn (`turn.moves.length == 0`) and the player has not clicked one of his or her opponent's pieces. If so, we return false to prevent the selection.

```
} else if (turn.moves.length == 0) {
  turn.moves.unshift(record);
  turn.piece = record;
  this.setCurrentTurn(turn);
  return true;
}
```

If we are at the beginning of a move and the user has clicked the correct piece, we add the record onto the beginning of our moves array.

> We store moves in reverse order so that the first move in the list is the
> last move made. This is because it makes it much easier to grab the first
> element in the array (which will always be `turns.moves[0]`), than it
> is to count the array elements to grab the one on the end of the array.

We then set the current turn with our new information and return true, so that the selection event fires and the square the piece is in highlights.

If this is not the first move (turn.moves.length is greater than zero), it means the user has previously selected a piece and is now selecting a square for the piece to move into. If this is the case, we move on to the next else statement, which checks to see if the move is legal under our game rules:

```
} else if (this.isLegalMove(turn.moves[0], record)) {
  turn.moves.unshift(record);

  if (this.isKingable(record)) {
   turn.kingable = true;
   this.setEndOfTurn();
   Ext.Msg.alert("King me!", "Landing here would cause you to be
kinged and end your turn.");
  }

  this.setCurrentTurn(turn);
  this.decorateCurrentTurn();
  return true;
 } else {
  return false;
}
```

If the move is legal, we also check isKingable() to see if the player has reached the opposite side of the board. If the move is legal, we set the turn appropriately and add the arrows for the move using the decorateCurrentTurn() function. We will take a closer look at how the decorateCurrentTurn() function works a little later, but first we want to cover the logic behind the isLegalMove() function.

Checking if a move is legal

The isLegalMove() function is called when the user has selected a valid piece and is attempting to move it to a new square. The move isn't actually committed in this function, we are just checking to see if the square the player taps is a valid move. If it is, we allow the DataView's select event to fire by returning true.

> The source code for this application includes extensive console logs inside this function. These will print out information to the console in Safari or Chrome and should help when trying to follow the logic inside this function. Try clicking on valid and invalid moves while looking at the console to see which pieces of the function are responding, and how the move is validated.

To make this determination, we follow the basic rules for checkers and examine the move with the following criteria:

- The destination square cannot be occupied
- The move must be in the correct direction (regular pieces can only move forward)
- The move can be one square away from the current position
- The move can be two squares away from the current position, *if* there is an opponent's piece in between the two squares

Since this is a rather large function, we will cover it in several parts, starting with the overall skeleton and filling in the details as we go.

We start our function by passing it values for our `from` and `to` locations for the move. We then grab the current turn and set some variables for later use:

```
isLegalMove: function (from, to) {
var turn = this.getCurrentTurn(),
fromID, toID, distance, intermediate;

if (to.get('occupiedBy') != 'none') {
 return false;
}

fromID = from.get('squareID').split('');
toID = to.get('squareID').split('');
// This makes the letter element 0, and the number element 1.

distance = Math.abs(toID[1] - fromID[1]);

if (distance == 1 && !turn.hasJumped) {
 // here we will check for our different piece types: king, black or red
}
if (distance == 2) {
 // here we will check for our different piece types: king, black or red
}

return false;
}
```

The first thing we check is if the destination square is occupied using
`to.get('occupiedBy')`. If the square is clear this variable should be `none`
and if it is occupied, it will be either `red` or `black`. If we get back `red` or `black`,
we immediately return false which will exit our `isLegalMove()` function.

Next, we use the `split` function to take our values for `to` and `from`, and split them
into an array. Since we `split` on `''`, it assigns the letter (A-H) to the first element
of the array (`fromID[0]` and `toID[0]`) and assigns the number (1-8) to the second
element of the array (`fromID[1]` and `toID[1]`).

We then use `Math.abs` to give us the distance between the two number values.
`abs` is an absolute value, which ensures that we get back a positive number even
if `fromID[1]` is greater than `toID[1]`.

> It is important to note that this distance is the row distance
> and not the actual number of squares between the start and
> the end of the move.

Next, we need to make sure our distance is one row (no jumping) or two rows
(jumping). If it's neither, we return false and do not allow the move. These two
sections are currently empty, so let's fill them out with some code.

As it turns out, these two options also have a few possibilities we need to account
for. We will start off with a possible move of one row:

```
if (distance == 1 && !turn.hasJumped) {
```

This checks our distance of one row and it also makes sure that the user does not jump
a piece and then attempt to move a single row afterwards as part of the same move.

Inside of this `if` statement, we need to check three possibilities:

- Is the piece a king?
- Is the piece red?
- Is the piece black?

These criteria determine which direction the piece can move and allow us to check
if the move is valid. For the king we check the following condition:

```
if (turn.piece.get('pieceType') == 'King') {
    if (toID[0] == this.nextLetter(fromID[0])) {
        this.setEndOfTurn();
        return true;
    } else if (toID[0] == this.previousLetter(fromID[0])) {
```

```
        this.setEndOfTurn();
        return true;
    }
}
```

Here we use our `nextLetter()` and `previousLetter()` functions as part of a check to see if the move is on the diagonal:

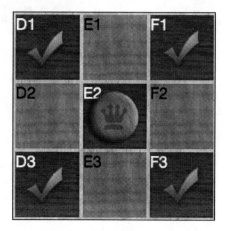

In the example above, a king located in the **2** row of the board can move to either the **1** row or the **3** row, in the **D** or **F** column. Since our previous `doSelect()` function already checked to make sure we did not select a light background, we know that these are all valid moves. This is true for a king of either color.

We then call `setEndOfTurn()` and return true to fire the select function and select the square.

For regular red and black pieces, we need to make sure the move is in the correct direction. For red, this looks like this:

```
} else if (turn.piece.get('occupiedBy') == 'red') {
 if (toID[1] < fromID[1]) {
  if (toID[0] == this.nextLetter(fromID[0])) {
   this.setEndOfTurn();
   return true;
  } else if (toID[0] == this.previousLetter(fromID[0])) {
   this.setEndOfTurn();
   return true;
  }
 }
}
```

Since our rows are numbered 1 - 8 from top to bottom and red moves from bottom to top, we need to make sure that the row number we are coming from is less than the row number we are going to (`toID[1] < fromID[1]`).

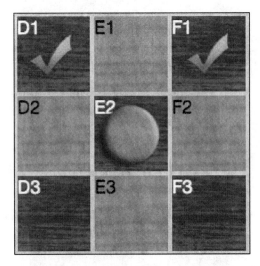

We also need to make sure we are going to the next or previous letter before calling `setEndOfTurn()` and returning true to select the square in the DataView.

For the black pieces, we will be moving from top to bottom, so we need to make sure our destination row is greater than our starting row. This will close out our `if` statement for distances of one row (no jumping):

```
  } else {
   if (toID[1] > fromID[1]) {
    if (toID[0] == this.nextLetter(fromID[0]))
     {
      this.setEndOfTurn();
      return true;
     } else if (toID[0] == this.previousLetter(fromID[0])) {
      this.setEndOfTurn();
      return true;
     }
   }
  }
```

As before, this checks our row letters to make sure we only move to the adjacent rows, calls `setEndOfTurn()` and returns true to select the square:

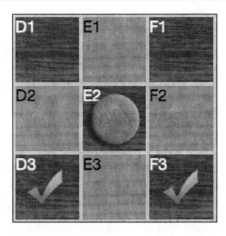

Now that we have our single row moves accounted for, we need to take a look at what happens when we try to move a distance of two rows.

From the user's perspective, they will select a piece by tapping on it, and then select an empty square with an opponent's piece in between the two squares. If additional jumps are available, the play will tap those squares as well before clicking on the **Finish Move** button:

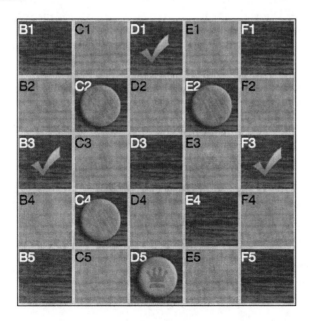

In this example, the player would tap the red king piece and then tap the three squares (shown here with check marks) before clicking on the **Finish Move** button. Let's take a look at how the code checks for this move.

This is where we fill out the second `if` statement inside of our `isValidMove()` function:

```
if (distance == 2) {
  intermediate = this.getIntermediateSquare(from, to);
```

This will check our row distance and grab the square located between the `from` and `to` locations using a `getIntermediateSquare()` function. In the preceding example, the move from **D5** to **B3** would grab **C4** as the intermediate square.

Much like before, we will also need to check and see if the piece is black, red, or a king so we can make sure the jump is in the correct direction. However, there are a few new wrinkles to allow for.

First, we have to make sure that there is an opposing piece in between the `from` and `to` locations. Second, we need to allow for multiple jumps.

If you remember back at the top of our controller, we had two variables for `currentTurn` and `previousTurn`. Inside of these were empty arrays for `moves` and `removedPieces`. We will use these arrays to store the multiple jumps.

For the king pieces, we open up a new `if` statement, right below where we grabbed the intermediate square:

```
if (turn.piece.get('pieceType') == 'King') {
   if (intermediate.get('occupiedBy') == 'red' && turn.piece.
get('occupiedBy') == 'black') {
    turn.moves.unshift(intermediate);
    turn.removedPieces.push(intermediate);
    turn.hasJumped = true;
    this.setCurrentTurn(turn);
    return true;
   } else if (intermediate.get('occupiedBy') == 'black' && turn.piece.
get('occupiedBy') == 'red') {
    turn.moves.unshift(intermediate);
    turn.removedPieces.push(intermediate);
    turn.hasJumped = true;
    this.setCurrentTurn(turn);
    return true;
   }
 }
```

Once we know that we have a `King` piece, we don't need to check for the direction of the jump, we just need to make sure that the `intermediate` piece is the opposite color from the piece that is moving (our `occupiedBy` piece). Once we have determined this is a valid king jump, we use `unshift` to add the move onto the beginning of our array of moves.

> Remember we need to add things to the beginning of the `moves` array, so we can quickly access the most recent of these moves later on by using `moves[0]` in our other functions. This is necessary for placing the arrow decorations correctly (as we will see later on). It is less critical for our `removedPieces` array, which places the negation symbol directly over the piece. So for `removedPieces`, we use the `push()` function instead.

We also add the `intermediate` location to our `removedPieces` array and set `hasJumped` to `true`. This lets us know that there are potentially more moves to be executed. Finally, we use `setCurrentTurn()` to record the location the user selected and return true to select the square in the DataView.

For moving a red piece, we run a check to see if the piece is jumping forward by checking to make sure that `toID[1] < fromID[1]`:

```
} else if (turn.piece.get('occupiedBy') == 'red') {
 if (toID[1] < fromID[1]) {
  if (intermediate.get('occupiedBy') == 'black') {
   turn.moves.unshift(intermediate);
   turn.removedPieces.push(intermediate);
   turn.hasJumped = true;
   this.setCurrentTurn(turn);
   return true;
  }
 }
}
```

We also check to see if the piece that was jumped is black. The rest of the code follows the same pattern as the code for the king jump.

We add the same basic code block to check the jump for a black piece:

```
} else {
  if (toID[1] > fromID[1]) {
   if (intermediate.get('occupiedBy') == 'red') {
    turn.moves.unshift(intermediate);
```

```
        turn.removedPieces.push(intermediate);
        turn.hasJumped = true;
        this.setCurrentTurn(turn);
        return true;
      }
    }
  }
```

Again, we check our direction using `toID[1] > fromID[1]`, and check our intermediate square for a red piece. The rest of the code follows the same pattern as the code for both the red and the king jumps.

At the bottom of our `isValidMove()` function, after all the `if` statements, we close out the function with `return false`. This covers us when the user does something totally outside of our set of `if...then` rules.

Once we have determined if the move is valid, we need to add the correct classes to our game board to let the user know they have chosen a valid move, and what will happen when the move is finished.

Decorating the move

Once the user has started a turn and clicked on a square, there needs to be some indication that a valid move was selected. This happens as part of the `doSelect()` function and it happens in two different ways.

The first way is that when we validate the selected move, we return either `true` or `false`. When we return `true`, that DataView fires the `select` event and the selected square is highlighted (this is the default behavior for a DataView).

When we return `false`, we actually prevent the `select` event from firing and the square is not highlighted.

As we mentioned earlier in the chapter, the highlight color is controlled with CSS styles and a class of `x-item-selected`. This class is automatically applied to any selected item in a DataView. We can use a similar methodology to add additional CSS decorations to our squares, which will give the user a better idea of what is happening in the game.

This happens in the `decorateCurrentTurn()` function.

Earlier in the chapter we talked about our decoration classes:

- `up_left`: This suggests an arrow in the upper-left corner
- `up_right`: This suggests an arrow in the upper-right corner
- `down_left`: This suggests an arrow in the lower-left corner
- `down_right`: This suggests an arrow in the lower-right corner
- `removed`: This suggests a negation center in the middle of the square

On the game board, they look like this:

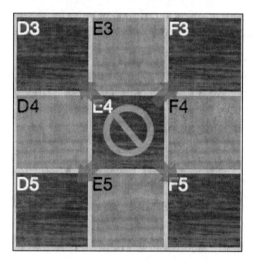

The `decorateTurn()` function will loop through our array of moves for a turn and apply the correct styles.

We start by getting the `fromID` and `toID` values for the move and splitting it into an array with two elements: a number and a letter. Then we compare them to create a class name that corresponds to one of our four arrows:

```
decorateTurn: function(turn) {
        var i, from, to, fromID, toID, cls;

        for (i = turn.moves.length - 1; i > 0; i--) {
            from = turn.moves[i];
            to = turn.moves[i - 1];
```

```
            fromID = from.get('squareID').split('');
            toID = to.get('squareID').split('');
            if (fromID[1] < toID[1]) {
                cls = 'down';
            } else {
                cls = 'up';
            }
            if (fromID[0] < toID[0]) {
                cls += '_right';
            } else {
                cls += '_left';
            }
            from.set('decoration', cls);
        }

        for (i = 0; i < turn.removedPieces.length; i++) {
            cls = turn.removedPieces[i].get('decoration');
            cls += ' removed';
            turn.removedPieces[i].set('decoration', cls);
        }

        this.getBoard().refresh();
    }
```

For example, let's assume we have a piece moving from **E4** to **D3**. If we split these values and check them in the preceding code, we would see that:

- 4 < 3 is false and we would set the value of cls to up

- D < C is also false and we would add the text _left to our cls value

This leaves us with a class of up_left applied to our square, and an arrow in the upper-left corner.

> Comparing greater than / less than for text values in JavaScript compares the ASCII values for the letters. This is fine if you are comparing single letters, all with the same case, but it can become problematic in many cases. For example, "Z" < "a" is actually true in JavaScript, because all uppercase letters have a lower ASCII value than lowercase letters. In this case we are comparing a single uppercase letter to another single uppercase letter, which works just fine.

Once we have set our arrow to indicate the direction using `from.set('decoration', cls);`, we need to account for any pieces to be removed. We handle this by looping through our `removedPieces` array that is part of our `turn` variable. We add `'removed'` to the class for all of the pieces in this array. The space in front of the string means that it will be added as an additional class on the square.

This means the CSS class would be something like `"up_left removed"`, if the turn jumps over a piece that is up and to the left of its current location. Both styles would be applied to the square, giving it an upper-left arrow and a negation symbol.

Once we have applied our styles for each move, we call `this.getBoard(). refresh();` to refresh the board and make everything show up.

The beauty of creating a separate function for `decorateTurn()` is that we can use it to decorate the previous turn as well as the current one:

```
decoratePreviousTurn: function() {
 var turn = this.getPreviousTurn();
 if (turn.player == null && turn.piece == null) {
  Ext.Msg.alert('Game not started', 'There is no previous turn to
show');
  return false;
 }
 this.getBoard().select(turn.moves, false, true);
 return this.decorateTurn(turn);
}
```

This function runs a check to see if we have a previous turn. If we do, we just pass it along to our decorate turn function and let it handle showing the appropriate decorations. If you were feeling particularly ambitious, you could store all the turns and replay every one of them by looping through and passing each turnoff to the `decorateTurn()` function.

However, before we get too ambitious, let's take a look at how we clear a move and its decorations.

Clearing the move

When we clear a move, we need to accomplish two main things: clear the data out of our currentTurn variable and clear the decoration values out of our store. We split this into two separate functions to make things easier to update and maintain. The first function handles resetting the values for our currentTurn variable and then deselects everything on the board:

```
clearTurn: function() {
 var turn = this.getCurrentTurn();
 turn.piece = null;
 turn.moves = [];
 turn.removedPieces = [];
 turn.endOfTurn = false;
 turn.hasJumped = false;
 turn.kingable = false;
 this.setCurrentTurn(turn);
 this.getBoard().deselectAll(true);
 this.clearDecorations();
},
clearDecorations: function() {
 var store = this.getBoard().getStore();
 store.each(function(square) {
   square.set('decoration', '');
 });
}
```

The second function clears all of the decorations from the store. You might remember from previously in the chapter, the decorations are the arrows that indicate movement and the negation symbols used to designate a jumped piece. These are all applied as CSS styles to the squares in our DataView. When we clear the value for decoration on each square in the store, the DataView will automatically remove the arrows and symbols from the display.

Going beyond the finished game

Playing through the finished game can lead to some interesting ideas for modifications and improvements.

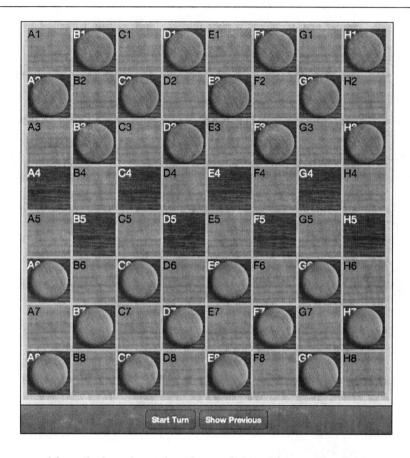

The squares could easily be adapted to the traditional hex grid used in most tabletop role-playing games.

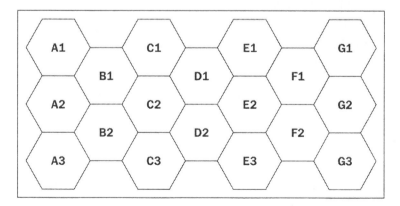

Even with a hex layout, the basic logic flow for the game still remains the same:

- The user selects a piece and we check if it is a valid selection
- The user selects a destination and we check if the destination is valid
- If it is a valid move we provide visual feedback through CSS to tell the user
- We determine the result of the move and remove or modify pieces as appropriate
- We check to see if the game has ended and if not, we repeat the process for the next player

The validation is also still a matter of math and some basic if...then logic. Granted, this logic can become much more complex, but the basic rules and game flow will remain the same.

Additionally, CSS transitions could be used to add a more visual appeal to the game play. A number of options can be found in the documentation at http://docs.sencha.com/touch/2-0/#!/api/Ext.Anim.

These variations allow you to take a simple game model and truly make it your own.

Summary

In this chapter we covered the creation of a basic game of checkers:

- We built the basic game board
- Explored the CSS and HTML structure to create our layout
- We built the basic game controller and covered the game board logic
- We showed you how to start, validate, decorate, and clear the moves on the board
- We also talked about some options for expanding the game and making it your own original idea

Index

interactions, Sencha Touch Charts
about 127
ItemCompare 127
ItemHightlight 127
ItemInfo 127
PanZoom 127
PieGrouping 127
Rotate 127
ToggleStacked 127
iOS Dev Center 86
iOS Provisioning Portal 86
isActive function 236, 237, 243
isComplete, boolean value 19
isCompleted, boolean value 39
isKingable function 302
isLegalMove() function 306
isValidMove() function 314
item array 56
ItemCompare 127
ItemHightlight 127
ItemInfo 127
item model
creating 183-185
.htaccess 185, 186
RewriteRule 185, 186
item store 186, 187
itemtap action 51
itemTpl 30
itemTpl config
exploring 295-298
itemTpl XTemplate
creating 61

J

JSON 176
JSON API plugin 247
JSONLint
about 204, 205
URL 204
JSONP proxy component
about 53
callback function 53
script tag 53
URL 53
JSONP store 246

L

launch function 26, 238
layout
creating, for TimeCop application 76-79
list component 105
lists
adding 28-30
list view
adding, to MainView 45
LocalStorage proxy 45
LocalStorage Proxy object 15

M

mainBtn function 300
main.js file 98
MainView
about 44
list view, adding 45
MainView container 46
main view controller
concluding 228-232
mainView.js controller
about 216
starting 217
mainView tab panel 29
marker section 125
media queries 260
model
defining 112
models
about 11
creating 144, 145
defining 112
model, task list
adding 16, 17
adding, to store 17
move
checking 306
clearing 318
decorating 314-317
MyApp.model.Task 24
MyFormPanel panel 36
MyModel 16
MyStore 15

Thank you for buying
Creating Mobile Apps with Sencha Touch 2

About Packt Publishing

Packt, pronounced 'packed', published its first book "*Mastering phpMyAdmin for Effective MySQL Management*" in April 2004 and subsequently continued to specialize in publishing highly focused books on specific technologies and solutions.

Our books and publications share the experiences of your fellow IT professionals in adapting and customizing today's systems, applications, and frameworks. Our solution based books give you the knowledge and power to customize the software and technologies you're using to get the job done. Packt books are more specific and less general than the IT books you have seen in the past. Our unique business model allows us to bring you more focused information, giving you more of what you need to know, and less of what you don't.

Packt is a modern, yet unique publishing company, which focuses on producing quality, cutting-edge books for communities of developers, administrators, and newbies alike. For more information, please visit our website: www.packtpub.com.

About Packt Open Source

In 2010, Packt launched two new brands, Packt Open Source and Packt Enterprise, in order to continue its focus on specialization. This book is part of the Packt Open Source brand, home to books published on software built around Open Source licences, and offering information to anybody from advanced developers to budding web designers. The Open Source brand also runs Packt's Open Source Royalty Scheme, by which Packt gives a royalty to each Open Source project about whose software a book is sold.

Writing for Packt

We welcome all inquiries from people who are interested in authoring. Book proposals should be sent to author@packtpub.com. If your book idea is still at an early stage and you would like to discuss it first before writing a formal book proposal, contact us; one of our commissioning editors will get in touch with you.

We're not just looking for published authors; if you have strong technical skills but no writing experience, our experienced editors can help you develop a writing career, or simply get some additional reward for your expertise.

Sencha Touch Mobile JavaScript Framework

ISBN: 978-1-84951-510-8   Paperback: 316 pages

Build web applications for Apple iOS and Google Android touchscreen devices with this first HTML5 mobile framework

1. Learn to develop web applications that look and feel native on Apple iOS and Google Android touchscreen devices using Sencha Touch through examples

2. Design resolution-independent and graphical representations like buttons, icons, and tabs of unparalleled flexibility

3. Add custom events like tap, double tap, swipe, tap and hold, pinch, and rotate

Sencha Touch Cookbook

ISBN: 978-1-84951-544-3   Paperback: 350 pages

Over 100 recipes for creating HTML5-based cross-platform apps for touch devices

1. Master cross platform application development

2. Incorporate geo location into your apps

3. Develop native looking web apps

Corona SDK Mobile Game Development: Beginner's Guide

ISBN: 978-1-84969-188-8   Paperback: 408 pages

Create monetized games for iOS and Android with minimum cost and code

1. Build once and deploy your games to both iOS and Android

2. Create commercially successful games by applying several monetization techniques and tools

3. Create three fun games and integrate them with social networks such as Twitter and Facebook

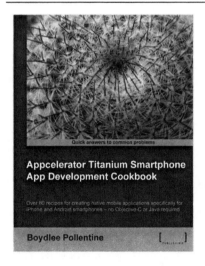

Appcelerator Titanium Smartphone App Development Cookbook

ISBN: 978-1-84951-396-8   Paperback: 308 pages

Over 80 recipes for creating native mobile applications specifically for iPhone and Android smartphones – no Objective-C or Java required

1. Leverage your JavaScript skills to write mobile applications using Titanium Studio tools with the native advantage!

2. Extend the Titanium platform with your own native modules

3. A practical guide for packaging and submitting your apps to both the iTunes store and Android Marketplace

Please check **www.PacktPub.com** for information on our titles

CPSIA information can be obtained at www.ICGtesting.com
Printed in the USA
LVOW110246110413

328594LV00005B/66/P